PRUDENT PRACTICE

PRUDENT PRACTICE:
A GUIDE FOR MANAGING
MALPRACTICE RISK

─────────────────── By ───────────────────

Mary Kay Houston-Vega and Elane M. Nuehring
with Elisabeth R. Daguio

CONTRIBUTING WRITERS
Robert H. Cohen, JD, ACSW
Elizabeth DuMez, ACSW
Loretta Sih Robinson, MA

COMMISSIONED BY
National Association of Social Workers Insurance Trust
Loretta Sih Robinson, MA, *Director*

NASW PRESS

NATIONAL ASSOCIATION OF SOCIAL WORKERS
WASHINGTON, DC

Jay J. Cayner, ACSW, LSW, *President*
Josephine Nieves, MSW, PhD, *Executive Director*

Linda Beebe, *Executive Editor*
Nancy A. Winchester, *Editorial Services Director*
Christina A. Davis, *Production Editor*
Louise Goines, *Copy Editor*
Beth Gyorgy, *Proofreader*
Bernice Eisen, *Indexer*

First printing November 1996
Second printing May 1998

Library of Congress Cataloging-in-Publication Data
Houston, Mary Kay.
    Prudent practice: a guide for managing malpractice risk / by Mary Kay Houston-Vega and Elane M. Nuehring, with Elisabeth R. Daguio; contributing writers, Robert H. Cohen, Elizabeth DuMez, Loretta Sih Robinson; commissioned by National Association of Social Workers Insurance Trust, Loretta Sih Robinson, Director.
    p. cm.
    Includes bibliographical references and index.
    ISBN 0-87101-267-7 (alk. paper)
    1. Social workers—Malpractice—United States. 2. Social work—United States. I. Nuehring, Elane M. II. Daguio, Elisabeth R. III. National Association of Social Workers Insurance Trust. IV. Title.
KF3721.H68   1996
344.73'0313—dc21   96-37035
                                                        CIP

Printed in the United States of America

We dedicate this work to "Topsy," Elsie Mae Houston, who encouraged us from the book's inception and whose memory inspired us. We also thank our families, who supported and encouraged us throughout the writing of this book—Juan A. Vega, Timothy C. Houston-Vega, Ronald Nuehring, Kawika M. K. Daguio, and Sarah M. E. Daguio.

M.K.H.-V., E.M.N., E.R.D.

CONTENTS

A CAUTIONARY NOTE

Prudent Practice: A Guide for Managing Malpractice Risk is a guide to help you manage your practice and increase your awareness of possible risks and potential solutions. It is not a substitute for the advice of legal counsel or local experts. Although the authors have attempted to make the book as current as possible, new developments occur frequently. Further, your practice is governed by laws and regulations set by federal, state, and local authorities. The authors, publisher, NASW, the NASW Insurance Trust, and any distributors are not responsible for actions taken in regard to your practice; they are not responsible for any loss incurred as a result of your use or application of information or materials contained in this book.

The guide offers suggestions and principles that you, as the reader, must shape to fit your particular situation, rather than specific diagnostic rules. The book also contains a large number of sample forms, which we hope will be useful to you in developing your own record-keeping and contractual arrangements. The forms are provided in the appendix and on disk so that you can adapt them to meet requirements in your geographic and practice areas. They are offered without any warranty, implied or explicit, that they are appropriate forms for use in your practice. We cannot and do not assume any responsibility for their use with any client. You must assume full responsibility for the use of these forms. You should review any forms that establish a contract between you and another individual with your legal counsel to be assured that they conform with local law and practice.

You may need additional information to manage a case or cases. In those instances, you should seek the advice of a competent professional consultant.

IMPORTANT NOTICE TO READERS

The intent of this work is to offer tools and practice techniques that may be helpful in improving practice as well as useful in reducing and managing social work malpractice risks; consequently, the book is generally a menu of recommendations for practitioners. In no way does this work constitute the setting of standards or guidelines.

Any narrative that speaks to social work principles, standards, guidelines, norms, precedents, strategies, techniques, forms, or recommendations stated or implied in this work are the opinions and thinking of the authors and do not in any way constitute standards or guidelines of the professional organization, NASW, unless expressly identified as an official NASW standard or guideline. NASW has set its own specific procedures for promulgating official standards and guidelines for the practice of professional social work through its Delegate Assembly and Board of Directors. That process and the NASW official standards and guidelines cannot be supplanted or superseded by the narrative of a text developed by individual authors.

PREFACE

As chair of the National Association of Social Workers Insurance Trust, I was sometimes asked why the Trust emphasizes risk management given the inherent imperfections in the arena of malpractice litigation. After all, "good" social workers are sued every day. Judges and juries may award damages in a seemingly arbitrary manner. Claims can be settled for reasons aside from the merit of the case. So why bother with a book to help social workers practice prudently?

Aside from the most obvious benefit of identifying and negotiating a solid social work professional liability product, the Trust is aiming to contain the cost of malpractice insurance for all social workers. As malpractice claims against social workers increase in frequency and severity, so do the premium rates for all social workers. Although statistically the average social worker will never be sued for malpractice, because of the nature of group malpractice insurance coverage, one's insurance premiums are going to reflect losses attributable to anyone and everyone in the group.

All social workers bear the penalty in insurance rates of negligent practice by colleagues and the high cost of the defense of both unfounded and legitimate claims. Moreover, a lawsuit for malpractice is only one of many adverse actions that can befall a social worker. As the authors point out, "a malpractice suit is often only one part of a wrenching experience that is likely to involve additional complaints to NASW and state professional regulatory agencies, as well as other civil or even criminal charges."

It is my opinion that the risk management strategies discussed in this book, if practiced religiously, will dramatically limit the social worker's exposure to malpractice litigation and other adverse actions. The reason behind my belief is quite simple. This book is a reference guide for social workers seeking to practice within the profession's standard of care. This concept of the standard of care can be a pivotal point in a social worker's defense against allegations of malpractice. All malpractice litigation requires that the professional breached the standard of care in a professional relationship and that the breach was the direct or proximate cause of the injury sustained by the plaintiff. In simple terms, if a social worker can prove that he or she practiced within the standard of care and within the norms of prudent practice for the profession, he or she is likely to prevail in malpractice litigation.

In theory, the function of malpractice litigation is twofold: (1) to compensate victims for injuries caused by the negligent behavior of another party and (2) to deter professionals from substandard practice. Of course, a significant number of malpractice suits do not involve any negligence on the part of the professional. As the authors of this book state, "anyone can be sued at any time for a variety of alleged wrongful conducts or negligent behaviors." Some clients sue in the event of a bad outcome rather than for an injury caused by negligence. This suggests that they may sue first and foremost because they are disappointed and dissatisfied. It must be emphasized that although not all service produces the desired results, the failure to achieve results does not necessarily mean that the social worker practiced negligently or committed malpractice. Clients who expect service to be the panacea for their problems may be very disappointed when reality fails to meet their expectations.

Although judges and juries determine the validity of the case as best they can given the facts presented to them, their decisions regarding malpractice will not necessarily be consistent or correct. Moreover, the compensation paid in malpractice litigation can best be characterized as often arbitrary and unpredictable. Certainly, it is fair that a plaintiff may receive compensation for injuries, lost income, and pain and suffering. However, comparable cases do not necessarily receive comparable compensation. Any number of factors influence the amount of compensation paid beyond the facts of the case, including the skill of the attorneys, the demeanors of the defendant and plaintiff, the characteristics of the jury, and the personality of the judge.

Another complication is that most social work malpractice claims are settled before going to trial. Although some settlements may acknowledge the validity of the claim or offer compensation in amounts large enough to suggest that the plaintiff had a legitimate complaint, most malpractice settlements do not admit any fault and do not involve large amounts of compensation. Settlements are pragmatic for both the defendant and the plaintiff because settlements expedite resolution while minimizing the costs associated with the dispute resolution process.

Yet society uses the tort system to determine the validity of any claim and the level of compensation, if any, that may accrue when a claim is found to be valid. As imperfect as the judicial system may be, it is the ultimate method of dispute resolution used in society. Until the time when we can change the system, we have to live with it and all of its imperfections. However, our acceptance does not have to be passive.

Malpractice cannot occur unless the profession's standard of care is breached. Staying within the standard of care would be easy if it were a clearly defined boundary. Unfortunately, it is not. The standard of care is in constant evolution. As the profession grows and changes with society, so does the standard of care. While the standard of care does include ethical standards, practice standards and guidelines, and laws and regulations, it also includes the daily actions of social workers in their practices.

A social worker's best protection is a solid understanding of the standard of care as it applies to practice. Professionals must make a concerted effort to practice within that standard of care and work consistently at remaining knowledgeable about changes in the profession. Therefore, professional education should be ongoing and unending.

Prudent Practice: A Guide for Managing Malpractice Risk, commissioned by the NASW Insurance Trust, is an invaluable reference for all social workers, whether in direct practice or other areas of social work. The book can help a social worker become a better practitioner, not only because it sensitizes one to malpractice issues, but also because the means of reducing one's risk are the same as improving and fine tuning the social work we conduct. In my opinion, this book begins to level the playing field for professionals facing the malpractice litigation system.

BARBARA W. WHITE, PhD, ACSW
Chair, NASW Insurance Trust, July 1993 through June 1996
Dean, University of Texas School of Social Work
Austin

ACKNOWLEDGMENTS

Special thanks for funding this work goes to the NASW Insurance Trust and National Union Fire Insurance Company of Pittsburgh, Pa.

CONTRIBUTING REVIEWERS

Mary Altpeter, MPA, ACSW
Linda Beebe
Donna DeAngelis, ACSW, LICSW
Richard C. Imbert, CIC
Vivian H. Jackson, ACSW
C. W. King, ACSW
Eric C. Marine
Carolyn I. Polowy, JD

NATIONAL ASSOCIATION OF SOCIAL WORKERS INSURANCE TRUST

Trustees

Special thanks for their assistance goes to Lynda Eubank, ACSW; Helen Northen, PhD, ACSW; Joan Parry, DSW, ACSW; Gwendolyn S. Prater, DSW, ACSW; and Mark S. Sioma, CPCU.

A large network of colleagues and friends have contributed to our knowledge of malpractice. Special thanks goes to those who contributed to Appendix C, including Dan Brady, LCSW; Larry Auerbach, LCSW; James Meyer, Jr., PhD; Ron Zimmett, Esq; Edward L. Zuckerman, PhD; and Irving P. R. Guyett, PhD.

INTRODUCTION

Prudent Practice: A Guide for Managing Malpractice Risk was commissioned by the National Association of Social Workers (NASW) Insurance Trust to assist social work practitioners in the reduction of risks for malpractice suits and other adverse actions arising from controversies with clients. This handbook explains malpractice and its consequences and offers a repertoire of approaches and tools to use in the prevention of both unsound practice and litigation. Echoing the views of many social work leaders, the book emphasizes that the best defense against malpractice litigation is competent, ethically conscientious, client-centered practice (Bernstein, 1981; Besharov & Besharov, 1987; Kurzman, 1995; Sharwell, 1979–80; Watkins & Watkins, 1989).

A malpractice suit is often only one part of a wrenching experience that is likely to involve additional complaints to NASW and state professional regulatory agencies, as well as other civil or even criminal charges. Depending on the malpractice insurance coverage owned, a practitioner's out-of-pocket expenditures can be very high. Even the best policy is unlikely to cover all the financial expenses and will not cover damage to reputation and standing among one's colleagues; license revocation; public ethical sanctions; and countless hours of time working with an attorney, preparing and delivering depositions, appearing in court, and seeking support and stress relief in therapy. Beyond the lost dollars are often psychological costs, including shame and self-recrimination; the deep sense of betrayal when a client one has attempted to help reciprocates with litigation; and the panicky fear that one's career, livelihood, and financial security are ruined.

The intent of this book is *not* to alarm practitioners nor to encourage the avoidance of "risky" clients and situations (Besharov & Besharov, 1987). The book's goal is to help equip social workers with knowledge and skills that minimize risk of harm to clients, resolve ethical and legal dilemmas, and foster evaluation of practice. For example, one essential safeguard against malpractice is the formulation and documentation of a rationale for the resolution of conflicting ethical principles, standards, laws, and agency policies (Houston & Northen, 1994). Specifically, the book

- addresses malpractice risks in each of the major phases of social work practice, in life-endangering situations, and in vicarious situations involving indirect responsibility for another's actions
- identifies, describes, and illustrates methods for enhancing practice and reducing legal and ethical risks.

How to Use This Book

This handbook was written to help reduce the risk of malpractice. Readers will gain a heightened awareness of the ethical and legal pitfalls of social work practice along with the knowledge of strategies that encourage competent, creative, liberal, and compassionate practice—all while reducing exposure to lawsuits and other adverse actions. *However, in no way does the book constitute legal advice,* nor is it a substitute for a solid working relationship with an attorney who is well versed in social welfare and mental health law, as well as in professional regulation and malpractice. Social workers should not wait for a lawsuit to choose an attorney but instead should identify a well-qualified, well-recommended individual and arrange an introductory consultation to acquaint him or her with the practice, especially areas of particular concern, and seek risk reduction advice. Practitioners should maintain contact with attorneys and seek a consultation whenever a legal dilemma surfaces. In addition, practitioners should confer with ethics experts or respected peers whenever an ethical dilemma arises.

There are no perfect plans that will unconditionally prevent one from being embroiled in a malpractice suit or complaint. Anyone can be sued at any time for a variety of alleged wrongful conducts or negligent behaviors; there are no prohibitions against someone in society filing a lawsuit if he or she feels aggrieved or sees an opportunity to realize a monetary gain. Although a court may dismiss a lawsuit as frivolous or the social worker ultimately may be found not guilty, many lawsuits are settled out of court to diminish financial and personal losses. Social workers should make every effort to avert malpractice suits, because you will never really win. Your best bet is prevention.

This handbook identifies in a comprehensive and extensive way many potential problem areas in social work practice; however, the intent is not to scare practitioners. The client's best interests are not served by an overzealous application of any and all of the guidelines mentioned in this book. The book is intended to provide comprehensive guidance, portions of which can be adapted to a practitioner's unique setting and clientele. Hence, the book can be used as a reference tool in seeking an answer to a question or in confronting a problem in practice. Discussions of particular practice considerations are continued throughout the book. For example, confidentiality is discussed as a general and legal principle in Chapter 2, as an issue in engaging clients and beginning service in Chapter 3, as an ongoing concern during service in Chapter 4, and as an issue in termination of service in Chapter 5. Confidentiality is further elaborated on in Chapter 6 in relation to life-endangering situations, in Chapter 7 in relation to vicarious liability, and in Chapter 8 in relation to responding to a client complaint or lawsuit.

In addition to the eight chapters that offer definitions and practical principles and ideas applicable to each stage of service, this book includes three appendixes. Appendix A is the *NASW Code of Ethics* as adopted by the 1996 Delegate Assembly, which will likely be the document, along with NASW standards applicable to a particular practice and state licensure laws and related rules, referred to most often in social work practice. All social work practitioners are encouraged to be familiar with the complete and current set of published policy statements that guide the profession, including the

- *NASW Code of Ethics* (NASW, 1996)
- *Standards for the Classification of Social Work Practice* (NASW, 1981a)
- *Standards for Social Work Practice in Child Protection* (NASW, 1981b)
- *Standards for Social Work Services in Long-Term Care Facilities* (NASW, 1981c)
- *Standards for Continuing Professional Education* (NASW, 1982)
- *Standards for Social Work in Health Care Settings* (NASW, 1987)
- *Standards for the Practice of Clinical Social Work* (NASW, 1989)
- *Standards for Social Work Personnel Practices* (NASW, 1990)
- *Standards for School Social Work Services* (NASW, 1992a)
- *Standards for Social Work Case Management* (NASW, 1992b)
- *Standards for the Practice of Social Work with Adolescents* (NASW, 1993)
- *Standards for Social Work Mediators* (NASW, n.d.).

Moreover, practitioners are advised to secure copies of the codes of ethics and practice standards of other professional groups with which they are affiliated through membership or certification. Social workers who profess expertise in a particular area—for example, family mediation—must be familiar with and abide by special guidelines, laws, and standards related to that area of practice and its credentials. In addition, practitioners should obtain from state regulatory bodies copies of the current licensure or certification laws for social workers, along with associated state rules and regulations.

Appendix B contains detailed information on locating laws, regulations, and court decisions germane to social work practice. Appendix C offers samples of materials to aid in the development of client information handbooks, brochures, fact sheets, and office signs. Also included are sample forms and letters. The materials in Appendix C can be customized to suit any practice setting and community. Accordingly, the contents of Appendix C are provided on a computer disk to enable practitioners to modify the items for a particular setting or clientele.

REFERENCES

Bernstein, B. E. (1981). Malpractice: Future shock of the 1980s. *Social Casework, 62*, 175–181.

Besharov, D. J., & Besharov, S. (1987). Teaching about liability. *Social Work, 32*, 517–522.

Houston, M. K., & Northen, H. (1994, May). *Reducing malpractice risks: A framework for resolving ethical–legal dilemmas and enhancing clinical practice.* Paper presented at the meeting of the Second National Clinical Social Work Conference for the National Federation of Societies for Clinical Social Work, Washington, DC.

Kurzman, P. A. (1995). Professional liability. In R. L. Edwards (Ed.-in-Chief), *Encyclopedia of social work* (19th ed., Vol. 3, pp. 1921–1926). Washington, DC: NASW Press.

National Association of Social Workers. (1981a). *Standards for the classification of social work practice.* Washington, DC: Author.

National Association of Social Workers. (1981b). *Standards for social work practice in child protection.* Washington, DC: Author.

National Association of Social Workers. (1981c). *Standards for social work services in long-term care facilities.* Washington, DC: Author.

National Association of Social Workers. (1982). *Standards for continuing professional education.* Washington, DC: Author.

National Association of Social Workers. (1987). *Standards for social work in health care settings*. Washington, DC: Author.

National Association of Social Workers. (1989). *Standards for the practice of clinical social work*. Washington, DC: Author.

National Association of Social Workers. (1990). *Standards for social work personnel practices*. Washington, DC: Author.

National Association of Social Workers. (1992a). *Standards for school social work services*. Washington, DC: Author.

National Association of Social Workers. (1992b). *Standards for social work case management*. Washington, DC: Author.

National Association of Social Workers. (1993). *Standards for the practice of social work with adolescents*. Washington, DC: Author.

National Association of Social Workers. (1996). *NASW code of ethics*. Washington, DC: Author.

National Association of Social Workers. (n.d.). *Standards for social work mediators*. Washington, DC: Author.

Sharwell, R. G. (1979–80). Learn 'em good: The threat of malpractice. *Journal of Social Welfare, 6*, 39–48.

Watkins, S. A., & Watkins, J. C. (1989). Negligent endangerment: Malpractice in the clinical context. *Journal of Independent Social Work, 3*(3), 35–50.

CHAPTER

1

SETTING THE STAGE

INCREASED VULNERABILITY TO MALPRACTICE SUITS

No comprehensive data exist on the number of malpractice suits filed against social workers, who are insured by various companies or may not be insured at all. However, since the establishment of the NASW Insurance Trust more than 25 years ago, malpractice suits against social workers insured by the Trust have increased dramatically (Besharov & Besharov, 1987; Reamer, 1994; Watkins & Watkins, 1989).

How can social workers understand their heightened exposure to malpractice suits? The profession has a long-standing and strong commitment to ethical principles, including a straightforward *Code of Ethics* (NASW, 1996; see Appendix A). Now social workers must operate within not only an ethical environment but also within a litigious environment (Kurzman, 1995). Moreover, changes in professional regulations and standards, mental health legislation, and court rulings have forced the profession to work within an increasingly complex legal structure. In turn, social workers are at greater risk for malpractice claims.

Several trends seem to explain the increase in malpractice complaints:

- State legislatures and courts are abolishing immunity from liability for social workers in public agencies and have expanded the legal concept of duty to protect and warn.
- In today's litigious society, consumers of human services are more aware of the available avenues of malpractice litigation.
- With declining resources and the advent of managed care aimed at cost-containment, clients are at greater risk of insufficient or prematurely terminated services as social workers respond to system requirements rather than to client needs.
- Finally, the profession has arrived. Social work's increased exposure to liability is an indicator of increased professional status, visibility, and sphere of responsibility. Signs of a recognized profession include consumers with clear expectations of providers and providers' accountability for their professional behavior (Kurzman, 1995).

Current literature and research suggest that social workers are aware of the malpractice risks but are not well informed about risk reduction (Bernstein, 1981; Besharov & Besharov, 1987; Reamer, 1987, 1994; Watkins & Watkins,

1989). Overall, the literature addresses selected legal issues, identifies at-risk populations and fields of practice, and describes the general features of malpractice and professional liability. Examples include discussions of privileged communication (Bernstein, 1978; Perlman, 1988; Watkins, 1989), child welfare and school liability (Barksdale, 1989; Besharov, 1985; Green & Hansen, 1989; Sharwell, 1982), informed consent (Parry, 1987; Reamer, 1987), supervisory and field practicum risks (Gelman & Wardell, 1988), misdiagnosis (Kutchins & Kirk, 1987), use of contracts (Kagle, 1984), duty to protect and warn (Fulero, 1988; Seelig, 1987; Weil & Sanchez, 1983), the fiduciary relationship (Kutchins, 1991), and legal issues with clients with AIDS (Abramson, 1990; Lamb, Clark, Drumheller, Frizzell, & Surrey, 1989; Reamer, 1991a, 1991b). In addition, a landmark comprehensive text about social work malpractice issues written by social work scholar Frederic G. Reamer was published in 1994.

All social workers are at risk and none are immune from the possibility of a lawsuit or other action being brought against them. Supervisors, child welfare workers, private practitioners, adult welfare workers, mental health workers, crisis workers, health care social workers, school social workers, and administrators must know how to keep their social work practice legally sound and ethical. Certain settings and situations tend to place practitioners at greater risk. For example, social workers involved in group practice may be held liable for the actions of the other members of the group. In managed care contexts, clinicians might be pressured by the reimbursement system to terminate service or not to choose the preferred service, only to find that a client whose best interests have not been served is litigating. Child protection settings create special risks for liability, including inadequately protecting a child, reporting suspected child abuse and neglect, and violating parental rights (Besharov & Besharov, 1987). Other areas of child welfare liability include failure to investigate adequately, unnecessarily intrusive investigation, failure to place a child in protective custody, wrongful removal or withholding of a child, returning a child to dangerous parents, failure to provide adequate case monitoring, faulty assessment and custody evaluation, and malicious prosecution (Besharov, 1985). In addition, clinicians who conduct child custody investigations and testify in court or practice as mediators are at greater risk if their findings do not concur with the family's expectations.

As social workers move farther into the arena of fee for service and away from the service ideal model, vulnerability to litigation increases. Clinical social workers in private practice face a higher probability of malpractice actions related to sexual impropriety, incorrect diagnosis and service, fee splitting, false imprisonment, failure to protect and warn, licensing irregularities, and improper or inappropriate referral (Jones & Alcabes, 1989).

As social work has become more specialized, detailed professional standards and licensing regulations have proliferated along with federal and state regulations, laws, and statutes. Increasingly, both public and private social services settings are expected to provide a higher standard of care that requires increased knowledge and skill. As the profession expands into the realms of private practice, managed care, proprietary services, for-profit agencies, and third-party reimbursement, social workers must know and adhere to additional regulations and standards for businesses and fair trade. Growing demands create many risks for social workers that might lead to dissatisfied clients with propensities to file lawsuits (Jones & Alcabes, 1989; Kutchins, 1991).

The best risk management for malpractice litigation is competent practice and accurate documentation of practice decisions and interventions (Bernstein, 1981; Besharov & Besharov, 1987; Watkins & Watkins, 1989). As Sharwell (1979–1980) advised,

> Examination of malpractice is important both because of its potential usefulness in saving the skin (or pocketbook) of the social work educator, student, or practitioner and because of the seemingly obvious relationship of malpractice to questions related to competent social work practice. Because they are opposite sides of the same coin, to learn about malpractice is to learn about competent practice as well. (p. 40)

Today's social work practitioner should be armed with an understanding of how malpractice liability occurs, the process for establishing liability, and the parameters of competent practice as set forth by codes of ethics, standards, and the law (Besharov & Besharov, 1987; Houston & Northen, 1994). In this chapter, we set the stage for protecting against malpractice. First, we discuss various professional liability risks, including malpractice and negligence, other civil violations, criminal actions, professional regulatory violations, and ethical violations. Second, we identify how a social worker can understand and access pertinent laws and regulations. A summary follows.

PROFESSIONAL LIABILITY RISKS

Good social work practice encompasses thorough assessment, accurate diagnosis, clearly defined service planning with client participation and informed consent, individualized and differential treatment, ongoing evaluation of the service process, regular consultation and supervision, referral to competent and appropriate resources, and timely transfer or termination (Houston & Northen, 1994). The NASW Code of Ethics (1996) and professional standards, as well as agency policy and federal, state, and local regulations and laws, set guidelines to determine competent practice and legal grounds for malpractice. However, these multiple, and at times conflicting or ambiguous, regulations of professional behavior, along with consequent lack of clarity about competent professional practice, discipline, and ethics, contribute to a growing rate of negligent acts, errors, omissions, and gross misconduct among social workers (Houston & Northen, 1994).

Increasingly, social workers are confronted with situations in which the NASW Code of Ethics and professional standards conflict with laws, statutes, and agency policies or in which there are few or no standards or guidelines. Social workers must contend with a baffling array of rules of conduct. Multiple factors may bear on how professional actions are judged:

- professional regulations, licensing, and disciplinary requirements
- professional ethics and standards
- agency regulations and policies
- a social worker's own sense of how to perform as a professional
- cultural and community standards of care
- relevant civil and criminal law.

Hence, it is possible to simultaneously violate one or more laws, regulations, and ethical codes. Any event or circumstance might crosscut the categories of liability. For example, criminal charges may be determined to be unfounded, but a malpractice complaint or professional violation may be found with the same evidence. Moreover, if a social worker is accused of malpractice, it is likely that the plaintiff's attorney will file as many levels of charges as possible.

The various legal and regulatory systems are designed for different purposes. *Civil law,* which dictates how disputes between two parties are resolved, includes contract law, laws that regulate businesses and commercial transactions, landlord–tenant disputes, real property law, family law, and tort law. Central to understanding malpractice, *tort law* includes "private" crimes such as libel, slander, false arrest, and malpractice. "A *tort* is a wrongful action which harms another in some legally recognized way, such as physical injury, monetary loss, emotional trauma, or damage to the reputation" (Meyer, Landis, & Hays, 1988, p. 13). *Criminal law* involves offenses against the government with fines and imprisonment as penalties. *State licensing laws and regulations* specify professional qualifications and identify people eligible to use certain titles such as "clinical social worker." Generally, such laws define the scope of permissible practice and incorporate a code of ethics or similar behavioral guidelines. *Codes of ethics* and *practice standards* established by professional organizations define how their members are expected to conduct themselves and provide guidance for professional conduct and action.

Various regulatory systems and professional associations have systems that determine whether a social worker is performing in an unprofessional manner. These differ in three areas: (1) the procedures used to determine professional misconduct; (2) standards of proof; and (3) consequences, such as sanctions imposed by a professional association or damages awarded by a civil court. *Standards of proof* are levels of evidence necessary for a party to comply with his or her burden of proof. First is proof beyond a reasonable doubt (applicable only in criminal cases), which precludes every reasonable hypothesis except that which tends to support and is wholly consistent with a defendant's guilt and inconsistent with any other rational conclusion. Second is clear and convincing proof or a preponderance of evidence, which is positive, precise, and explicit evidence that directly establishes the point to which it is adduced. Third is evidence that is of greater weight or more convincing than the evidence offered in opposition to it (applicable in civil cases). A preponderance of evidence or clear and convincing proof is required in professional disciplinary hearings.

Several classes of professional liability can be identified and differentiated: malpractice or negligence, other civil violations, criminal liability, infractions of professional regulations, and ethical violations.

Malpractice or Negligence

SAM

Sam was a clinical social worker in an inpatient substance abuse unit. He was assigned to provide individual counseling to a married female client with a history of substance abuse and sexual acting out. During her 21-day stay in the inpatient unit, the client mentioned that she was very dissatisfied in her marriage. Also, she made obvious verbal and nonverbal sexual overtures to Sam; she frequently complimented him on his "bedroom eyes" and indicated that she thought they would have a great time together if they met socially. The client was later discharged from the inpatient unit and referred to a relapse prevention group led by Sam. The client asked Sam to have coffee with her after the group, and he accepted. After several weeks, Sam and the client began seeing each other on weekends and began a sexual relationship. Shortly after the client completed the relapse prevention program, her husband discovered that she was having affairs with several other men, and the client ended her relationship with Sam. To repair their marital relationship, the client and her husband began counseling with Mary, another clinical social worker. During counseling, the client confessed that she had had an affair with Sam. The client's husband was outraged, and Mary encouraged the couple to consider reporting Sam's behavior to the state professional regulatory board and to consult an attorney. The couple filed a malpractice suit for sexual misconduct and mismanagement of the service relationship.

Malpractice is "any professional misconduct, unreasonable lack of skill or fidelity in professional or fiduciary duties, evil practices, or illegal or immoral conduct" (Black, 1979, p. 864). Professional malpractice relates to negligence by a practitioner, who is required to perform in a manner consistent with how ordinary, reasonable, and prudent professionals would act under the same or similar circumstances within their profession (Cohen & Mariano, 1982; Gifis, 1991). A social worker may be potentially liable when a client is harmed because his or her performance did not meet the profession's standard of competence and conduct. Intentionally or unintentionally doing nothing or doing wrong may cause potential liability (Berlinger, 1989; Besharov & Besharov, 1987).

A malpractice suit is a tort law action. Tort law is determined by common (court) law rather than statutory law; therefore, the court determines whether a wrongful act involves tort liability and under what circumstances. Tort liability is determined by court precedents as well as court rulings. Because tort action does not include criminal liability, damages sought are monetary and are received as compensation for injury or harm. Torts are designed not only to indemnify plaintiffs but also to serve educational functions by disciplining negligent professionals and by stimulating responsible behavior by other professionals who may cause harm (Prosser, 1971).

Tort law includes two categories. An *intentional tort* involves a deliberate or voluntary action aimed to do that which the law has declared wrong. An *unintentional tort* involves negligence. *Negligence* is the careless failure to take reasonable and prudent measures to ensure that others are not harmed by one's actions (Bennett, Bryant, VandenBos, & Greenwood, 1990). Negligence includes not doing what one should have (omission) or doing something incorrectly (commission) (Stromberg et al., 1988). A social worker may be found liable for negligence, owing to ignorance in his or her professional role, that causes harm to a client (Bennett et al., 1990).

Most malpractice actions involve negligence or failure to meet a standard of care. From 1969 through 1995, 53 percent of all malpractice claims in the NASW-sponsored occurrence program were filed for incorrect treatment, sexual misconduct, breach of confidence or privacy, and suicide or attempted suicide of a client (NASW Insurance Trust & American Professional Agency, 1996).

The legal finding of negligence and an award of damages for malpractice require four elements (Prosser, 1971; Rothblatt & Leroy, 1973):

1. professional duty or obligation recognized by the law and requiring the professional to perform based on a particular standard of conduct, for example, the practice standard precluding sexual relations with a client
2. a dereliction of duty involving a failure to conform to the required standard, for example, a practitioner becomes sexually involved with a current or former client
3. measurable harm, loss, or damage of some kind to the client or significant others, for example, the sexually involved client attempts suicide
4. legal and proximate cause in which the damage must be a result of something that the defendant did or did not do, for example, a suicide attempt occurs following the client's chance meeting with the practitioner's spouse and children at a school function, which leads to a discussion during a service session of the practitioner's intent to remain in her marriage.

Professional Duty

Professional duty, or obligation, may be established explicitly or implicitly. An explicit duty of care occurs, for example, when a social worker establishes a working agreement, bills a client, or places his or her name in a client's record. A practitioner might implicitly establish a duty of care by providing counseling over the telephone or emergency back up for a colleague. If the person knows that the practitioner is a social worker and assumes that the practitioner has delivered professional services, the practitioner will have to prove that he or she did not establish professional duty. However, this may be difficult. For example, if a social worker lectures to a community group and speaks to a group member alone during a break, the practitioner may have established duty of care. If the person assumes that the practitioner has provided expert services, he or she will more than likely be found to have established a duty of care because the practitioner's actions spoke for themselves (Bennett et al., 1990). A social worker's initial contacts, including screening and intake, are key to establishing a duty of care (for further discussion, see Chapter 3).

Dereliction of Duty

Dereliction of duty, or failure to meet the standard of care, is more difficult to determine. Courts tend to determine a standard of care based on what a reasonable, average, and prudent professional of similar training and theoretical orientation would do in similar circumstances. If a social worker practices an approach not typically used in the profession, the courts tend to find it acceptable if a "respectable minority" of the profession uses the approach (Schutz, 1982).

In addition, how a practitioner advertises himself or herself and his or her experience and theoretical orientation is considered in establishing the standard. If a social worker professes to have special expertise, his or her professional actions will be judged by an elevated standard of care. Also, if a practitioner professes two sets of education and expertise (for example, hypnotist and social worker), he or she will be held to the standards of care in both areas (Woody, 1988).

Case law on standards of care differs across the country as to whether it uses acceptable or customary practices to determine the standard (Woody, 1988). Also, case precedents may influence what a social worker's professional duties are, as in the case of *Tarasoff v. Board of Regents of the University of California* (1976), which established a legal duty to warn potential victims when a client threatens harm.

Professional codes of ethics and practice standards and licensing regulations set forth minimum criteria of conduct by which a social work practice may be judged. Liability for malpractice may be established based on the grounds of failure to follow a professional ethical standard or practice regulation. Current professional literature and research also may be used to establish the standard and failure to conform. Moreover, malpractice charges may arise from failure to adhere to an administrative rule, state statute, policy or procedure, criminal law, or civil law. Increasingly, state laws are making sexual relationships between a clinician and client a crime. In these cases, the civil court may need only the fact that a practitioner has been found guilty to determine negligence. Also, if a practitioner's negligent or wrongful actions directly or indirectly contributed to another's erroneous decision, the practitioner may be found liable. Lack of knowledge of a rule as well as inadequate supervision or training are not sufficient defenses (Stromberg et al., 1988; Woody, 1988).

Proving that a practitioner breached the duty of care is the responsibility of the plaintiff–client. Some deviations are easily proven, for example, if the practitioner engages in a sexual relationship with a client or shares confidential information with a friend. However, when professionals disagree about the standard of care, it is more difficult to prove that the practitioner deviated from that standard. This is particularly the case when determining if a practitioner had a duty to warn a sexual partner of a client who is HIV positive and who has not informed that partner and continues to engage in risky behaviors (Reamer, 1994). (Duty to warn others about HIV-positive clients is discussed in Chapter 6.) Typically, a malpractice suit has not been upheld if the practitioner substantiates that he or she followed a reasonable standard of care. Reamer (1994) presented two perspectives of the standard of care in social work. The first view emphasizes the practitioner's professional duty in his or her actions or decisions, such as protecting third parties and confidentiality and seeking informed consent. The second view involves the following of procedures, processes, and steps in determining a course of action and making a controversial decision (for example, using reasonable and acceptable assessment guidelines, seeking supervision and consultation, and maintaining clear documentation).

Malpractice is proven based on a *fair preponderance of the evidence*, meaning that evidence presented by one party is somewhat more believable than that presented by the other party. The court will determine with at least a 51 percent (majority) certainty that evidence of one party is more convincing (Stromberg et al., 1988). The court will examine a client's clinical record to determine if a practitioner's actions were correct and performed according to the appropriate procedures and if he or she met the standard of care. Not having records or maintaining incomplete records deviates from the standard of care and may increase culpability. Clinical records can be a social work practitioner's best defense (Stromberg et al., 1988; Woody, 1988).

Measurable Harm

Measurable harm, loss, or damage can be placed in one of three categories:

1. An indisputable physical injury or death has either befallen or been inflicted by the client. If such damage [has occurred], the emphasis will shift to proving that the practitioner's actions [constituted] proximate and legal cause.
2. The injuries cited (for example, loss of wages . . . divorce) [are] consequent to the act in question. The plaintiff must show that these injuries were the result of behavior directed or caused by the [practitioner].
3. The injury claimed may be largely subjective, that is . . . the harm may consist primarily of mental effects on the client, commonly referred to as "pain and suffering." (Bennett et al., 1990, p. 40)

Of these three, pain and suffering is the most difficult to quantify. Courts tend to award the most monetary damages in these cases.

Legal and Proximate Cause

The plaintiff–client must prove legal and proximate cause of the harm, loss, or damage. Proximate cause involves three criteria:

1. Legal cause must be established. Unless the alleged negligence of the practitioner occurred, the client would not have been harmed.
2. The professional's actions must be proved to be "the direct and reasonably foreseeable cause" and the "primary cause" of the harm.
3. The client must prove that there was an unbroken chain of events (Bennett et al., 1990).

Moreover, the complaint must be filed within the statute of limitations (time limits), which varies from state to state. For adults, the statute of limitations begins at the point of discovery or realization of the harm. The time limit for minors to sue begins at the point they achieve majority age. Only competent clients can sue. If a client was incompetent at the time of the harm, the statute of limitations begins when competency resumes (Stromberg et al., 1988). However, attorneys can be very innovative in finding ways to extend the statute of limitations.

Other Civil Violations

Civil law encompasses, among other areas, both tort law, which includes but is not limited to malpractice, and contract law. The same situation may give rise to several types of legal action.

Nontort civil complaints may be made against a social worker who violates a civil statute, a regulatory code, a client's civil rights, or a contract.

Statutes that can be violated include procedures for release of client records, reporting requirements for mentally ill people judged dangerous to others, and requirements for client access to records. Civil rights violations are most likely to occur in residential, mental health, and correctional settings where situations that have the potential to violate a client's rights to privacy, to refuse medication and service, to receive service, and so forth may arise. A breach of contract may be established regardless of whether the contract is written, verbal, or implied. A promise about service may establish a warranty, or guarantee, that a client may invoke. It must be shown that service did not achieve its promised purposes (Stromberg et al., 1988). Also, a third-party payer may initiate a breach-of-contract suit if a practitioner agrees to require a copayment with an insurance company and fails to bill or attempt to bill a client.

Criminal Liability

GEORGE

George, a social worker in private practice, provided treatment to a 33-year-old woman who had been fired from her job as a teacher's aide. The client's depression and anorexia had sapped her energy and creativity in working with the children. The course of treatment was supplemented with informal, experiential events such as joint attendance at cultural events and weekend travel. Eventually, the social worker and client developed a sexual relationship, and service ended. A few months later, George told the client he did not want to continue their relationship. The client became very upset and pursued legal action. George faced criminal charges for engaging in a sexual relationship with a client (which was illegal in his state).

The consequences of being found guilty of breaking criminal law may include a practitioner's loss of liberty and a possible fine. In criminal cases, the judicial system is responsible for presenting evidence. The standard of proof is that the evidence must be *beyond a reasonable doubt*, the most stringent criteria of proof, meaning that those in judgment must have less than a trivial doubt that the practitioner is guilty. In some states, criminal charges can be brought for sexual misconduct or for other violations that might be civil violations in other states. The misdemeanor and felony statutes of violations also vary with the jurisdiction. In some cases, criminal charges are filed in addition to a malpractice suit. Defense of a criminal charge cannot be covered by professional liability insurance.

Infractions of Professional Regulations

JOHNSON & ASSOCIATES

Johnson & Associates is a group practice of five licensed clinical social workers. In addition, the group employs six individuals, who recently received MSW degrees, whom the group is supervising toward licensure. Because Johnson &

Associates also does a notable amount of pro bono work with homeless and battered women, the local school of social work has developed a field placement with the group. Hence, at least one social work student is present on a regular basis. Johnson & Associates advertises its practice as offering the services of "professional, fully licensed, experienced clinical social workers." The group reasons that this statement is true, because all nonlicensed clinical staff are carefully supervised by an LCSW. A client, who was a battered spouse, on learning that her therapist was not yet licensed, complained to her attorney, who recommended that she file a malpractice suit. The attorney advised the state professional regulatory agency that the practice misrepresented itself in its printed literature and then filed a malpractice suit alleging improper service.

There are several types of professional regulatory laws including title protection laws, practice regulation acts, registration laws, and certification codes. *Title protection laws* define who may use a professional title such as "clinical social worker," "certified social worker," or "registered social worker." *Practice regulation acts* define the services and activities of a profession. Most state professional regulation acts incorporate part or all of the provisions of a profession's code of ethics. Thus, a breach of the *NASW Code of Ethics* (1996) is likely to be simultaneously a violation of a state's professional regulations for social work.

The Disciplinary Action Reporting System (DARS) is in place through the American Association of State Social Work Boards (AASSWB). Currently, 42 states report social workers against whom disciplinary action has been taken, and this information is shared bimonthly with the other states. An annual subscription to DARS is available to other organizations from AASSWB (personal communication with Donna DeAngelis, Executive Director, AASSWB, January 26, 1996).

In the event of a complaint against a practitioner, the state board, department, or agency responsible for enforcing professional regulations reviews the complaint and determines if it is legally sufficient. Then, probable cause is determined by either a preponderance of the evidence or clear and convincing evidence. Disciplinary actions may include denying, suspending, or revoking a license; probation; requiring the professional to retake the licensure examination or receive supervision; or restricting practice. If the professional found guilty does not comply with the disciplinary action, he or she may be fined or jailed. (See Chapter 8 for recommendations on how to respond to disciplinary procedures.)

Ethical Problems

Professional ethics are rules reflecting the values and goals of the profession. The *NASW Code of Ethics* (1996) sets forth the ethical foundation of social work. On the other hand, *professional standards* are model responses or actions set forth by custom or an authority, such as NASW, which fulfill the intent of the ethical principles. Professional standards summarize or delineate procedures or actions necessary to perform at the level set forth by the standard (Bennett et al., 1990). NASW has developed several statements of professional practice standards, such as the *Standards for the Practice of*

Clinical Social Work (NASW, 1989) and *NASW Guidelines on the Private Practice of Clinical Social Work* (Robertson & Jackson, 1991), both of which are available from NASW state chapters or the national office.

Social workers are urged to request additional copies of the *NASW Code of Ethics*, a full set of standards, and a copy of the state professional regulations for social work to add to the reference material provided in this book. We recommend comparing the state professional regulations code with the *NASW Code of Ethics*, standards, and guidelines. Normally, they are not in opposition, and state codes typically incorporate the recognized professional code of ethics and relevant standards. However, should a conflict between state law and professional criteria surface, the practitioner should seek legal advice.

Ethical Dilemmas

Because ethics are framed as broad, abstract principles, they give rise to differing interpretations and, moreover, may clash with other directives originating in law, administrative policy, or even service goals. Ethical dilemmas identified by Reamer (1995a, 1995b), Corey, Corey, and Callanan (1993), and others that practitioners are likely to face include

- defining and maintaining professional boundaries with a client so the service relationship is cleanly separated from business, personal, social, and especially sexual domains
- fully informing a client of the policies of the provider's setting, clinician and client responsibilities, and service risks, even when such information could discourage the client from starting service
- conflicts between professional values and an organization's settings and policies that interfere with social work functions
- limits to confidentiality
- duty to report a potentially dangerous client, duty to warn and protect potential victims, and conflict over disclosure of HIV status to a client's partner
- competing rights of family members
- a client's need for and inadequacy or unavailability of resources
- a client's need for access to the practitioner versus the practitioner's legitimate need for personal privacy
- conflict between the duty to aid and personal attitudes and values around issues such as abortion, cocaine-addicted infants, and child abuse
- withholding of potentially traumatic information from some family members at the request of others
- a client's access to his or her clinical records
- bioethical issues concerning abortion, organ transplantation, end-of-life decisions, folk remedies, and non-Western practices
- termination versus retention in service of a client who defaults on fees or is noncompliant
- discharge of a client from the hospital or termination of service regardless of his or her needs.

Some ethical issues are addressed in state professional regulatory codes and rules. Regardless of their articulation in formal, legal policy, any of the above-mentioned ethical dilemmas could be occasion for a malpractice suit, as well as other civil suits and possibly criminal actions.

Ethical Violations

A complaint of an ethical violation can be made by anyone with knowledge of the alleged violation, and it may be made to the state professional regulatory agency or to one or more professional associations espousing the code of ethics that is believed to have been breached and under which a practitioner is responsible. When a violation is found by a state professional regulatory agency, several disciplinary actions may be taken, including revocation of the social worker's license. Allegations of ethical violations may also be reviewed by professional associations, and these may impose corrective actions and sanctions. For example, NASW has set forth procedures and criteria for addressing grievances and determining ethical violations. (Contact any NASW chapter or the national office to obtain a free copy of *NASW Procedures for the Adjudication of Grievances* [NASW, 1994].) Once a social worker is found in violation of the *Code of Ethics*, NASW may take two types of disciplinary action: corrective actions and sanctions. Typically, a combination of these actions is recommended.

Corrective actions are designed to restore or bring a social worker to an appropriate level of competence and ethical functioning. The social worker may be required to seek supervision or consultation, follow a course of study, correct a record, or provide restitution by returning fees. Rectifying activities may include giving a client access to records or correcting a biased letter, evaluation, or report.

Sanctions may include suspension or expulsion from NASW, notification of the state regulatory board, publication of the name of the sanctioned member in the *NASW News* or chapter newsletter, notification of the social worker's employer, and notification of other credentialing bodies. Typically, corrective actions are requested first. Maximum sanctions are determined in grievous cases or cases in which the social worker does not comply with the corrective measures.

The types of ethics complaints filed vary, with any one category representing a relatively small percentage of incidents filed. According to a study of trends in NASW's adjudication of ethics violations (Kaplan, 1993), of 300 sampled cases, the largest category involved sexual activity with a client. Other comparatively frequent alleged violations are

- dishonesty, fraud, deceit, and misrepresentation
- compromised professional discretion and impartial judgment
- relationships or commitments in conflict with client interest (dual relationships)
- inappropriate withdrawal of services.

One-third or more founded allegations were associated with the following complaints (Kaplan, 1993):

- not keeping current with emerging knowledge
- private conduct that compromised professional role
- not treating equitably clients seeking temporary or emergency service
- acceptance of responsibility beyond the social worker's competence
- sexual activity with a client
- exploitation of the professional relationship for personal gain or advantage

- not obtaining informed consent to tape, record, or observe
- not seeking appropriate consultation
- terminating services improperly
- accepting something of value for making a referral
- misrepresenting education, experience, affiliation, or qualifications.

UNDERSTANDING AND ACCESSING LAWS AND REGULATIONS

Three Scenarios

Unfortunately, there is no one definitive answer to the questions posed in the following three scenarios. The answers reside largely in state statutes and rules, as well as case law, all of which vary by jurisdiction.

Child Abuse and Neglect

School social workers are often faced with suspected child abuse and must report it. Increasingly, social workers are asked to testify in court. What constitutes abuse? What constitutes neglect? How, when, and to whom does one report? If the state child protective services is already involved, is further reporting in order? State laws and administrative regulations spell out child abuse (as well as adult and elder abuse) reporting requirements: who must report abuse or neglect, to whom abuse or neglect must be reported, how the report must be filed, who will investigate, and how soon investigation will take place.

School social workers should obtain copies of relevant state codes and rules and become familiar with them. Troublesome aspects of the codes and rules should be discussed with a supervisor and the school district's legal counsel. (See Chapter 6 for more information on child maltreatment.)

Client Depression

Social workers in private practice furnish a large volume of services to depressed clients, who may also evidence suicidality. When a client appears to be a danger to self but refuses to seek voluntary admission to a hospital, what steps can a practitioner take? How is involuntary hospitalization accomplished? What steps are required? Who must be involved and in what ways? Again, state law and administrative rules are guidelines for matters concerning involuntary commitment. Social workers should consult these laws and rules with an attorney for needed clarification. (See Chapter 6 for more information on suicide.)

Client Anger or Threats

Social workers in community-based mental health programs may encounter clients who divulge extreme anger toward other people and threaten to harm those individuals. Where does client confidentiality fit with a need to protect potential victims? What are the practitioner's responsibilities to the dangerous client as well as to those he or she is threatening? Most states have codified the duties to warn and protect and the limits of confidentiality when the safety of the client or others is at stake. These laws are often referred to as the *Tarasoff* principle or rule. Social workers must know these laws and consult a supervisor and legal counsel when the duty to warn and protect is at issue. (See Chapter 6 for more information on duty to warn.)

Legal Interpretation

Like all tort law, malpractice law has evolved largely as case law, that is, court rulings can be determined based on common or case law set forth by how other courts have made decisions or interpreted statutes or constitutional law. In malpractice cases, a judge can set a new precedent or create a new law (Hogan, 1979). Case law is ever changing, creating new forms of liability (Reamer, 1994).

Accountable and effective practitioners must know the codes of ethics and practice standards as well as the law, key court precedents, and derivative regulations that apply to clients and the parameters of social work practice. However, practitioners should not inadvertently slip into the practice of law on their own behalf. An attorney must be responsible for legal interpretation. In researching a legal issue, practitioners should first pose the legal questions to an attorney. In addition, practitioners should confer with experienced colleagues and consult with the local area offices of pertinent state agencies, where copies of germane statutes and regulatory codes can be obtained. For example, the local area office of a state mental health program can provide the state laws and administrative rules governing mental illness determinations, voluntary and involuntary hospitalization, and so forth. The local area office of a state child welfare program can provide the codes related to abuse reporting, investigations and child protective services, custody, foster care, and so forth. Copies of a state's licensure law and regulations are available from the state department charged with professional regulation of social workers.

Practitioners should read the *NASW News* and newsletters of other professional associations, which are increasingly discussing ethical issues and malpractice. Local reference librarians can point out a number of newsletters that review case law and suits germane to social work practice (for more information, see *Newsletters in Print, 1994–1995*).

In addition, practitioners are encouraged to talk with local colleagues and agencies and consult with attorneys to develop their own understanding of the legalities of a situation. Practitioners' personal knowledge will enrich what information an attorney and other sources provide, better prepare them for a conference with an attorney, and ensure that they have examined the issue fully. However, identifying applicable laws and regulations may be intimidating and baffling for those who have never done legal research. Appendix B clarifies the types of laws, regulations, and court opinions that bear upon social work practice and identifies the sources of laws, regulations, and court opinions, as well as important secondary sources of information.

BEFORE ESTABLISHING A PROFESSIONAL RELATIONSHIP

Incorporating suggestions of Bernstein (1981), Besharov (1985), Besharov and Besharov (1987), and Watkins and Watkins (1989), before a social worker establishes a professional relationship with a client, he or she must

- understand malpractice and professional liability
- be aware of potential problems and high-risk areas and take action to avoid exposure to liability
- be familiar with professional standards and rules and regulations that apply to social work practice and the profession, such as the *NASW Code of Ethics*
- know and adhere to written and implied agency policies and procedures
- understand and adhere to relevant federal, state, and local statutes and administrative regulations that bear on social work practice.

REFERENCES

Abramson, M. (1990). Keeping secrets: Social workers and AIDS. *Social Work, 35,* 169–174.

Barksdale, A. (1989). Child abuse reporting: A clinical dilemma. *Smith College Studies in Social Work, 59,* 170–182.

Bennett, B. E., Bryant, B. K., VandenBos, G. R., & Greenwood, A. (1990). *Professional liability and risk management.* Washington, DC: American Psychological Association.

Berlinger, A. K. (1989). Misconduct in social work practice. *Social Work, 34,* 69–72.

Bernstein, B. E. (1978). Malpractice: An ogre on the horizon. *Social Work, 23,* 106–112.

Bernstein, B. E. (1981). Malpractice: Future shock of the 1980s. *Social Casework, 62,* 175–181.

Besharov, D. J. (1985). *The vulnerable social worker: Liability for serving children and families.* Silver Spring, MD: National Association of Social Workers.

Besharov, D. J., & Besharov, S. (1987). Teaching about liability. *Social Work, 32,* 517–522.

Black, H. C. (1979). *Black's law dictionary* (5th ed.). St. Paul, MN: West.

Cohen, R. J., & Mariano, W. E. (1982). *Legal guidebook in mental health.* New York: Free Press.

Corey, G., Corey, M. S., & Callanan, P. (1993). *Issues and ethics in the helping professions* (4th ed.). Pacific Grove, CA: Brooks/Cole.

Fulero, S. (1988). *Tarasoff:* 10 years later. *Professional Psychology: Research and Practice, 19,* 184–190.

Gelman, S. R., & Wardell, P. J. (1988). Who's responsible? The field liability dilemma. *Journal of Social Work Education, 24,* 70–78.

Gifis, S. H. (1991). *Law dictionary* (3rd ed.). Hauppauge, NY: Barrons.

Green, S. L., & Hansen, J. C. (1989). Ethical dilemmas faced by family therapists. *Journal of Marital and Family Therapy, 15,* 149–158.

Hogan, D. B. (1979). *The regulation of psychotherapists: Vol. I-A. Study in the philosophy and practice of professional regulation.* Cambridge, MA: Ballinger.

Houston, M. K., & Northen, H. (1994, May). *Reducing malpractice risks: A framework for resolving ethical–legal dilemmas and enhancing clinical practice.* Paper presented at the meeting of the Second National Clinical Social Work Conference for the National Federation of Societies for Clinical Social Work, Washington, DC.

Jones, J. A., & Alcabes, A. (1989). Clients don't sue: The invulnerable social worker. *Social Casework, 70,* 414–420.

Kagle, J. D. (1984). Restoring the clinical record. *Social Work, 29,* 46–50.

Kaplan, K. O. (1993, October). *The adjudication trends study.* Washington, DC: National Association of Social Workers, National Center for Social Policy and Practice.

Kurzman, P. A. (1995). Professional liability. In R. L. Edwards (Ed.-in-Chief), *Encyclopedia of social work* (19th ed., Vol. 3, pp. 1921–1926). Washington, DC: NASW Press.

Kutchins, H. (1991). The fiduciary relationship: The legal basis for social workers' responsibility to clients. *Social Work, 32,* 106–113.

Kutchins, H., & Kirk, S. A. (1987). DSM-III and social work malpractice. *Social Work, 32,* 205–211.

Lamb, D. H., Clark, C., Drumheller, P., Frizzell, K., & Surrey, L. (1989). Applying *Tarasoff* to AIDS-related psychotherapy issues. *Professional Psychology: Research and Practice, 20,* 37–43.

Meyer, R. G., Landis, E. R., & Hays, J. R. (1988). *Law for the psychotherapist.* New York: W. W. Norton.

NASW Insurance Trust, & American Professional Agency. (1996). *NASW Insurance Trust Professional Liability Insurance Program: Claims experience—Individual policies. Occurrence form, 1969–1995.* Unpublished manuscript, Washington, DC.

National Association of Social Workers. (1989). *Standards for the practice of clinical social work* (rev. ed.). Silver Spring, MD: Author.

National Association of Social Workers. (1994). *NASW procedures for the adjudication of grievances* (3rd ed.). Washington, DC: Author.

National Association of Social Workers. (1996). *NASW code of ethics.* Washington, DC: Author.

Newsletters in Print. (1994–1995). Washington, DC: Gale Research.

Parry, J. (1987). Informed consent for whose benefit? *Social Casework, 62,* 537–542.

Perlman, G. L. (1988). Mastering the law of privileged communication: A guide for social workers. *Social Work, 33,* 425–429.

Prosser, W. L. (1971). *Handbook of the law of torts* (4th ed.). St. Paul, MN: West.

Reamer, F. G. (1987). Informed consent in social work. *Social Work, 32,* 425–429.

Reamer, F. G. (1991a). *AIDS and ethics.* New York: Columbia University Press.

Reamer, F. G. (1991b). AIDS, social work, and the "duty to protect." *Social Work, 36,* 56–60.

Reamer, F. G. (1994). *Social work malpractice and liability: Strategies for prevention.* New York: Columbia University Press.

Reamer, F. G. (1995a). Ethics and values. In R. L. Edwards (Ed.-in-Chief), *Encyclopedia of social work* (19th ed., Vol. 1, pp. 893–901). Washington, DC: NASW Press.

Reamer, F. G. (1995b). *Social work values and ethics.* New York: Columbia University Press.

Robertson, H. W., & Jackson, V. H. (1991). *NASW guidelines on the private practice of social work.* Washington, DC: NASW Press.

Rothblatt, H. B., & Leroy, D. H. (1973). Avoiding psychiatric malpractice. *California Western Law Review, 9,* 260–272.

Schutz, B. M. (1982). *Legal liability in psychotherapy.* San Francisco: Jossey-Bass.

Seelig, J. M. (1987). Legal and ethical issues for independent social workers. *Journal of Independent Social Work, 2,* 81–86.

Sharwell, G. R. (1979–1980). Learn 'em good: The threat of malpractice. *Journal of Social Welfare, 6,* 39–48.

Sharwell, G. R. (1982). Avoiding legal liability in the practice of school social work. *Social Work in Education, 5,* 17–25.

Stromberg, C., Haggarty, D. J., Leibenluft, R. F., McMillan, M. H., Mishkin, B., Rubin, B. L., & Trilling, H. R. (1988). *The psychologist's legal handbook.* Washington, DC: Council for National Register of Health Service Providers in Psychology.

Tarasoff v. Board of Regents of the University of California, 551 P.2d 334 (1976).

Watkins, S. A. (1989). Confidentiality and privileged communications: Legal dilemma for family therapists. *Social Work, 34,* 133–144.

Watkins, S. A., & Watkins, J. C. (1989). Negligent endangerment: Malpractice in the clinical context. *Journal of Independent Social Work, 3*(3), 35–50.

Weil, M., & Sanchez, E. (1983). The impact of the *Tarasoff* decision on clinical social work practice. *Social Service Review, 57,* 112–124.

Woody, R. H. (1988). *Fifty ways to avoid malpractice.* Sarasota, FL: Professional Resource Exchange.

2

PRIMARY PRINCIPLES OF MALPRACTICE PREVENTION

E very social work practitioner should implement good practice safe-guards and risk management strategies before problems surface. If specific steps are taken before the social worker–client engagement, vulnerability to malpractice claims can be greatly reduced. This chapter summarizes general procedures and preparatory risk management actions that can organize the practice setting at the administrative level.

As noted in Chapter 1, practitioners should be informed about relevant statutory and case law and professional regulations; administrative regulations; and applicable ethical codes. Additional safeguards, which can mitigate the risks of malpractice and ethical violations and also enhance services to clients, include

- understanding privacy, confidentiality, and privileged communication
- developing practice policies and procedures for dissemination to clients
- developing documentation and record-keeping systems.

UNDERSTANDING PRIVACY, CONFIDENTIALITY, AND PRIVILEGED COMMUNICATION

LINDA

Linda specializes in employee-related problems and is a pre-ferred provider for several self-insured businesses. A client who worked on an assembly line was referred to Linda for symptoms of stress and job burnout. During the sessions the client revealed that she had been addicted to cocaine. How-ever, since receiving treatment two years ago, the client had relapsed on only two occasions during a vacation. Linda reported to the client that she appeared to be depressed, did not discuss any other diagnoses, and treated her for depres-sion. Linda then sent the necessary information to receive reimbursement for services to the client's employer, who managed all of the insurance claims. However, after five weeks Linda still had not received any reimbursement, so she called the employer. The employer indicated that he needed to have more information about the severity of the employee's condition before determining eligibility for coverage. Linda then discussed the client's treatment and problems in greater detail and mentioned that the client had been treated for cocaine addiction and had relapsed only twice. Following the conversation with Linda, the employer fired the client on grounds of using drugs on the job. The client discovered that Linda had revealed information about her addiction and sued for breach of confidentiality and defamation of character.

The concepts of privacy, confidentiality, and privileged communication cause frequent conflicts among the mandates of professional ethics, laws, and agency policies. Practitioners can expect to confront dilemmas associated with these principles. A clear understanding of each can facilitate the resolution of such predicaments.

Privacy

Privacy, guaranteed by the Fourth and Ninth amendments to the U.S. Constitution, is understood to mean that an individual can determine what and how much of personal data, actions, beliefs, and attitudes will be made known to others. Schutz (1982) discussed actions that might violate a client's privacy, including

- telephone calls to a client's place of work identifying the caller as a therapist
- bills and correspondence sent to a client identifying the therapist in a manner that others might see
- nonessential staff members present during a client interview
- discussion of a client in a case conference or as part of a class discussion
- a waiting area or treatment room that does not protect a client's privacy
- support staff or other people with easy access to a client's records.

Discussing even complimentary client information can be an invasion of privacy if the client has not granted permission to do so (Schutz, 1982). Other ways to invade a client's right to privacy include publishing material about a client without his or her permission, discussing a client in public, revealing client information to the media, and using a client's name in advertising.

The work setting poses special concerns. Because employers are responsible for ensuring the safety of their employees, a client's employer may "need to know" about an employee who is potentially dangerous. However, except for compelling professional reasons, such as when the client has made a threat to harm someone in the work setting, a signed release of information form is necessary before talking with the employer (for more information on informed consent, see later in this chapter and Chapter 3). Also, issues related to confidentiality and privileged communication are relevant to maintaining a client's right to privacy.

Confidentiality

Confidentiality is "the obligation of a social worker or other professional not to reveal records of or communications from or about a client obtained in the course of practice" (Saltzman & Proch, 1990/1994, p. 392). This ethical principle is a cornerstone on which the therapeutic relationship is built, obliging professionals to protect information obtained from a client and not to disclose information obtained in the professional relationship. As stated in the *NASW Code of Ethics* (NASW, 1996; see Appendix A), "Social workers should respect clients' right to privacy . . . and should protect the confidentially of all information obtained in the course of professional service, except for compelling professional reasons."

The concept of confidentiality is broader than privileged communication and generally is a legal right authorized by the state and an ethical tenet mandated by the *NASW Code of Ethics.* Social workers maintain confidentiality except in certain compelling situations in which statutes or ethics permit breach of a client's confidentiality (Watkins, 1989). For example, some state statutes and case laws mandate a breach of confidentiality to protect people threatened by a client or a client who is a danger to himself or herself. Another exception requires or permits social workers to advise authorities of maltreatment of designated populations (for more information about these situations, see later in this chapter and Chapter 6).

It is important to clarify the legal limits of confidentiality and legal privilege with all parties concerned in a given service plan. However, confidentiality parameters are not always straightforward and can be conflicting. Practitioners may wrestle with the question, To what degree can confidentiality be preserved in this case? If a compelling professional reason to breach confidentiality arises, the social worker should be able to articulate a legal or ethical justification for the breach and keep careful records of the decision, how the decision was made, and with whom the practitioner conferred about the decision.

A confidentiality policy for a clinical practice setting should be made a part of the administrative or personnel policies. All support staff and professionals should sign an agreement to maintain client confidentiality, and this agreement may be indicated in the client information (Woody, 1988) (see Appendix C for a sample staff confidentiality policy). In addition to allaying client fears, a confidentiality policy heightens the awareness of all staff that client confidentiality is a responsibility with legal ramifications for violations.

Intentional Breach of Confidentiality

State laws and professional standards identify situations that allow or require intentional breach of confidentiality. The information released must be only that necessary to address the purpose of the inquiry. Depending on the circumstances and the requirements of state law, intentional breach of confidentiality might occur in the following examples:

- The client harmed or threatened to harm another person, including the practitioner or people close to the practitioner.
- The client is a danger to self.
- The client is a minor (the definition varies among states) and is a victim of a crime.
- Known or suspected maltreatment or exploitation of a child or legally protected adult has occurred.
- Certain information in the client's records is made available to others in a practice setting for the purposes of service, supervision, consultation, teaching, quality assurance, program evaluation, research, filing, or billing, with the client's informed consent.

- A client's records are released to referral sources, third-party payers, employee assistance programs (EAPs), and so forth with the client's informed consent.
- The practitioner's services are sought to assist the client with committing or planning to commit a crime.
- A court orders an evaluation or report, and the practitioner is appointed or retained to provide these services (however, only the records required to prove the case should be revealed).
- Breach of contract or duty is alleged by either the practitioner or client (for example, if the client sues for abandonment, and the practitioner counter-sues for uncollected fees).
- The client requests his or her records or grants informed consent for release of his or her file.
- The client's delinquent account with minimal information is turned over to small-claims court or to a collection agency (the client was informed of this possibility at the initiation of service) (Stromberg et al., 1988).

Confidentiality issues can be complicated for specific populations, including minors, elderly people, individuals with disabilities, and residents of institutions. Most states do not make a distinction between minors and adults when providing guidelines for confidentiality; all are entitled to privacy. However, state statutes do require breach of confidentiality with minors when they are a danger to self or others or a victim of a crime, maltreatment, or exploitation. Similar statutes apply to elderly people and, depending on the state, other vulnerable adults such as those with disabilities. All 50 states and U.S. territories except Puerto Rico have maltreatment reporting laws for elderly people. In most cases, reporting is mandatory for human services, health care, and law enforcement professionals (Elder Abuse Project, American Public Welfare Association, & National Association of State Units on Aging, 1986; Tatara, 1995).

Providing service to children without parental consent is controversial, but some states allow this practice. States typically specify the age and conditions under which a minor can consent to service. In situations in which a child's right to consent to treatment is not clearly established, practitioners should notify and involve the child's parents or legal guardian unless it is not in the best interest of the child and can be appropriately justified and documented. Regardless of whether parents consent to social work services, parents in many situations will have the right to inspect their child's service records unless the interests of the child will be harmed or the child is of sufficient maturity to make decisions about his or her own file. The situation is further complicated for a child whose parents are separated or divorced. Unless parental rights have been terminated, both parents generally have a right to information. This becomes complicated when one parent wants to release the clinical records as evidence in a child custody hearing but the other parent does not. Confidentiality in these situations may be set forth in family law. Practitioners should consult an attorney or the agency's counsel to help determine a state's family laws and should always inform the custodial parent of potential problems regarding information access.

Confidentiality issues can be complicated when providing social work services to couples, families, and groups. Practitioners should emphasize good clinical practice and should not participate in private conversations with any one member of a couple, family, or group about other members.

Stromberg et al. (1988) proposed that family members and couples sign a statement specifying who is authorized to release information. However, it is best to obtain signed releases of information from all clients in a family unit. In individual interaction with one member of a group, practitioners should focus on the individual's issues rather than those of other people or the group in general.

Clients with HIV/AIDS have additional confidentiality issues. States are struggling with legislation to protect HIV-tested patients' rights to confidentiality as well as the duty to protect others from possible threat of infection. More than half of the states have passed laws mandating warning partners of HIV-infected people (Landers, 1993). According to NASW's policy on HIV/AIDS, "practitioners and agencies may perceive a responsibility to warn third parties of their potential for infection if their spouses, other sexual partners, or partners in intravenous drug use are HIV infected and the partners refuse to warn them" (NASW, 1994, p. 24). Reamer (1991a, 1991b) suggested that social workers must aim to protect the rights of both HIV-positive clients and third parties by documenting how the social worker has dealt with a case, by knowing the laws specific to the reporting of sexually transmitted diseases and HIV infection, and by clarifying the limits of confidentiality verbally and in writing.

The decision to intentionally breach confidentiality must be based on an accurate assessment of all the facts surrounding a particular situation and the ability to articulate a statutory or ethical basis for the breach. Wherever feasible, if confidentiality must be breached, the client should be notified of the decision to release information and the basis for doing so.

Unintentional Breach of Confidentiality

Unintentional breach of confidentiality includes incidents in which the practitioner mentions a client's name in public, discusses a case with a friend or colleague, negligently leaves confidential papers in view, or does not dispose of confidential papers carefully. Modern technology has created new ways of accidentally breaching client confidentiality—for example, a computer screen with client data is left in view when the worker is out of the office, a conversation with a client is overheard on a mobile telephone, faxed material is received by the wrong person, or computer files are not protected by a password.

Electronic breach

Because information is generated, transmitted, and stored electronically, it is necessary to anticipate novel threats to confidentiality. If client records are maintained on a computer, the practitioner should provide for security with passwords and should remember to log off the computer when leaving the room. Files should be backed up diligently and the back-up tapes or disks secured.

Practitioners should ensure that the use of fax, electronic mail, and file transfers is carefully controlled when these means are used to send confidential client information. For example, the practitioner should call before sending a fax to make certain that the intended recipient personally receives the information. If possible, practitioners should have a fax machine dedicated to the transfer and receipt of client information. Faxed materials should carry a statement stipulating that the information is confidential and should not be received by or released to anyone other than the intended recipient. Reamer (1994) suggested the following message:

The documents accompanying this facsimile transmission contain confidential information. The information is intended only for the use of the individual(s) or entity(ies) named above. If you are not the intended recipient, you are advised that any disclosure, copying, distribution, or the taking of any action based on the contents of this information is prohibited. If you have received this facsimile in error, please notify us immediately by telephone at the above number to arrange for return of the original documents. (p. 62)

If analog systems that transmit conversations via radio frequencies are used, mobile telephone conversations can be scanned and overheard. Even with digital equipment that purports to be secure, practitioners should be sensitive to the surroundings when using a mobile telephone. People often talk on their telephones while shopping; eating in restaurants; or waiting in lines, reception rooms, and public transportation terminals. Practitioners should not conduct conversations with or about clients in any public place or in a private place in the presence of friends, family members, or professional colleagues.

Social workers should be sure to retrieve and erase without delay messages left on telephone answering machines at the office or home. Messages should not be replayed in the presence of others or in circumstances in which bystanders can listen. Practitioners should have separate telephone lines for clients who call them at home or in a home–office situation and should be the sole person with access to the answering machine. If a telephone answering service is used, office personnel should be trained in handling mental health clients and confidential material. Practitioners should use answering services trusted by other practice settings.

It is risky for practitioners to release clinical information over the telephone, even with a client's informed consent. However, in an emergency situation or utilization review, social workers should verify the telephone number and name of the person to whom they are speaking and document their effort to do so.

Inattentive conversations
Practitioners must be aware of inadvertent disclosures of confidential information to unauthorized people in the context of routine conversation. Although other professionals in the practice setting or in other settings are bound by the same ethical principles in relation to clients and although they are highly likely to respect confidential information, nevertheless, they do not have a legal duty to protect the confidentiality of another social worker's client if it is breached in their presence. Other nonprofessionals, including friends or family members, have neither the ethical commitment nor the legal duty to keep the client's confidences. Clients are within their rights to allege malpractice if a practitioner discloses their identities or details of their cases to colleagues or to anyone else without their informed consent, regardless of how low the risk of further damaging disclosure. Adhering to the following guidelines will reduce risk:

- Avoid gossip, story swapping, flippant remarks, banter, and other conversations with colleagues or significant others that implicate an individual, identifiable client.

- Do not discuss a client with supervisors or formally designated consultants unless in private settings, and avoid identifying the client by name when possible.
- Never discuss a client within the hearing of anyone not intended to receive the information (for example, in the office with the door ajar; in the waiting room of the practice setting; in hallways, elevators, or restrooms; and in any public environment). Even if a client's name is not stated, personal details may be sufficient for people to "put two and two together."
- Avoid using a client's name when with him or her and in the presence of others, especially in a populated waiting room. If the practitioner knows a client by sight, simply approach the person or signal and say, "Please come in." For a client's first visit, ask, for example, "Who is here to see Ms. Smith for a 3:00 appointment?"
- Be heedful of the physical environment. Even appropriate, private conversations with others about a client or a client session can be overheard in inadequately soundproofed rooms. A client may recognize another client in the parking lot, waiting room, or hallway. Although practitioners cannot always control situations in which unauthorized people recognize a client, they should inform the client about the risk and take steps to improve sound containment in the office or arrange for separate entry and exit doors that would minimize encounters.

Careless information handling

Just as client information can be disclosed inadvertently via electronic media, information can be made known through careless management of records and paperwork. A client's identity can become known to unauthorized people if telephone messages or the message book or appointment log kept by a secretary are accessible, especially to other clients, mail carriers, and product vendors. File cabinets containing confidential information should be locked and maintained with restricted access, and records kept in the office should not be easy to access on a desktop, or in an in-box or unlocked desk drawer. Confidential material to be destroyed should be properly shredded and not simply discarded in a trash can. Old records stored in a warehouse should be secure. In the event of a disaster (for example, fire, earthquake, flood, or hurricane), client records should be safe not only from destruction but also from the vantage point of confidentiality.

Practitioners should consider the consequences of misfortunes such as automobile accidents, disaster damage to the home, and simple household misadventures such as spills and encounters with small children and pets and therefore should never take client records home to work on them. In these situations, client records may be damaged, and others may have occasion to view them. Even in the absence of an accident, moving client records from one location to another increases the risk that they will be misplaced or lost and, as a result, accessible to others.

Privileged Communication

Privileged communication, or legal privilege, defines a client's right to restrict the social worker from revealing in a legal action information given in confidence (Saltzman & Proch, 1990/1994). The client is the holder of the privilege unless he or she is legally incompetent or is a minor; in such instances, the holder of privilege might be a parent, legal guardian, or conservator.

The law with respect to legal privilege is generally found in state statutes, usually as a component of the law that regulates the practice of clinical social work or the laws of evidence. In June 1996, the U.S. Supreme Court ruled in *Jaffee v. Redmond* that confidences in therapy between licensed social workers and their clients are protected from disclosure in federal courts: "The ruling extends to psychotherapists a federal rule that allows client communications to be 'privileged,' and it specifically extends that privilege to licensed social workers" ("Therapy Privilege Upheld," 1996, p. 7). Social workers should be informed about the law and should consult with an attorney about legal privilege issues if subpoenaed for confidential client records or information.

Responding to subpoenas and court orders requires special care. A social worker receiving a subpoena should first determine whether the client has provided a written release or waiver of privilege. A practitioner should indicate to the source of the subpoena that a signed release of information from the client or a court order may be necessary for the social worker to be able to produce the records lawfully or testify about client information. A practitioner who receives a court order may have to release the necessary client information and should contact an attorney. Austin, Moline, and Williams (1990) summarized the following guidelines for responding to subpoenas:

- In general, no information should be released unless the practitioner is authorized to do so in writing by the client, including information to the client's attorney.
- The social worker who does not know whether legal privilege has been waived by the client must claim the privilege to protect the client's confidentiality.
- Even a registered assistant or trainee should claim legal privilege, although the court might rule that unlicensed practitioners are not included.
- The practitioner must determine who served the subpoena and arrange for any witness and travel fees before going to court or giving a deposition.
- At a deposition, where there is no judge, the practitioner can have an attorney present or can review the issues with the client's attorney.
- The practitioner must appear at the location stated in the subpoena unless he or she can work out a reasonable alternative or there is a legal basis for providing the client's records and only the records are required.

If a client is involved or is likely to be involved in a court action, the practitioner should discuss the court's access to client records and requiring a deposition. Clients should be assured that if the practitioner or any person associated with the practice setting receives a subpoena for information, the client will be contacted immediately to discuss the situation and his or her willingness to release information. Lacking a signed release from a client, one course of action is to write a letter to the judge stating that the practitioner wishes to comply with the request but that the client has not waived legal privilege. In these instances, a court order may be issued to release the information (Stromberg et al., 1988). Practitioners should consult with an attorney to determine the appropriate course of action when responding to a court order because of the *Jaffe v. Redmond* decision that protects the confidentiality of therapy discussions.

Certain clients or their survivors are concerned about the disposition of sensitive information after the client's death. Some states transfer the right of waiving legal privilege to the designated next of kin or personal representative in the event of a client's death (Stromberg et al., 1988). In these cases the practitioner should consult with an attorney.

DEVELOPING PRACTICE POLICIES AND PROCEDURES FOR DISSEMINATION TO CLIENTS

MARTHA

Martha recently quit her job at a major medical facility and established a private practice. In the first few months of her practice, Martha treated a client who indicated that he desperately wanted Martha's services but had financial problems and could not pay the $25 copayment required by his insurance plan. In the initial contact, Martha told the client not to worry about the copayment; she had always been uncomfortable in negotiations about money and had no experience in setting client fees. During the next five months, Martha began to have financial problems because of unpaid client bills. She hired a financial adviser who suggested that she use a collection agency. The collection agency contacted the client regularly at his job and at home, leaving messages about his unpaid bills and reported his lack of payment to a credit agency. The client sued Martha for violation of his privacy and negligence in meeting the standard of informed consent.

Legal and ethical hazards can be reduced by educating clients about services and setting clearly defined policies. Clients have sued practitioners for

- not informing clients of the limits of confidentiality
- invasion of privacy for the use of collection agencies
- using undue influence or coercion to get clients into therapy
- false advertising
- making false promises
- negligence for practicing outside one's area of expertise.

For the most effective client education and orientation, practitioners should develop written documents that can be disseminated to and discussed with clients. The information should be sensitive to diverse languages, literacy levels, and eyesight capabilities and should be informative but not intimidating. Practitioners should arrange for translations; have items read by people of different ages and backgrounds; and have materials assessed by a professional who can help adjust the level of reading comprehension, aiming for a sixth-grade level at most.

The first step is to review existing policies and procedures and establish new ones as needed. The second step is to determine what aspects of these policies and procedures clients need to know. Some practice policies and procedures are general and lend themselves to a written format useful for all clients—for example, a client handbook or a brochure. Other client information applies selectively and may be unduly alarming if presented to new clients or to clients to whom the information does not apply, such as information about sexual impropriety or termination against professional advice. In these cases, letters or fact sheets can be distributed depending on a client's needs.

Setting policies and providing written information to clients serves a number of purposes essential for informed consent, including

- informing clients about the practitioner's credentials, areas of expertise, professional affiliations, and professional codes of ethics
- orienting clients to the practice setting
- discussing confidentiality, legal privilege, and release of information
- writing a working agreement and service contract
- informing clients of their rights
- explaining the boundaries of the service relationship
- obtaining consent to use client information for research
- preparing clients for emergency situations.

Some practitioners and settings rely on an oral orientation for clients; others rely on printed information and signed agreements. A combination of written material and thorough discussion and clarification is strongly recommended.

In developing client information and forms to document understandings, the goal is to reduce malpractice risks while avoiding discouraging clients with an overly legalistic, procedural impression of the practice setting. Information should be relayed during initial contacts and with sensitivity to the client's culture, mental state and receptivity. Clients in a crisis situation or a state of consuming mental or emotional preoccupation may be unable to receive or understand the information.

In addition to distributing client orientation information, several forms, signed by the client and in most cases the social worker, serve to further advise the client of his or her rights, responsibilities, and risks. These include

- working agreements—informed consents to initiate service and abide by the standard operating procedures of the setting
- fee agreements—information clarifying fees, billing, and collection methods
- service contracts—informed consents for individualized service plans
- informed consents to procedures related to audiotaping or videotaping or research activities
- releases of information.

Well-placed signs in the setting can reinforce client rights, codes of ethics, and policies concerning fees and cancelled and missed appointments. (See Appendix C for sample fact sheets and forms.)

Zuckerman and Guyett (1992) advocated a client brochure that explains therapy as a process, the practitioner's professional background and approach, risks and benefits of treatment, appointments, emergencies, financial matters, and confidentiality. In addition, they recommended a loose-leaf binder kept in the office waiting room containing an assortment of orientation and education materials that the client can browse through at his or her leisure. The binder should include exceptions to confidentiality; the inappropriateness of sex and other dual relationships in the service relationship; copies of forms a client might be asked to sign; and notifications the clinician might send if indicated, such as follow-ups of missed appointments or past-due account reminders.

If the practice setting can provide private viewing space, a videotape can help orient clients to the practice setting; the service process; and the roles, rights, and responsibilities of clients and clinicians. This approach can be especially helpful with children and any adults who have difficulty with reading. However, the videotape orientation should keep its content informational and focus on the policies and procedures of the setting; it should not demonstrate the service process or give clinical advice. Also, no one should be filmed, who has been in the past, is currently, or could become a client in the future or who works on the staff.

Many matters are too variable or complex to be stated adequately in a written handout or captured on videotape. Instead, they can be clarified by follow-up discussion in client sessions (see Chapter 3 for more information).

Practitioner Credentials, Areas of Expertise, Professional Affiliations, and Codes of Ethics

Clients have the right to know about practitioner credentials, areas of expertise, professional affiliations, and codes of ethics of the profession. In disseminating this information, practitioners should consider who the clients are and what they need to know. Materials should indicate degrees, licenses, other special credentials (for example, certifications and diplomates), and experience. Publications and professional memberships (and offices held) should also be listed. Practitioners should indicate that, because they are professional social workers, the NASW Code of Ethics (1996) applies to the practice. The code should be given to clients on request as well as posted in the waiting room. Information about civic, social, personal, or political achievements, characteristics, or commitments should not be included in the materials. If the setting is a training practicum site, the presence of graduate interns, their disciplines, and the supervision provided to them should be indicated as well.

Practitioners should accurately represent themselves and the practice setting and not exaggerate capacity or mislead clients to expect specialized skills or services that are not available. False advertising is grounds for a malpractice suit. If specialized expertise is claimed, higher standards will be applied in a lawsuit.

Practice Setting and Approach

Practitioners should describe the agency or practice setting, including the general mission or purpose, history, auspices and governance, funding, size (number of staff and clients served), organizational structure, and locations. The material should explain the types of clients served—for example, court-ordered clients, children, mentally ill individuals, substance abusers, families, people needing divorce mediation or custody evaluations, or clients from EAPs.

Practitioners should inform clients about the practice approach and nature of the services to help reduce clients' anxiety about beginning therapy and to engage clients in the therapeutic process. Based on the model or approach of the practice setting (for example, behavioral, solution focused, crisis intervention, short term, psychosocial, ecological, psychodynamic, cognitive, or a combination of approaches), practitioners should identify the general aims of service, describe the treatment process, indicate how goals are set, develop service plans, and evaluate client change and the practice process. Practitioners should clarify what is expected of clients, such as honesty and homework. A description of the models used and the services available (for example, group, family, couples, or individual therapy; child welfare services; custody evaluations; divorce mediation; forensic evaluations; elderly services; home-based services) is helpful. Practitioners should identify any special procedures such as audiotaping or videotaping sessions and explain how such tapes are used.

As appropriate, practitioners should indicate that the practice setting involves more than just being seen by a primary clinician. Clients are served indirectly by clinical supervisors, consultants, graduate interns, and staff assigned to monitor how things are done, ensure quality of care, evaluate the program, file records, and handle billing. Practitioners should assure clients that anyone associated with the setting who is authorized to gain access to confidential client information is as obligated as the primary clinician to preserve client privacy and protect confidentiality.

Confidentiality, Legal Privilege, and Release of Information

Written client materials should acknowledge the sensitive nature of information shared in a professional relationship and the legal and ethical codes that protect client confidentiality (see discussion earlier in this chapter). Practitioners should identify the steps involved in protecting client confidentiality as well as the circumstances in which there may be a breach of or waiving of confidentiality. The materials should emphasize that the client will normally have the opportunity to discuss intentional breaches of confidentiality and will be asked to sign a time-limited release of information form specific to each situation, except in emergency situations in which information is released as needed based on permission obtained at the initiation of service to cover such circumstances (see discussion later in this chapter). The materials should describe what happens to client information once a release is signed and indicate that a copy or description of what was released is placed in the client's files.

The written materials should state that client information must be released to third-party payers if the client is to receive a health benefit and should explain how and when this information will be used (for example, for continuity of care and utilization review). Clients should know that the information may be released during a telephone conversation with a utilization review worker. In addition, clients should be advised that EAPs require feedback from the practitioner. Clients should know of any existing computerized client database and its uses and their rights to inspect their own data (Caputo, 1991; Gruber, Meenaghan, & Caputo, 1984). Furthermore, the materials should state that in the client's interest the practitioner may ask for confidential information from other sources with the client's written consent. If possible, the client should collect the information and forward it to the practitioner.

In selected circumstances the law requires that information be released even without permission. The written materials should explain that client's privilege is waived for certain clients and should clarify the nature, content, and uses of the reports required by the court. Clients should be aware of their opportunity to review the reports (Stromberg et al., 1988). The materials should state that in some cases courts may subpoena or otherwise order client records or require a practitioner's deposition if a client is involved in court action. If it is likely that court proceedings will occur, practitioners should use a client session for a detailed discussion of how subpoenas and court orders are handled.

Furthermore, clients should be alerted to other limits of confidentiality and legal privilege, including the difficulties posed in couples, family, and group sessions and the limitations of confidentiality with minors and people who are legally incompetent. The risks to confidentiality posed by modern technology should be explained.

Minimally, a valid release of information form includes (see Appendix C for a sample form)

- name and professional title, auspices, or affiliation of the person or entity receiving the information and of the party releasing the information
- name and unique identifiers (for example, social security number, date of birth) of the client, including verification that the client is of legal age
- date of the release
- purpose for which the information may be used
- description of the type of information to be released, such as summary, diagnosis, service plan, and session notes
- notice that the information is not to be shared with anyone other than the individuals listed on the form and is not to be released to other agents without the client's written consent
- consequences of refusal to release records (for example, inability to proceed with a placement plan, loss of health benefits)
- length of time for which the release is valid
- indication that the client can revoke permission at any time and the steps for doing so
- the client's (or legally authorized other's) valid and legible signature, the date, and the signature of a witness (Stromberg et al., 1988).

Releases of information should always be examined by an attorney. Information should not be released in response to a request unless a completed release of information form is presented. Practitioners should respond to inappropriate requests and invalid releases by explaining that they are unable to cooperate in the absence of a valid release and then stating the requirements of a valid release (see Appendix C).

Working Agreement and Service Contract

Informed consent to service is a two-tiered process. Initially, clients must be oriented to the general and standard operating procedures of the setting. Next, practitioners should provide a mechanism—known as a "working agreement"—for clients to indicate their informed consent to initiate service under these conditions.

As soon as clinically feasible and in keeping with applicable managed care service plan requirements, individualized goals, objectives, and indicators of progress and outcomes should be established mutually and a service contract written and signed by both client and practitioner to document consent to the service plan. The practitioner should advise clients that they can review and amend the service contract at any time. (See Appendix C for samples of a working agreement and a service contract.)

Some practitioners argue that the use of contracts interferes with the helping relationship by limiting service to the stated goals and objectives and may also offend the client (Barker, 1986, 1992). Some attorneys argue that service contracts are actually only general commitments, not legally binding and not enforceable by law (Barker, 1992; Croxton, 1988). Those who agree with the use of contracts point out that the practitioner relationship is a fiduciary relationship built on trust (Kutchins, 1991). Contracts reinforce this trust and specify the obligations and terms of the relationship. "Private social work practitioners can significantly reduce their risk of legal problems with written contracts" (Barker, 1992, p. 118), because, in malpractice suits, written substantiation may be the best defense.

Fee Setting and Bill Collection

Fee setting and bill collection, sensitive and potentially volatile issues that involve a number of legal risks (see Chapter 4), should be addressed in the client materials. Also, a pleasantly stated office sign summarizing the setting's financial policy is useful.

Part of the service contract should be the client's written consent to a fee agreement that has been thoroughly discussed and agreed on. The fee agreement should state that the client should immediately advise the practitioner of difficulty with payment. The agreement should indicate that delinquent payment of fees will first involve efforts to resolve the payment problems but may lead to termination of services and collection efforts allowed by state law. Also, the client materials should state the setting's policies on forms of payment, third-party payments, sliding fee scales, charges for missed appointments, payment due expectations, consequences of nonpayment, bartering and pro bono work, and fee splitting.

Forms of payment
Does the setting accept cash, checks, money orders, or credit cards as forms of payment?

Third-party payments
Does the setting accept third-party payments, or are clients asked to pay first and await reimbursement from the insurance company? In the latter case, who bills the insurer? Because third-party payers require practitioners to release confidential client information to document eligibility, clients should sign an information release for this information.

Practitioners who have contracts with preferred provider organizations, health maintenance organizations, or managed care firms are obligated to fulfill certain billing requirements; these should be stated in the client materials. For example, the information should state that copayments cannot be waived and that the practitioner will comply with the payer's eligibility requirements, such as precertification, exclusions, and reimbursement procedures. Clients should know that third-party payers may limit service sessions. For a group practice, social workers should keep in mind that "signing off" (one professional signs the insurance forms as if he or she provided the service) is fraudulent. The fee structure for clients with or without insurance coverage should be the same.

Sliding fee scales

Has a sliding fee scale been established? What are the client criteria for the fee schedule and what documentation (for example, tax returns) is required to establish the criteria? Independent practitioners should weigh the costs and benefits of using a sliding fee schedule. It can invite bargaining and negotiating entanglements that can subvert arriving at a working agreement and can lead to continued struggles over fees as service progresses. In small agencies and independent practices, it may be advisable to set fees uniformly for all clients and occasionally make special arrangements, such as payment plans or pro bono work.

Charges for missed appointments

How does the practitioner charge for sessions that are delayed and thus shortened because of the client's late arrival? How does the practitioner charge for sessions that are due to the clinician's inability to start on time? Are missed appointments billed with or without notice? How much notice is necessary for a client to avoid being billed for a missed session? A client billed for a missed session should understand that the third-party payer may not reimburse a missed appointment and therefore he or she is responsible for the payment. (Practitioners should mark on the bill that the charge is for a missed appointment and not for services rendered.)

Payment due expectations

When are payments from clients expected? Is credit extended and clients billed later, or are clients to pay when services are rendered? The safest course of action is to expect payment at the end of every session and not let an unpaid balance accumulate. In addition, billing adds to service costs. Furthermore, mailing bills involves some risk to client privacy. A bill can be misdelivered or can come to the attention of others. However, if there is no bill, there should be a way to document contacts, services, charges, and payments so that clients have a record.

Consequences of nonpayment

What are the consequences of returned checks? Of unpaid accounts? Is service halted to the client with a delinquent account? How large must the unpaid balance be before service is stopped? Is a collection agency or a small-claims court used to collect payment? When are collection actions taken? Practitioners should decide carefully what steps will be taken to collect unpaid bills and state these procedures in a written policy. It is also wise to mention that a collection agency or a small-claims court may be used for delinquent accounts.

Practitioners should choose collection methods based on consideration of potential harm to the client and guarding confidentiality. First, practitioners should try gentle communications to collect outstanding payment, including written notes and oral reminders. If these methods fail, practitioners should weigh the risks and benefits of turning the account over to a collection agency or a small-claims court. Collection agencies can be aggressive and irritating. To the extent that payment default is often associated with client dissatisfaction, an unpleasant encounter with a collection agency might trigger an already piqued client to file a malpractice suit. The best course of action may be to write off the debt, the loss of which is minor compared to the potential costs of a malpractice suit.

Bartering and pro bono work
Practitioners should understand that bartering and pro bono work can increase malpractice risk because such arrangements can be ambiguous, can create a dual relationship, and can cause disputes. Bartering arrangements, particularly those involving services and not goods, create the potential for conflicts of interest; exploitation; and insufficient boundaries in the professional relationship, including allowing the client access to personal aspects of a practitioner's life. Other questions should be considered as well. How will equivalent payment be determined? Will a client's time be considered equal to the practitioner's time, or will a client be expected to complete work that is equal to the fee? How will a client's not completing the barter be handled?

As stated in the *NASW Guidelines on the Private Practice of Clinical Social Work* (Robertson & Jackson, 1991):

> Some social workers include in-kind exchange as an option for payment for services. These arrangements require careful thought and planning. It is essential that the arrangement not interfere with the therapeutic relationship between the social worker and the client and that it not put the client at risk for exploitation. In general, personal services arrangements (which inherently establish a parallel role relationship) are to be avoided. Alternative arrangements, in which services are essentially *pro bono* but an in-kind exchange allows for the maintenance of client self-esteem, are more acceptable. Similarly, an in-kind exchange for services may be more acceptable in communities that have a tradition of such practices. (pp. 11–12)

Most professionals and agencies provide pro bono services selectively. Because the number of clients experiencing financial constraints is likely to exceed the capacity of most practice settings to provide nonreimbursed services, guidelines for pro bono work should be developed. Without guidelines, clients whose service was terminated for delinquent bills can argue that they have been abandoned, possibly in a discriminatory manner. Practitioners should decide what client circumstances will be considered for pro bono services; how many pro bono sessions will be provided to a client; and how many pro bono clients or client hours can be sustained in, say, a fiscal quarter.

Fee splitting
In 1990, NASW revised the *Code of Ethics* to remove the concept of fee splitting. The *NASW Guidelines on the Private Practice of Clinical Social Work* (Robertson & Jackson, 1991) addressed key factors to consider when developing a policy for the division of income:

- The client should benefit from all parties with whom income derived from the client is shared. Examples of services include information, referral, treatment, problem solving, supervision and consultation, facilities, administrative support, and program activities.
- All parties should feel comfortable informing clients of the general framework of income distribution.
- Income distribution should take into account discrete, quantifiable costs for tangible services received such as office space, administrative services, and supervision and consultation.
- The arrangement should reflect a reasonable relationship between the amount paid and the value of the service received.
- The social worker should assess the potential influence of the income distribution plan on treatment decisions.

Fraudulent billing or "kickbacks" for referrals are never acceptable and may subject the offender to criminal liability.

Appointments and Length of Service

Clients need to know the length and frequency of service sessions and how long the therapy is expected to continue. Client materials should state that these details will be worked out individually and clarified at the beginning of the service contract.

Other arrangements lend themselves to standardized policies and procedures, such as cancellations, missed appointments, and late arrivals by clients. Is there a charge for appointments that are cancelled in less than 24 hours of their scheduled time? Are routine follow-up telephone calls made to determine the reason for unexcused absences? If the client is late, is he or she seen for the allotted time? If the practitioner is late, is the client seen for the allotted time, or is the appointment cut short? In this event, what reimbursement adjustments are made? It is good practice to post a sign in the waiting room explaining the policy for missed and cancelled appointments.

It is helpful to indicate whether clients may bring children or other family members to the waiting room while the session is taking place. In determining this policy, practitioners should consider space limitations, supervision and amenities for children, and the confidentiality of other clients. Also, practitioners should advise clients about parking arrangements and public transportation resources.

The practitioner's availability by telephone should be made known to clients. When and in what circumstances may a client have access to the practitioner in a professional capacity? Is telephone counseling conducted? If so, what is the fee?

Furthermore, the role of the third-party payer in determining the length of services should be specified in the client materials. It should be indicated that continuation of service beyond the practitioner's allowed limit of sessions may be determined by the client's ability to pay.

Risks and Benefits of Service

Clients should be aware that changes for both better and worse may lie ahead. Risks and benefits of service, along with consequences of refusing service, are clinically specific to each situation. Client information materials should describe the concept of risks and benefits of services in general.

Information might indicate that service can evoke difficult or painful emotions such as anxiety, anger, and guilt; can put stress on relationships; and can sometimes involve grappling with difficult life decisions. Materials should state clearly that service may not effect change as hoped and may contribute to additional problems, but they should also offer the assurance that counseling and psychotherapy have been found helpful in a long tradition of scientific research and that an individual would not be treated if the belief existed that he or she would not benefit. Furthermore, client information should indicate that part of service is its ongoing evaluation; without indication of positive progress, the course of service will be changed or service will be terminated. If one or more of the available strategies is used to evaluate the practice empirically (Bloom, Fischer, & Orme, 1995), the information should explain the procedures and emphasize that the process of data gathering and interpreting is shared with each client in determining progress and benefits of service.

In initial sessions with a client, the practitioner should thoroughly discuss and include in the service contract and working agreement the risks and benefits of service that apply to the client's case, along with service alternatives, the rationale for selecting the agreed-on approach, and the prognosis with and without service. This step is essential in obtaining informed consent to service (see Chapter 3). However, the practitioner should not promise a cure; an unfulfilled promise or a perceived disappointment can increase the risk of a malpractice suit.

Termination, Referral, and Follow-up

Woody (1988) proposed that a termination policy clarify when, why, and how termination should occur. The termination policy should emphasize the importance of a mutually agreed-on termination, based on the satisfactory completion of a service contract and attainment of service goals. However, recognizing that not all terminations are mutually agreed on, the client materials should also clarify both client and practitioner responsibilities at the end of service in a way that prevents abandoning the client during a time of need or crisis. For example, the materials might state that the client has a right to terminate service at any time; however, he or she should schedule at least one termination appointment. This is particularly important in families and groups in which other members might not wish to terminate or might need the opportunity for closure.

The client materials should clarify practitioner responsibilities in referring the client for further help or evaluation, including having the client sign a release of information, helping locate appropriate help, and following up to ensure the referral was satisfactory. Follow-up efforts must be planned and systematic. These efforts are evidence that the standard of care is being met.

The *NASW Guidelines on the Private Practice of Social Work* (Robertson & Jackson, 1991) can be used to set forth the conditions under which the practitioner is sanctioned to end the professional relationship without the client's agreement. For example, service to a client can be terminated for lack of payment if the client is not at risk or if appropriate services can be arranged. This group includes clients whose insurance becomes depleted or whose third-party payer sets limits on service sessions. However, in the latter case, if the social worker is convinced that continued service is needed, he or she is obliged to advocate for the client with the managed care firm.

Service to a client who harms or threatens to harm a practitioner or people close to the practitioner can be terminated; the practitioner should make an effort to secure alternative help for such clients. Service to a client who no longer needs service but is reluctant to say good-bye and a client who does not comply with the service contract by breaking or missing appointments or refusing to abide by an agreed-on service plan can be terminated as long as the involuntary termination does not place the client in jeopardy and the practitioner offers assistance in securing alternate services. If a client does not make progress or has needs that surpass the practice expertise or scope of services, the practitioner must help him or her find appropriate services and facilitate transfer accordingly. Likewise, termination of service and referral or transfer of a client must occur in the event that a conflict of interest or a dual relationship develops, unless it can be resolved quickly or, with the assistance of a supervisor and the input of the client, the conflict is determined to pose no foreseeable risk to the client (see discussion later in this chapter).

Appendix C contains suggestions for letters of understanding to clients for whom service was terminated under specified circumstances and also includes a sample referral form, along with a format for communicating with a managed care firm when a dispute exists over a decision to restrict further service. Chapter 5 examines practice guidelines and criteria for transfer, referral, and termination.

Client Rights

Client Bill of Rights

Many agencies and practices post a client bill of rights, and some reiterate these rights in written client materials. Zuckerman and Guyett (1992) presented a useful list of client rights, including the right to

- accept, refuse, stop, and return to service
- be treated with dignity and nondiscrimination regardless of gender, age, race, ethnicity, or culture
- have privacy and self-determination respected
- grieve or complain
- know the name of the practitioner's supervisor
- request access to one's clinical files.

(A sample client bill of rights is included in Appendix C.) The processes of signing the working agreement and releases of information should be clearly linked to these rights.

Client Grievances

Initial client information should include procedures for dealing with a client's dissatisfaction with the social worker's services or for handling client complaints. Clients should be encouraged to bring problems directly to the practitioner or, if this arrangement is unacceptable, to the supervisor. If the matter cannot be resolved, clients should be aware that they can request transfer to another practitioner or terminate and seek referral to another setting.

Social workers should consider providing information about state or NASW complaint procedures as a part of a general information notebook available to all clients. In this way, a client can refer to a full range of dispute resolution mechanisms. Under this circumstance, it is not necessary to give all of the complaint resolution information at the beginning of service.

Client Access to Files

As set forth in the *NASW Code of Ethics* (1996), clients should be provided reasonable access to their files, and due care should be taken to protect the confidences of others. Saltzman and Proch (1990/1994) noted that records can be considered the property of clients. Moreover, under the Freedom of Information Act (1974) and many state laws, records kept in public agencies are for the most part open to clients. However, securing clients' access to their records can be complicated. Cohen (1994) proposed that client access to records involves ethical, clinical, and legal considerations. When clients request their records, practitioners should consider the latent and manifest meanings of the request. Does the client want to read the record or be provided with a copy of it? Is the client communicating that he or she is dissatisfied and wants to file a lawsuit? Does the client fear or mistrust the practitioner? When does the client want to see the file? Is there an urgent need? Can the contents of the file be harmful to the client? Does the file include information about others and require a signed information release from the third parties?

Practitioners should seek legal counsel if the request for records is coupled with a threat of a lawsuit or anger toward the social worker or practice setting. Practitioners should use discretion and consult the supervisor before releasing a record to a client.

Written client materials should inform clients of how to gain access to their clinical records and include the state code on their rights of access to their files. Most states extend a doctrine of professional discretion if a client asks to see his or her record. In these jurisdictions, the professional can refuse to disclose the information when such disclosure would be detrimental to the client. Some state regulations or statutes may pre-empt professional discretion and give access to records to all clients. According to the Freedom of Information Act, if a person is served in a federal or other government-sponsored facility, the individual can request and read his or her psychiatric and medical records with responsible supervision (Cohen & Mariano, 1982; Saltzman & Proch, 1990/1994).

Practitioners who are legally able to deny clients access to their records and choose to do so should remember that the NASW *Standards for the Practice of Clinical Social Work* (1989) and the *NASW Code of Ethics* (1996) specify the client's right to see his or her records, with the social worker available to supervise and assist the client during the process. In a malpractice suit the practitioner could be challenged to defend why he or she invoked professional discretion and acted contrary to general professional ethics.

Also, the records must maintain the confidentiality of other people and collateral contacts such as family members. Client materials should state that portions of their records that would breach collateral confidentiality will be removed unless the third party grants a release of information. In addition, the materials should advise clients of the emotional risks in reading sensitive information in their records.

Boundaries of the Service Relationship

Dual and multiple relationships evolve when clinicians adopt additional roles in relation to a client: friend, employer, business partner, sexual partner, neighbor, teacher. Although sexual relationships with clients are off limits and well established as grounds for legal action, all dual or multiple relationships can compromise the therapeutic helping relationship, are potentially exploitative of the client, and are potentially unethical. Written client materials must emphasize the singular focus of the professional relationship and the reasons for it. Clients must know about the limits of the relationship; that the relationship is professional and fiduciary; and that although it is to be friendly and responsive, the relationship is not a friendship. The practitioner must emphasize that he or she is the client's social worker and nothing else.

A sexual relationship with a current client is never acceptable. Given the risks of sexual involvement in service relationships, the client materials should state clearly that sexual overtures by either client or practitioner are not tolerated. The information should indicate the immediate steps a client should take if sexually approached by a professional. In addition, practitioners should consider making available for selective use as a fact sheet a more detailed discussion of sex in the service relationship, such as the publication by the American Psychological Association's Committee on Women in Psychology (1989), *If Sex Enters into the Psychotherapy Relationship*.

Some examples of dual relationships are not straightforward and should be explained. For example, a client may decide to enroll in a school of social work where the practitioner is an adjunct faculty member teaching one course a year in supervision. Several other instructors also teach the course, which is an elective. The social worker, the client, and the supervisor all judge that the client's presence in the program will mean little or no additional involvement with the social worker and, if the client takes the course in supervision, he or she will have a wide choice of instructors. Agreement is reached that the client will not enroll in the class and that both the client and social worker will actively avoid contact with each other in the university setting. If the scenario were such that there were only one course and instructor, then duality and potential conflict of interest would exist. Could the social worker give a failing grade to the client, knowing that it would be devastating? Could the social worker address the failure objectively in treatment?

Written client materials should clarify logistics such as how to handle casual meetings when either practitioner or client is in the company of other people and introductions would normally be in order. For example, the information should state that it is common practice not to acknowledge knowing the client unless the client first acknowledges the social worker and that any conversation is minimal. The practitioner should emphasize that talk about the professional relationship is prohibited outside the practice setting (see Chapter 4 for further discussion of boundary issues).

Consent for Research

Increasingly with managed care, client data, including psychological and social-functioning scales and behavioral measures, are used to document individual service outcomes and, in aggregate form, to establish program effectiveness. The client materials should explain these procedures. Informed consent should be obtained for routine, administratively required practice and program evaluation uses of client data. Clients should be advised that if such data result in professional publications, only aggregate data without identification of individuals will be reported.

In some settings academic research is carried out using existing client information, typically in aggregate form with records identified only by code numbers. If code numbers cannot be linked with individual clients, informed consent to use client records for research is not required from human research participants in federally funded studies (45 C.F.R., §§46.101, 1991). If the data derived from clinical records could be linked with individual clients, informed consent to participate voluntarily is required.

If a federally funded research design called for access to clients for interviews or the completion of questionnaires or psychological tests, informed consent to participate voluntarily is required unless at least one of two conditions prevails: (1) participants are totally anonymous (that is, participants are impossible to identify directly or through codes linked to their identities) and (2) material from records is not of a sensitive or potentially damaging nature. In a practice setting it is safe to assume that most information, including the fact of the client's presence in the caseload, is sensitive.

Clients may be asked to complete anonymous questionnaires on a voluntary basis and, in so doing, provide implied consent. If self-administered questionnaires are not anonymous, then informed consent is indicated. If the research involves direct researcher–client contact facilitated by the social worker, then informed consent is required for the breach of confidentiality involved in releasing client information to the researchers.

Following federal law for the protection of human study participants (45 C.F.R., §§46.116, 1991), informed consent for research activities should include the following elements (see Appendix C for a sample consent form for research):

- the purpose of the research, expected duration of participation, and a description of procedures
- foreseeable risks, discomforts, or negative consequences of participation
- expected benefits of participation to the participants and others
- alternatives to participation that might benefit the participant (for example, in a study of residential service effectiveness, nonparticipants might have access to support groups and case management)
- confidentiality or anonymity assurances and any limits to their protection
- provisions for compensation or treatment in the event of harm or injury
- contact people available to respond to questions about the research, participants' rights, and complaints.

If the research is federally funded and involves non-anonymous, sensitive information, investigators may be obliged under requirements of federal law (45 C.F.R., §§46.101, 1991) to have the research procedures reviewed by a formally appointed body—an institutional review board (IRB). IRBs typically exist in universities, large hospitals, and other organizations engaged in funded research. Many researchers insist on seeking or are required by their employers to seek IRB review regardless of funding. IRB review provides additional protection for research participants. Social workers who agree to cooperate with an external research project that involves clients or client data or who are collaborating investigators should seek an IRB regardless of whether they are technically required to do so. In addition, a study may pose risks to the well-being of the participants, and an IRB can review the protocol to see how it affects human safety. Where problems are detected, the IRB will suggest remedies. Ultimately, the written approval of the IRB documents compliance with the stringent protection of human participation and informed consent measures of federal law.

Emergency Situations and Interruptions in Service

Practitioners

Both unanticipated and anticipated absences can be perceived as abandonment. Malpractice claims for abandonment tend to focus on negligence occasioned by not giving clients notice of pending absences and failing to provide professional "back up." The social worker should normalize absences by advising clients that occasional absences are to be expected, establishing general procedures, and providing back-up arrangements. When not available to the client, the practitioner should make explicit arrangements for competent coverage by a professional who is well informed about the client. Practitioners should ensure that clients understand the back-up procedure and the importance of their granting permission to share information so that another professional can effectively step in (see Appendix C for a sample information release form).

Clients

Practitioners should develop and disseminate in written form policies and procedures for client emergencies, including contacting the practitioner, receiving and returning messages, and receiving consultation and supervision. Client emergencies can be provided for in a variety of ways; some of these measures can be specified in written client information, whereas others are best discussed with clients on a case-by-case basis. General written information should

- assure clients that they may need, and should immediately seek, emergency services. Clients should know that the practitioner wants to hear from them when crises occur and should know what to do when the practitioner is not available.
- advise clients to sign an information release for other professionals, agencies, and hospitals, specifically for emergencies. Clients should know that a contact person will be notified if there is concern about the client's safety or well-being.

- provide a system for receiving emergency messages from clients, such as an answering service or machine. Clients should know how to use the message system. The system should be checked regularly; failure to respond in a timely manner could jeopardize a client and cause him or her to perceive abandonment.
- educate clinical staff, colleagues, and other back-up professionals to respond to client emergencies and clarify the procedures to follow in the event that the practitioner is unavailable.
- arrange for back-up assistance from colleagues with relevant professional expertise and credentials. Notify the back-up professional of any recognized fragile or at-risk clients in the caseload. With the client's permission, the professional should be familiar with the client's record and kept informed of the client's situation.
- provide clients with a secondary safety net in the event that they are unable to contact not only their clinician but also the back-up professional. Clients should have the names, addresses, and telephone numbers of available community mental health centers with crisis units, hospital emergency rooms, and crisis hotlines.
- clarify the contractual arrangements for emergencies and urgent situations when joining a provider network. Make certain the managed care organization has an adequate policy for providing for emergencies. Most managed care standards indicate that an urgent situation must be seen in three days, an emergency in 24 hours, and a regular appointment in one week. Clients should know their third-party payer's procedures for managing emergencies and urgent situations (Austin et al., 1990).

DEVELOPING DOCUMENTATION AND RECORD-KEEPING SYSTEMS

DAVID

David, a clinical social worker for more than 20 years, believed that keeping any kind of client records other than basic identifying data placed him at greater risk if he were sued for malpractice. Two years ago, David provided counseling to a family with problems related to their teenager, who had run away. The parents had revealed in family sessions that they were considering a divorce. After consulting with his supervisor, David indicated to the couple that he did not have sufficient expertise to treat them as a couple and felt that he should terminate service. The parents concurred, and he gave them three referrals. Recently, the wife filed a malpractice suit against David for abandonment and causing her divorce. David's supervisor moved out of state and could not be located. During his court testimony, David indicated that he could not remember all of the details of the issues addressed in service or the names of the three referrals. The wife's attorney argued that David's liability included lack of records and failure to follow a standard of care regarding termination and record keeping.

Client Records

Record keeping is a clinical, ethical, and legal activity that provides evidence of how the standard of care is met. Accurate and meaningful record keeping is essential to maintaining an ongoing assessment, formulating an accurate diagnosis and effective service plan, evaluating the service process, and determining future service. Documentation can help clients meet eligibility requirements for insurance reimbursements; can provide a means of communication in interdisciplinary practice; and can be a source of information for supervision, evaluation of service outcomes, and quality assurance. Clinical judgment is supported by documentation, and the lack of competent documentation will undermine a practitioner's legal defense.

> Recordkeeping is especially critical in situations that involve the potential for social worker liability or the possibility of involvement of other parties who may have a legal right to case information or who may need recorded information to assist the client. Special circumstances involve suicidal, homicidal, or violent clients; child abuse (especially sexual or physical abuse); family violence (including battering); elder abuse; sexual assault; divorce; child custody; supervision/consultation; and peer review or utilization review. (Robertson & Jackson, 1991, pp. 13–14)

Inaccurate, insufficient, or nonobjective documentation can lead to a variety of malpractice suits, including defamation of character, use of derogatory words, wrongful reporting, and liability for the actions of others who based their decisions on negligent or inaccurate assessment or record keeping. Poor documentation also can lead to client harm. Having no documentation does not protect practitioners from a lawsuit. Instead this places them in a vulnerable position because there is no evidence to support their professional actions or demonstrate their competence (Reamer, 1994; Stromberg et al., 1988; Woody, 1988).

The content of the records will vary by type of client, setting, and service approach. Records should reflect professional activity beginning with the first contact through the time of termination and follow-up. In general, records should include a core set of 10 items suggested by Robertson and Jackson (1991), which are supplemented below with malpractice risk management in mind:

- identifying information, including the client's name, address, telephone number, age, sex, ethnicity, and significant others
- professional assessment of the client, including diagnosis as appropriate
- dates of the client's visits
- the client's treatment plan, including objectives or goals, and the relationship of the plan to assessment and diagnosis
- the practitioner's treatment modality
- treatment interventions, including the rationale for selection of interventions in lieu of other alternatives
- treatment outcome
- referrals and collaborations
- fee information, including charges and payments

- closing note and letter to the client documenting reasons for termination.

In addition, the records should include copies of

- working agreement and service plan
- fee agreements
- signed informed consent and release of information forms
- risks and benefits expected from service
- prognosis with and without service
- client contact log and progress notes, including the substance of each session, new problems and needs that develop, interventions, referrals, and recommendations
- collateral contact log
- consultations and notes from supervision
- follow-up notations
- copies of all correspondence sent and received
- court documents.

Practitioners should develop a system for organizing records (Bennett, Bryant, VandenBos, & Greenwood, 1990; Kagle, 1991, 1993, 1995; Zuckerman & Guyett, 1992). If possible, practitioners should set aside time each day to do record keeping and record impressions while they are fresh. Practitioners should review records regularly and update new information that has influenced professional actions. However, practitioners should never alter earlier notes and recordings.

Basic Information and Assessment

Practitioners should develop or select an assessment and basic information form that fits each client situation. The form should include the service plan, goals and objectives, modality and service approach, responsibilities of other professionals, outcomes, and referrals. Practitioners should keep a record of each contact with a client, specifying date of session, types of services provided, significant actions taken, the client's response, and decisions made. Practitioners should also record casual contacts with clients and all contacts with consultants, supervisors, referral sources, other professionals, and the significant others of clients. Discussions with supervisors and consultants should include their recommendations (Kagle 1991, 1993, 1995; Woody, 1988).

In record keeping there is no place for prejudices, the use of derogatory words, moral judgments, subjective convictions, and countertransference issues. Practitioners should not record identifying information about people with whom the client has had illegal or illicit involvements and should curtail recording of a client's past illegal activities or other current incriminating information unless it is central to the present service effort. In record keeping practitioners should avoid any unnecessary detail and should not leave gaps or falsify information. They should separate facts, inferences, and hearsay. In hearsay the origin of the information, such as teacher or parent, should be noted.

In client records practitioners should make only substantiated conclusions. If enough information is not collected to verify the social worker's conclusions, records should include a statement such as, Symptoms are consistent with _____, but are not verified. Practitioners should record with a "third eye" (Cohen, 1994), maintaining records with a wider audience in mind, because many people in addition to the client may have authorized access to the information.

Some social workers advocate keeping separate files, one for formal objective information and the other for subjective and process information. The subjective records may place a practitioner at greater risk for malpractice because subjective impressions are difficult to defend. However, if client records are defined only in terms of formal, objective material to the exclusion of any professional impressions and subjective observations, the records may be judged inadequate and incomplete. Furthermore, they may be insufficient to justify and document professional judgments and decisions as service progresses. It is inadvisable to maintain secret notes that contain important but sensitive data regardless of their subjective or objective nature. Practitioners should write progress notes for family, individual, and group contacts on separate sheets. Doing so may help protect others' rights to confidentiality.

As noted earlier, practitioners should carefully record high-risk situations. Records should include data that substantiate practitioner conclusions and describe the rationale for the selection of the service approach and intervention, particularly with decisions to breach confidentiality, to warn or not warn third parties who may be harmed, and to seek or not seek involuntary hospitalization. Information about high-risk situations should include objective information, such as direct quotes from the client, others' interpretations of the client's behavior, and the practitioner's observations.

Financial Records

Financial records will vary based on the nature of the practice. An agency setting will have financial forms and collection procedures in place along with the expertise of a financial officer or accountants. In an independent practice the social worker will develop a fee-setting, billing, and financial accounting system with an accountant and, perhaps after considering the wide variety of computerized financial systems available, adopt an accounting program. Regardless of the accounting system in place, the main objective is to record client charges and fee payments regularly and accurately and to disseminate regularly to clients a summary of the transactions. Financial records should include any correspondence sent to third-party payers or reminders of unpaid balances. If third-party payments are accepted, complete information on the client's policy, including policy number, vendor, insurance administrator or managed care contact, and mental health benefits should be recorded (Stromberg et al., 1988).

Records Disposition

The length of time clinical records must be retained varies by practice setting and state law. A state licensure statute or the rules of the professional regulatory body might stipulate the minimum amount of time necessary to retain closed case records; practitioners may want to increase that minimum or elect to keep closed files indefinitely. When making that decision, practitioners should consider the statute of limitations (the legal time limit during which a lawsuit may be filed) for malpractice suits. In most states the time frame specified for malpractice begins at the time the aggrieved person realizes or discovers the error or omission and extends for at least two years. In alleged sexual misconduct cases, discovery may occur years after the alleged events occurred. Stromberg et al. (1988) recommended retaining full client records for 12 years for adults and 15 years after a child achieves the age of majority. Others have recommended keeping records in perpetuity ("Don't Throw Away Your Records Yet," 1993). The disposition of business and financial records is governed by federal and state laws.

Practitioners should not destroy a record at a client's request. If personal items submitted by a client have been retained by the practitioner as a part of the record, they should be returned if the client requests them. Practitioners should consult an attorney before destroying or transferring client records, particularly for

- disposition of client records in case of a social worker's death
- disposition of client records in case of a social worker's termination of practice
- disposition of client records in case of transfer or sale of a practice
- disposition of client records in case of a client's death
- disposition of client records when a minor reaches the age of majority
- the length of time to maintain records (Robertson & Jackson, 1991).

Those who decide to destroy client records should use a shredder.

Practitioners should secure both clinical and financial records by keeping them in a locked file cabinet, limiting access to as few individuals as possible, having client records stored in computers protected by a password, and locking computer disks in a cabinet (Robertson & Jackson, 1991). Security is not just a matter of precluding unauthorized access to records; practitioners should also provide for computer failures or system crashes, natural and human-made disasters, and crime.

Other Practice Documents

In addition to clinical and financial client records, three additional areas of documentation can assist in malpractice risk management:

1. client inquiries that do not result in a service contract and the initiation of service
2. practitioner credentials
3. internal policies and procedures in effect in the practice setting but not included in general client information.

Prospective Client Inquiries

Initial telephone and in-person discussions with clients who have sought services may uncover problems with potential dual relationships, client needs beyond the clinician's ability, or client inability or unwillingness to accept the policies of the practice setting. If contact with a prospective client results in a decision not to initiate service, practitioners should maintain a record of the inquiry, the decision not to treat and its rationale, and suggestions for alternative services offered to the individual. (See Chapter 3 for the importance of screening clients before establishing a service agreement and initiating service.)

In some cases the practitioner will agree to see a client, but the client will fail to keep the initial appointment. At this point, the practitioner has not established a professional duty to the prospective client. Nevertheless, it is good practice to make one nonpressured follow-up attempt to express interest in the client's well-being and to offer to reschedule the appointment (see Appendix C for a sample note to a client failing to keep the first appointment).

Practitioners should maintain these types of information with the same attention to confidentiality and for the same duration as applied to clinical records.

Professional Credentials and Development

Practitioners should maintain well-organized files of transcripts of degrees; background materials relating to professional licenses, certifications, and diplomates; continuing education activities; and any supervision and consultation. For supervision and consultation, the social worker and the supervisor or consultant should keep notes on their sessions, including dates, clients discussed (without identifying client information), and recommendations. Ideally, the supervisor or consultant should sign a confirmation of the session. A follow-up thank-you letter may be sent to the consultant. Although this is not the same as a confirmation, it can provide some evidence of what transpired.

Internal Policies and Procedures

The written policies and procedures of the practice setting vary with the type of organization. On the one hand, some areas of policy and procedure have little obvious bearing on malpractice risk reduction and management (for example, personnel policies governing benefits). On the other hand, having a well-considered written policy condemning sexual contact between staff and clients, censuring other dual relationships, forbidding fee splitting, clarifying a position on bartering for services and pro bono work, and detailing bill collection procedures is helpful in the event of a lawsuit. These policies can demonstrate the integrity of the practice and counter arguments that a client was singled out for unusual or capricious handling.

REFERENCES

American Psychological Association, Committee on Women in Psychology. (1989). *If sex enters into the psychotherapy relationship.* Washington, DC: Author. (Available from the Women's Programs Office, American Psychological Association, 750 First Street, NE, Washington, DC 20002-4242; 202-336-6044; e-mail: txb.apa@email.apa.org)

Austin, K. M., Moline, M. E., & Williams, G. T. (1990). *Confronting malpractice: Legal and ethical dilemmas in psychotherapy.* Newbury Park, CA: Sage Publications.

Barker, R. L. (1986). Spelling out the rules and goals. The worker–client contract. *Journal of Independent Social Work, 1,* 67–78.

Barker, R. L. (1992). *Social work in private practice* (2nd ed.). Washington, DC: NASW Press.

Bennett, B. E., Bryant, B. K., VandenBos, G. R., & Greenwood, A. (1990). *Professional liability and risk management.* Washington, DC: American Psychological Association.

Bloom, M., Fischer, J., & Orme, J. G. (1995). *Evaluating practice: Guidelines for the accountable professional* (2nd ed.). Boston: Allyn & Bacon.

Caputo, R. K. (1991). Managing information systems: An ethical frame-work and information needs matrix. *Administration in Social Work, 5,* 53–64.

Cohen, R. H. (1994, October). *Legal dimensions of clinical social work practice.* Paper presented at the NASW Annual Meeting, Nashville, TN.

Cohen, R. J., & Mariano, W. E. (1982). *Legal guidebook in mental health.* New York: Free Press.

Croxton, T. A. (1988). Caveats on contract. *Social Work, 33,* 169–172.

Don't throw away your records yet. (1993, July). *Mental Health Legal Review,* p. 1.

Elder Abuse Project, American Public Welfare Association, & National Association of State Units on Aging. (1986). *A comprehensive analysis of state policy and practice related to elder abuse.* Washington, DC: Authors.

Freedom of Information Act, P.L. 93-502, 88 Stat. 1561 (1974).

Gruber, M. L., Meenaghan, T., & Caputo, R. K. (1984). Information management. In F.P.D. Perlmutter (Ed.), *Human services at risk* (pp. 127–146). Lexington, MA: Lexington Books.

Kagle, J. D. (1991). *Social work records.* Belmont, CA: Wadsworth.

Kagle, J. D. (1993). Recordkeeping: Directions for the 1990s. *Social Work, 38,* 190–196.

Kagle, J. D. (1995). Recording. In R. L. Edwards (Ed.-in-Chief), *Encyclopedia of social work* (19th ed., Vol. 3, pp. 2027–2033). Washington, DC: NASW Press.

Kutchins, H. (1991). The fiduciary relationship: The legal basis for social workers' responsibility to clients. *Social Work, 36,* 106–113.

Landers, S. (1993, January). AIDS deepens duty to warn dilemma. *NASW News,* p. 3.

National Association of Social Workers. (1989). *Standards for the practice of clinical social work* (rev. ed.). Silver Spring, MD: Author.

National Association of Social Workers. (1994). AIDS/HIV. In *Social work speaks: NASW policy statements* (3rd ed., pp. 19–26). Washington, DC: Author.

National Association of Social Workers. (1996). *NASW code of ethics.* Washington, DC: Author.

Protection of Human Subjects, Part 46. (1991). 45 C.F.R., §§46.101, 46.116.

Reamer, F. G. (1991a). *AIDS and ethics.* New York: Columbia University Press.

Reamer, F. G. (1991b). AIDS, social work, and the "duty to protect." *Social Work, 36,* 56–60.

Reamer, F. G. (1994). *Social work malpractice and liability: Strategies for prevention.* New York: Columbia University Press.

Robertson, H. W., & Jackson, V. H. (1991). *NASW guidelines on the private practice of clinical social work.* Washington, DC: NASW Press.

Saltzman, A., & Proch, K. (1994). *Law and social work practice.* Chicago: Nelson-Hall. (Original work published in 1990)

Schutz, B. M. (1982). *Legal liability in psychotherapy.* San Francisco: Jossey-Bass.

Stromberg, C., Haggarty, D. J., Leibenluft, R. F., McMillan, M. H., Mishkin, B., Rubin, B. L., & Trilling, H. R. (1988). *The psychologist's legal handbook.* Washington, DC: Council for National Register of Health Service Providers in Psychology.

Tatara, T. (1995). Elder abuse. In R. L. Edwards (Ed.-in-Chief), *Encyclopedia of social work* (19th ed., Vol. 1, pp. 834–841). Washington, DC: NASW Press.

Therapy privilege upheld. (1996, July). *NASW News,* p. 7.

Watkins, S. A. (1989). Confidentiality and privileged communications: Legal dilemma for family therapists. *Social Work, 34,* 133–144.

Woody, R. H. (1988). *Fifty ways to avoid malpractice.* Sarasota, FL: Professional Resource Exchange.

Zuckerman, E. L., & Guyett, I.P.R. (1992). *The paper office 1* (rev. ed.). Pittsburgh: Clinician's Toolbox.

CHAPTER

3

BEGINNING SERVICE

During the beginning phase of service, the practitioner identifies the client's needs, orients the client to the practice setting and sets expectations, begins a psychosocial assessment and formulates a diagnosis, and plans a course of service. The beginning phase of service provides the practitioner with many opportunities to clarify conditions that could lead to a malpractice suit, including the risks and benefits of service, alternative approaches to service, confidentiality and legal privilege, fees and bill collection, and the rights and responsibilities of being a client.

Jones and Alcabes (1989) found that nearly half of all social work malpractice claims were made by clients who had not been adequately acquainted with the norms of being a client. Besharov (1985) further substantiated the importance of socializing clients to service and securing their informed consent to the service plan. The malpractice risks most evident in the beginning phase of service are a practitioner's failure to

- adequately screen the client for service
- adequately orient the client to the assessment and service process
- secure an adequate working agreement, service contract, and release of information
- make an adequate assessment or diagnosis
- formulate a service plan consistent with the assessment and diagnosis (Houston & Northen, 1994).

This chapter discusses four key factors of malpractice risk:

1. client screening
2. informed consent
3. assessment and differential diagnosis
4. service planning.

CLIENT SCREENING

JULIE

Julie recently quit her job as a health care social worker and started a private practice. A client called asking for help dealing with her abusive husband. During the conversation, Julie counseled the client, exploring the dynamics of the husband–wife relationship. The client related that she was isolated and depressed and afraid of her husband. Julie encouraged the client to "stand up for herself" and scheduled an appointment for the next week. However, several days later, Julie realized that she had booked another client for that time and left a message on the woman's answering machine canceling the appointment and rescheduling it for the same time the following week. During the interim, the client murdered her husband and attempted suicide. The client later filed a malpractice suit alleging abandonment because of the appointment cancellation and incorrect treatment because Julie advised her to "stand up for herself."

As set forth in NASW's *Standards for the Practice of Clinical Social Work* (1989), the client's well-being is paramount in the practice process. Thus, beginning with the first contact with a prospective client, practitioners should take steps to protect the client's welfare while also reducing exposure to malpractice allegations. Before accepting a client, practitioners should consider three questions:

1. Can the client's request be responded to in a timely manner given the urgency of the client's need?
2. Does the social worker have the expertise necessary to work with the client?
3. Does the client meet the criteria for services?

Practitioners who answer no to any of these questions must be prepared to refer the client to another agency staff member or to a professional in another setting.

In many settings a prospective client seeking services will have contact first with a receptionist or secretary. Support staff must be skilled in understanding incoming referrals, maintaining client confidentiality and privacy, dealing with urgent requests, and recognizing and handling potential emergencies. Optimally, social workers return prospective clients' calls (recording name, address, and telephone number) and schedule first appointments themselves. This arrangement provides an opportunity to determine the urgency of each client's needs and whether the client will be at risk if he or she must wait to see the practitioner.

During the first contact with a potential client, practitioners should determine why the client is seeking services and offer information about skills and credentials, the practice setting, general service approaches, fees and payment plans, and office hours (see Chapter 2 and Appendix C for more information about client materials). Practitioners who provide more than factual information and begin the counseling process during this initial conversation have accepted the client and have established a duty to provide professional services, placing them at risk for malpractice until they screen the prospective client in person.

During initial contacts practitioners should determine if the client has any special needs and whether they have the skills, knowledge, and resources to serve the client. For example, can the practitioner speak the client's language fluently? Is the practitioner knowledgeable about and comfortable with the client's culture and value system? If the situation seems to warrant family or group therapy, is the practitioner competent to provide it?

Practitioners must determine if accepting a client will pose any conflict of interest or create a dual relationship. For example, is the practitioner likely to enter into a student–teacher association with the client in the future? Is the client a resident of the same neighborhood and therefore likely to be encountered in local shops or during social or community events? Is there an existing professional, business, or social relationship or other association with the client's family members or significant others? Has there been a past professional, business, social, sexual, or other personal relationship with the client? (Bennett, Bryant, VandenBos, & Greenwood, 1990).

In the event of a dual relationship, the practitioner must end the initial meeting with the prospective client after a candid discussion of the concerns about preserving the integrity and singularity of the service relationship, carefully document the decision to do so, and provide a referral to an appropriate service provider. However, avoiding dual relationships is not always realistic in certain situations such as in small communities. If the possibility of a dual relationship cannot be circumvented, the practitioner should discuss the issues thoroughly with the prospective client and possibly the supervisor and then carefully document the discussion, the mutual decision to initiate the service relationship, and the rationale for doing so (Bennett et al., 1990) (see Chapter 4 for more information on dual relationships).

If the practitioner determines that he or she cannot meet the needs of the prospective client or that the client does not qualify for the practitioner's services, the practitioner should take steps to protect the person's well-being. The practitioner should explain why the client cannot be accepted and then provide several referrals who can offer the needed services and expertise, based on the urgency of the client's need. Hence, practitioners should be knowledgeable about other professional human services providers and community services and refer to competent and appropriately licensed and certified professionals (see Chapter 5 for guidelines on making appropriate referrals). A practitioner can be found liable for referring a client to an incompetent professional if it can be determined that the practitioner should have known the reputation of incompetence (Reamer, 1994).

Practitioners who are members of a managed care provider network should carefully explain to the client the steps to obtain service set forth by the provider. For example, the client may be required to return to his or her primary caregiver for a new referral.

In addition, practitioners should maintain a confidential filing system for inquiries for service and referrals, retaining files for the same time period as clinical treatment records.

INFORMED CONSENT

EVA

Eva, a private practitioner and play therapy specialist in a group practice, had been seeing a six-year-old in play therapy for several months. When the client's mother signed the consent for service, she indicated that she did not want her estranged husband to know about the help her son was receiving (the couple was involved in divorce proceedings). In the second month of service, the child refused to see his father and when he did, was aggressive toward his father.

The father discovered Eva was seeing the child and filed a malpractice suit alleging service without parental consent.

Informed consent to service proceeds at two levels. First, informed consent is based on the client's clear understanding of the services provided, including practitioner credentials and experience, the nature of the services provided and the practice setting, confidentiality and legal privilege, the length and frequency of sessions, fees and bill collection, arrangements for missed appointments, provisions for crisis situations and practitioner absences, and the boundaries of the client–practitioner relationship (Barker, 1992; NASW, 1989; Reamer, 1987; Schutz, 1982). Second, informed consent to service must reflect the client's comprehension of his or her individual service plan, the risks and benefits of service, alternatives to service, anticipated length of service, and prognosis without service (Barker, 1992; Kagle, 1984; Reamer, 1994).

It is important to clarify the difference between the working agreement and the service contract. Both are contracts that are accepted by the practitioner and the client, and both reflect the client's informed consent to service. However, the service contract, which is the individualized service plan, cannot precede a period of assessment and goal setting, which are done after the working agreement is completed.

Underpinning informed consent are the ethical principles of fostering client self-determination and participation. Informed consent is intended to guarantee the client's freedom, privacy, and safety (Parry, 1981; Reamer, 1987, 1995; Wilson, 1978). The basic standard for informed consent is what a reasonable client would need to know to make an informed decision. Practitioners should determine for each client what is reasonable and should avoid providing too much information or using excessively technical or legal language. As well, information should be presented with consideration to the client's culture and unique needs.

Malpractice allegations related to informed consent to service can stem from the social worker's failure to discuss the limits of confidentiality, including the

- duty to warn others to protect them from harm
- compromises that occur when a client is seen in a group or family
- legal requirement to report abuse and neglect of children, elderly people, and other vulnerable adults
- possibility of court orders for records or depositions
- requirements of managed care utilization review.

Malpractice allegations also can occur when there is a breach of confidentiality, with the practitioner giving information to staff, colleagues, supervisors, consultants, evaluators, interns, and agencies without the client's consent.

In general, valid informed consent must meet the following standards:

- The client must be competent and have the capacity to give consent.
- Consent should be given voluntarily and without undue influence.
- Consent should be based on a clear understanding of the nature of the services, including specific interventions and procedures and

awareness of the right to withdraw or refuse consent at any time (Reamer, 1987).

The practitioner should obtain informed consent by finalizing a working agreement before beginning assessment and service. However, this may not always be possible. For example, in a life-threatening emergency, the practitioner's duty to treat the client can precede the requirement for informed consent. The practitioner's actions will be guided by the client and the situation.

Four steps are involved in obtaining informed consent:

1. determining client competence
2. providing service information
3. ensuring client understanding
4. documenting informed consent.

Determining Client Competence

The assessment of client competence is basic to the determination of ability to give informed consent for service. Competent clients understand the procedures to which they are agreeing, both in the abstract and concretely as they apply to them in the present. However, there is little agreement about what constitutes competency. Most state laws and statutes use criteria to define competence based on mental illness, mental retardation, age, and physical condition. "Despite the unsettled debate about determining competence, practitioners seem to agree that incompetence should not be presumed absolutely for any particular client group, such as children, the mentally ill, or mentally retarded, except for those who are unconscious" (Reamer, 1987, p. 426). Reamer also proposed the use of minimal standards, such as the mental status examination, history of mental illness, ability to make reasoned judgments and comprehend abstract ideas, and remote and recent memory.

Social workers must know the laws when working with minors or people who are unable to give voluntary informed consent. Treating children without parental consent in some states is permissible. Typically, the age and conditions under which a minor can consent to service are specified by law. Some states allow minors to give informed consent to services for pregnancy, abortion, sexual assault, birth control, and drug and alcohol abuse, whereas other states mandate parental consent for all services to minors.

It is prudent to contact and involve the parent or legal guardian unless the situation expressly dictates against doing so and the reasons can be documented. With respect to legal cases about the rights of minors and their involuntary commitment to mental institutions, courts recently have ruled that the interests of the child and parent are inextricably linked. Therefore, minors have the constitutional right to have a neutral fact finder decide whether the parent or guardian may commit the child to a state mental institution.

Divorce and child custody cases require particular vigilance and knowledge of state laws. Unless parental rights have been terminated, each parent has the right to waive confidentiality and consent to the service of their child regardless of which parent has custody (see Chapter 2). Practitioners should discuss these rights with both parents before beginning service with their child and clarify the social worker's role and who is being served. If the parents are in litigation, the practitioner should establish rules about whether he or she will testify as an expert witness for one or the other or only testify objectively with a court order or should seek to have the parents agree before service that neither will attempt to elicit testimony or subpoena records.

Providing Service Information

As set forth in the *NASW Code of Ethics* (1996; see Appendix A), "Social workers should use clear and understandable language to inform clients of the purpose of the services, risks related to the services, limits to services because of the requirements of a third-party payer, relevant costs, reasonable alternatives, clients' right to refuse or withdraw consent, and the time frame covered by the consent." Practitioners use a variety of methods to explain services to clients and obtain informed consent; some use written material, others verbally present the necessary information, and some use a combination of both. Clients should be provided with written information—a handbook, brochure, or set of fact sheets (see Chapter 2)—that discusses

- practitioner credentials, areas of expertise, professional affiliations, and professional codes of ethics
- the nature of the practice setting and service approach
- confidentiality, legal privilege, and release of information
- fee setting and bill collection; appointments and length of service; risks and benefits of service; and termination, referral, and follow-up
- client rights, including a client bill of rights, client grievance procedures, and client access to files
- boundaries of the service relationship
- consent for research
- practitioner and client absences and emergencies.

In addition to the general points that apply to all clients, issues particular to specific clients should be addressed in the orientation. For example, if the client expresses discomfort with the back-up and emergency procedures, the practitioner should examine these feelings and reactions. If the client has financial constraints and raises the possibility of bartering services, the practitioner should clarify the setting's bartering policy.

Family and group members should be oriented to the terms of their participation; the purpose of the sessions; the expectations about sharing information; and the differences between individual, family, and group service. This discussion should examine the complex confidentiality issues surrounding couples, family, and group service.

In a multimodality approach (seeing the client in a group, individually, and with his or her family), the practitioner should clarify the purpose of each and the relationships among individual, group, and family sessions and discuss the risks and benefits of each modality.

If applicable, practitioners should discuss the rights of custodial or noncustodial parents to obtain access to their child's records and waive confidentiality. Service to minors whose custodial parents disagree about consent to service and releases of information requires an attorney's consideration. Similarly, practitioners should discuss the rights of a guardian or family member of an adult who is not considered legally competent, or other legally authorized person to access client records and waive confidentiality.

Ensuring Client Understanding

Simply providing written materials and having clients sign a form stating that they understand the contents and agree to service is insufficient for obtaining informed consent; clients must also demonstrate understanding of the information provided (Barker, 1992; Reamer, 1987). Written material must be in a language and format and at a reading level that clients can understand and discuss. In addition, both the verbal and written information should be presented and discussed with cultural sensitivity. Cultural groups may differ in their beliefs and responses related to consent, self-determination, and autonomy. For example, some groups may find direct communication offensive. Others might be suspicious of written agreements and materials. Some cultural groups may appear to be compliant based on the value of deferring to authority and not on a clear understanding of their choices. Other groups might expect information to be provided in an egalitarian and noncondescending manner (Reamer, 1994).

After the client is provided with written information, the practitioner should follow up with a detailed discussion, making certain that the client understands the content and documenting in the client's records the discussion and the clarification of any points about which the client indicates lack of understanding or agreement. The discussion should refer to the areas delineated in the client materials and should address all key areas (Hofling, 1981; Kagle, 1984; Reamer, 1987; Schutz, 1982; Simon, 1982; Watkins, 1989; Watkins & Watkins, 1989).

After discussing the service information, the practitioner should give the client the opportunity to ask questions and demonstrate his or her understanding of the information by reiterating key areas. A number of strategies can be used to ensure that the client reads the written material. The practitioner can give or mail the material to the client before the first meeting or discuss the information and give the material to the client to take home after the first meeting.

Documenting Informed Consent

Once the decision is made to accept a client and the client is apprised of the details of the practice setting, the practitioner and client enter into a contractual agreement to embark on the processes of assessment and service. One way to document informed consent is the working agreement, which is intended to reflect the client's understanding of roles, rights, and responsibilities and should include the statement that the client understands the orientation material (see Chapter 2). The working agreement should be signed by everyone seeking service, including couples, families, members of a group, and children who have achieved the "age of reason" and who accept the invitation to participate in the formal consent process. Woody (1988) suggested a contract that states, "The professional shall exercise his or her learned judgment about what will be the preferred treatment for the best interests of the client, and the client shall make a good-faith effort to fulfill the treatment recommendations and to make payment of service in a timely fashion" (p. 120).

ASSESSMENT AND DIAGNOSIS

MANUEL

Manuel, a clinical social worker in a private for-profit hospital with both psychiatric and substance abuse service programs, completed an intake form on a patient who presented himself at the emergency room. The chief presenting problem was clearly polydrug abuse, which required hospitalization, and there was indication that the patient may have used drugs in part to cope with situational depression. The patient's insurance did not cover substance abuse service but did provide for inpatient psychiatric care. The patient was very motivated, and payment was the only obstacle. Manuel was faced with a dilemma: He could record drug abuse, knowing that the client would not be authorized for hospitalization, or he could record a diagnosis emphasizing depression that would lead to an authorized hospitalization. Manuel weighed the benefits of getting the client into inpatient care as the preferred course of treatment against the risks of misdiagnosis for himself and the client. Manuel recorded a diagnosis of depression, and the patient was hospitalized. Because the hospital did not immediately recognize the patient's symptoms of physical drug withdrawal, they were not properly addressed. After discharge from the hospital, the patient sued Manuel for misdiagnosis.

Competent practice is predicated upon an accurate, differential, multi-dimensional, and individualized assessment (Houston & Northen, 1994; Northen, 1995). The ongoing process of assessment is guided by the practice setting's purpose, functions, and policies and, above all, the client's needs. "In accordance with the value of the right to privacy, [assessment] should be limited to what is essential to achieving agreed-upon goals" (Northen, 1995, p. 81). However, certain areas of assessment that social workers are legally and ethically responsible to identify, report, and act on may appear to violate the client's rights to privacy; self-determination; confidentiality; and in an era of restricted services, access to needed service (Houston & Northen, 1994; Northen, 1995).

Malpractice claims may be made against practitioners for improper diagnosis because of conscious distortion aimed at protecting the client or at accessing services or because of clinical error. Grounds for a lawsuit may include the practitioner's failure to

- make an accurate diagnosis of mental disorders and substance abuse when these are a possibility
- assess accurately the environmental situation, such as the suitability of a family or residential setting for the placement of a child or adult with disabilities

- consider biological factors that influence psychosocial functioning
- refer a client to a physician for a medical diagnosis when indicated
- consider physiological factors, such as response to substance abuse or medication
- gather or read collateral information or records of past history and service
- make a diagnosis
- make an accurate diagnosis, leading to harm or inappropriate service or fraudulent reporting to insurance companies
- use objective professional language in assessment and diagnostic reports, leading to charges of defamation of character
- identify, document, report, or warn of potential dangerousness and violence to self or others.

A variety of assessment and prediction risks occur with clients who are potentially dangerous to self or others; victims or perpetrators of child, spouse, or elder abuse; incompetent; or gravely disabled. The crisis situations involving such clients are discussed in Chapter 6.

A number of social work authors and commentators on the topic of malpractice (Alexander, 1983; Besharov & Besharov, 1987; Kirk & Kutchins, 1988; Kutchins & Kirk, 1987; Watkins & Watkins, 1989) have warned that misdiagnosis is a major litigation threat. "In reviewing the literature on psychiatric malpractice as it applies to psychotherapy, faulty diagnosis and inappropriate treatment are foremost among the potential dangers" (Bernstein, 1978, p. 108).

Misdiagnosis, both underdiagnosis and overdiagnosis, is encouraged by contemporary practices of third-party payers, managed care corporations, and employee assistance programs. On the one hand, clinicians are increasingly concerned about the guarantee of confidentiality when reporting diagnoses for insurance reimbursement and to government agencies. In some instances, insurance forms are not processed with confidentiality as a priority, and employers and other staff may gain access to the practitioner's assessment. Jobs and reputations can be endangered when clinically sensitive information leaks to coworkers and supervisors. Sharfstein, Towery, and Milowe (1980) and Kirk and Kutchins (1988) reported that studies of the use of mental health benefits indicated the diagnostic information submitted on insurance claims forms is often inaccurate and concluded that legitimate concerns about client confidentiality influence practitioners' decisions to submit inaccurate information. On the other hand, practitioners may increase the severity of the diagnosis so the client can qualify for services or third-party reimbursement (Kutchins & Kirk, 1987; Sharfstein et al., 1980; Watkins & Watkins, 1989).

However, not all misdiagnosis is strategic; at times misdiagnosis reflects the questionable competency or judgment of practitioners. In an analysis of social work malpractice claims, Alexander (1983) found that half of the claims related to misdiagnosis involved presentation of psychiatric symptoms with underlying physical conditions that required medical service and that were missed by mental health practitioners. If an inappropriate or inadequate diagnosis harms a client, the practitioner can be held professionally liable and be found to be practicing medicine without a license (Alexander, 1983; Besharov & Besharov, 1987; Watkins & Watkins, 1989).

Furthermore, practitioners who are not attuned to the side effects of medications or to the physiological risks of substance abuse and withdrawal are also at risk for a malpractice claim. For example, practitioners should know that elderly clients may be taking a variety of medications that can interact, causing symptoms of mental illness. In addition, given the increased number of substance-abusing clients, practitioners must be able to inquire skillfully about substance use and identify clues to physiological dependence on and withdrawal from alcohol and other drugs that could lead to life-endangering conditions.

Kutchins and Kirk (1987) recommended the following procedures to help practitioners maintain ethically and legally sound practice and diagnosis with appropriate referrals to physicians:

- Make all diagnoses with scrupulous regard for correct procedures.
- Report every diagnosis accurately to the client and insurer.
- Give careful attention to organic conditions.
- Routinely consult a physician about the medical aspects of a diagnosis.
- Refer clients to physicians for the evaluation of a suspected or apparent medical condition.
- Advise clients, preferably in writing, that a diagnosis is not meant to indicate a definitive judgment about any physical condition.

SERVICE PLANNING

SANDY

Sandy, who works for a youth services program providing counseling to high-risk adolescents, was seeing a 13-year-old client who was referred by a local minister because of family problems. The client had many strengths, including A grades and participation in school activities. In the initial interview, it was evident that family counseling was the preferred choice of service. Because Sandy strongly believes that all family members must be present to provide successful family counseling, she will not provide family counseling if one family member refuses to attend. The client and her mother were very eager to start family counseling; however, the father and another sibling emphatically refused. Sandy decided she would not see the mother and client conjointly and decided to see the client in a group for youths at high risk for dropping out of school. Sandy used the same "fast food" service plan for all the group members. After two months of attending the group, the client began to act out at school and joined a gang with one of the members in the group. The client's parents sued Sandy for incorrect service.

Service planning is the bridge between assessment and intervention. Planning, a mutual endeavor between the client and practitioner, is influenced by setting parameters (for example, policies and procedures regarding length and type of service) and is predicated on the practitioner's professional judgment as to the

- needs and problems of the client that will become the focus of treatment
- goals for successful outcomes and an evaluation plan

- service means to be undertaken, such as the modalities or unit of attention, service structure, number and types of providers, and length of treatment (Northen, 1985).

The service plan and resulting service contract reflect the decisions that a practitioner makes based on client participation, professional judgment, and the parameters set forth by the practice setting.

The service contract should include the risks and benefits of service, alternatives to service, rationale for choosing a particular approach, and prognosis with and without service. The exploration of the risks and benefits of service will be individualized for each client. Clients should know that change is not easy and may involve recalling uncomfortable or sad memories or experiencing anger and grief. As well, clients may decide to undergo major life changes such as divorce. Clinical risks such as regression, psychosomatic conditions, dysfunctional periods, and transference are more difficult to describe. Clients should understand that often the prognosis without service is difficult to determine, because many unforeseen life factors can affect the course of a problem.

Service contracts must be kept current. If new problems and issues develop or the course of service changes, the service contract, and, if applicable, the working agreement should be revised. Even without changes in the service protocol, the service contract should be renewed at regular intervals, at least every 90 days.

Typically, malpractice risks evident in the planning process are related to

- promising and then failing to cure
- not clarifying the risks and benefits of service
- providing negligent service
- not developing a mutually agreed-on or individualized service plan in which the objectives and planned interventions fit the assessment and instead developing a practitioner- or insurance-driven plan that does not meet the client's needs
- not developing a plan for evaluating the outcome of the intervention.

Explaining Risks and Benefits of Service

During the planning, contracting, and informed consent processes, practitioners should clarify alternative approaches to and risks and benefits of service. Malpractice suits for breach of contract and failure to cure have been successful if the practitioner has made a promise to cure, guaranteed the results, promised a specific level of success, or agreed to a plan that the practitioner could not or would not implement. However, courts have tended to rule that the practitioner's opinion that the service is likely to help is not an enforceable promise (reassurance is not contractual) (Stromberg et al., 1988). Practitioners should not withhold information about potential service risks (Stromberg et al., 1988).

Meeting the Standard of Care

Negligent service can occur if appropriate professional judgment is not exercised when service duration, modality, or approach is determined. Given the pressure of time and a setting's demands, practitioners may use the same fast food service plan for a category of clients. If this plan does not reflect the client's individual needs, the assessment, and what is done in service, the practitioner may be found liable for both breach of contract and negligent practice because he or she did not meet an appropriate standard of care.

In addition, negligent service can occur when the practitioner is not appropriately trained or selects the wrong approach based on poor professional judgment (that is, the practitioner's judgment deviates from what a reasonable, prudent practitioner would do in similar circumstances) (see Chapter 4). Practitioners should not implement a service plan with an approach or modality for which they are not properly trained; instead, practitioners should refer the client to another qualified service provider.

Developing a Client-Driven Plan

A client-driven plan is built upon the social worker's understanding of the client's individual needs and respect for the differences related to age, gender, sexual orientation, race, ethnicity, and differential abilities. Practitioners should not select an approach or modality or determine duration of service because it is convenient, represents a favorite approach, or meets the third-party payer's requirements. Doing so could place the practitioner at risk for a malpractice suit because the plan does not reflect responsible professional judgment. Also, practitioners should not allow idealistic, purist, and unrealistic beliefs to interfere with providing the necessary care (for example, refusing to use a family approach unless all family members participate).

In today's world of managed care, practitioners are struggling with requirements and protocols that do not sufficiently match client problems or needs. Third-party payers are increasingly limiting the duration of service and dictating the modality and approach. Practitioners should not respond to these limits by committing fraud (for example, writing an individual service plan and then providing family service). Instead, a number of strategies can be used. To respond to a limit on the number of sessions, practitioners can provide episodic services, seeing the client for a specified number of sessions and developing a plan for when and how the client returns later for additional services. If the managed care organization denies the necessary number of sessions or appropriate modality, practitioners can act as advocates for the client by appealing the decision, documenting that the necessary and appropriate plan of intervention, based on professional judgment, is not congruent with the provider's decision. If the appeal is denied, practitioners can consider service alternatives such as a referral to a less-expensive provider.

Evaluating Outcome

Increasingly, the social work standard of care includes evaluating client outcome. Practice evaluation tells both practitioner and client if the service is working. Practitioners who do not develop a plan for evaluation might continue services beyond the point they are needed or might provide incorrect service. A regular review of goals and objectives and systematic evaluation of the practice with the client and supervisor can enhance effectiveness, ensure client participation, justify to the provider the need for continued services, and reduce malpractice risks. Practitioners should formulate measurable service goals and objectives, select an appropriate single-system design and evaluation measures (for example, rapid assessment instruments, self-anchored rating scales, behavioral indicators measured with structured client logs or clinician ratings), administer the measures, and chart and review progress.

BEGINNING SERVICE

The beginning phase of service is dynamic. Clients are likely to be uncomfortable and in pain, and their expectations are high and sometimes unrealistic. Mistakes by the practitioner at this stage can cause a sharp client reaction. Clinical social work, practiced competently and ethically, is in its essence a form of risk management.

REFERENCES

Alexander, C. A. (1983, November). *Professional liability insurance: Jeopardy and ethics.* Paper presented at the NASW Professional Symposium, Washington, DC.

Barker, R. (1992). *Social work in private practice* (2nd ed.). Washington, DC: NASW Press.

Bennett, B. E., Bryant, B. K., VandenBos, G. R., & Greenwood, A. (1990). *Professional liability and risk management.* Washington, DC: American Psychological Association.

Bernstein, B. E. (1978). Malpractice: An ogre on the horizon. *Social Work, 23,* 106–112.

Besharov, D. J. (1985). *The vulnerable social worker: Liability for serving children and families.* Silver Spring, MD: National Association of Social Workers.

Besharov, D. J., & Besharov, S. (1987). Teaching about liability. *Social Work, 32,* 517–522.

Hofling, C. K. (1981). *Law and ethics in the practice of psychiatry.* New York: Brunner/Mazel.

Houston, M. K., & Northen, H. (1994, May). *Reducing malpractice risks: A framework for resolving ethical–legal dilemmas and enhancing clinical practice.* Paper presented at the Second National Clinical Social Work Conference for the National Federation of Societies for Clinical Social Work, Washington, DC.

Jones, J. A., & Alcabes, A. (1989). Clients don't sue: The invulnerable social worker. *Social Casework, 70,* 414–420.

Kagle, J. D. (1984). Restoring the clinical record. *Social Work, 29,* 46–50.

Kirk, S. A., & Kutchins, H. (1988). Deliberate misdiagnosis in mental health practice. *Social Service Review, 62,* 225–237.

Kutchins, H., & Kirk, S. A. (1987). DSM-III and social work malpractice. *Social Work, 32,* 205–211.

National Association of Social Workers. (1989). *Standards for the practice of clinical social work* (rev. ed.). Silver Spring, MD: Author.

National Association of Social Workers. (1996). *NASW code of ethics.* Washington, DC: Author.

Northen, H. (1995). *Clinical social work knowledge and skills* (2nd ed.). New York: Columbia University Press.

Parry, J. (1981). Informed consent for whose benefit? *Social Casework, 62,* 537–542.

Reamer, F. G. (1987). Informed consent in social work. *Social Work, 32,* 425–429.

Reamer, F. G. (1989). Liability issues in social work supervision. *Social Work, 34,* 445–448.

Reamer, F. G. (1994). *Social work malpractice and liability: Strategies for prevention.* New York: Columbia University Press.

Reamer, F. G. (1995). *Social work values and ethics.* New York: Columbia University Press.

Schutz, B. M. (1982). *Legal liability in psychotherapy.* San Francisco: Jossey-Bass.

Sharfstein, S., Towery, O., & Milowe, I. D. (1980). Accuracy of diagnostic information submitted to an insurance company. *American Journal of Psychiatry, 137,* 70–73.

Simon, R. I. (1982). *Psychiatric interventions and malpractice.* Springfield, IL: Charles C Thomas.

Stromberg, C., Haggarty, D. J., Leibenluft, R. F., McMillan, M. H., Mishkin, B., Rubin, B. L., & Trilling, H. R. (1988). *The psychologist's legal handbook.* Washington, DC: Council for National Register of Health Service Providers in Psychology.

Watkins, S. A. (1989). Confidentiality and privileged communications: Legal dilemma for family therapists. *Social Work, 34,* 133–144.

Watkins, S. A., & Watkins, J. C. (1989). Negligent endangerment: Malpractice in the clinical context. *Journal of Independent Social Work, 3,* 35–50.

Wilson, S. J. (1978). *Confidentiality in social work.* New York: Free Press.

Woody, R. H. (1988). *Fifty ways to avoid malpractice.* Sarasota, FL: Resource Exchange.

CHAPTER

$$4$$

ONGOING SERVICE

Assessment of the client's needs is ongoing, and as service progresses, the nature and goals of the helping process require continued clarification and updating. The practitioner's aim is to create a relationship and system in which the client can make and maintain changes (Northen, 1985).

The middle phase of service is vulnerable to malpractice and other actions for several reasons. Unrealistic and strong emotions and reactions (that is, transference and countertransference) of both practitioner and client emerge. As the service relationship develops, clients may experience a corrective emotional experience based on the social worker's unconditional regard and objectivity. As this occurs, the client may respond to the social worker as he or she has responded to people in the past. Client resistance and noncompliance may emerge. As well, the clinician's own values, past experiences, and current needs can influence the client and interfere with the helping process (Houston & Northen, 1994; Northen, 1995). For the practitioner, workload pressures may corrupt performance. Professional impairment may undermine the practitioner's ability to serve the client, and poor or poorly used continuing education and supervision and professional isolation may compromise judgment and skill.

In the middle phase of service, most malpractice suits and other actions are occasioned by the practitioner's omissions and commissions in three general areas:

1. improper service, including failure to report maltreatment of or by a client; failure to warn and protect potential victims from harm by a client; failure to protect a client from harm and death; assault and battery; treatment not indicated by diagnosis; harmful advice; practicing medicine without a license; improper child placement or removal; inadequate foster care; failure to provide for adoption of a foster child; failure to be available when needed; abandonment; failure to refer, consult, transfer, or terminate service when indicated; unnecessary continuation of treatment; and using treatment methods without adequate training and credentials
2. dual relationships and failure to maintain boundaries in the client–clinician relationship, leading to allegations of sexual misconduct, intentional infliction of mental distress, client exploitation, and undue influence and coercion
3. fiscal malfeasance, which can take many forms (Stromberg et al., 1988), including paying or receiving kickbacks for referrals, billing

more than one payer for the same services and receiving double payment, billing for services excluded from coverage, routinely waiving copayments or deductibles, colluding with a client by overcharging a third-party payer, billing the client or payer at more than the agreed-on fee, billing for services not actually rendered, billing for services of people not being reimbursed, providing misleading information on the nature of service or the identity of the provider of service, and providing unnecessary services and seeking reimbursement.

IMPROPER SERVICE

PATRICIA

Patricia, who last year attended a half-day experiential workshop on techniques to discover the "inner child," had been treating a 29-year-old client diagnosed with a borderline personality disorder. On several occasions, the client had vague recollections of sexual abuse as a child. Patricia thought that the client would benefit from inner-child work. She recognized that she was a novice with the inner-child approach and considered the risks and benefits of the approach and her need to receive adequate training and supervision. She studied the books and articles recommended in the workshop bibliography. Patricia discussed her interest in using inner-child work with her client, and she and the client agreed on a revision of the existing service plan and contract. During the third session, the new approach was particularly evocative, and the client deteriorated to the point of active psychosis requiring emergency hospitalization. The client later accused Patricia of "emotional punishment" and told her, "I don't think you know what you're doing." The client initiated a lawsuit for improper treatment and use of influence.

Improper service can occur when the practitioner

- fails to intervene adequately and appropriately
- uses techniques that he or she is not properly trained to use
- uses an innovative or radical treatment approach
- physically intervenes with a client
- suffers with the effects of subjective responses, work overload, burnout, and impairment.

Intervention

Matching the service approach to the client's diagnosis and assessed needs, the mutually defined service goals, and the practitioner's capacity and credentials is essential to legal, ethical, and competent practice. The implementation of appropriate service is further dictated by regulations and standards governing the practice setting. For example, mental health law requires client placement in the least-restrictive setting and establishes criteria for involuntary psychiatric hospitalization for evaluation, treatment, and discharge (Houston & Northen, 1994; Northen, 1995). Therefore, whenever residential, inpatient, or day treatment care is provided to a child or adult, the treating mental health professionals are exposed to malpractice claims owing to failure to provide the least-restrictive form of service consistent with the client's circumstances, to false imprisonment, and to failure to provide adequate care for a client in a residential facility. In addition, child welfare settings have legally and administratively prescribed standards for child placement or removal. Accordingly, child welfare work exposes professionals to allegations involving inadequate or harmful foster care, failure to facilitate adoption, and wrongful child removal (Besharov, 1985).

Practitioners have been sued for recommending, for example, that a client get a divorce or change jobs on the basis that the advice was harmful. Practitioners should remember professional norms and emphasize client self-determination and participation, avoiding at all costs undue influence or coercion. Practitioners have been sued for practicing medicine without a license for not immediately referring clients who have physical or psychosomatic complaints to a physician or for suggesting that a client decrease or increase an amount of medication (Austin, Moline, & Williams, 1990; Schutz, 1982).

Practitioners have been sued for prolonging unsuccessful service. The practitioner who is not making progress with a client should seek and document supervision. If there is still no improvement, the practitioner should seek an objective evaluation of the client by another professional. If indicated, the practitioner should refer the client elsewhere, taking care to make an effective, well-informed referral (Austin et al., 1990; Reamer, 1994).

Adequate intervention also includes explicit back-up instructions and arrangements for when a practitioner is not available because of planned absences or emergencies. Back-up coverage should be provided by professionals who are well informed about the client's problem, history, diagnosis, service, and risks for danger to self and others (see Chapter 2). The client should sign a form indicating that he or she understands and received the back-up instructions, and a copy should be included in the client's record. Malpractice suits alleging abandonment or failure to be available when needed are relatively frequent (Reamer, 1994).

Training and Knowledge

Practitioners who profess to specialize in a particular form of service, such as hypnosis, gestalt, family therapy, or biofeedback, should provide service consistent with other specialists in the area who are treating similar clients in similar situations. Moreover, service must comply with additional credential requirements and standards. Practitioners who become specialized in and wedded to one approach or a narrow range of techniques should guard against misapplication with all clients.

Practitioners should realize educational, personal, and professional limitations and seek to remedy knowledge and skill deficits. Wherever possible, social workers should become formally certified and should always be thoroughly trained in the methods they use. They should engage in related ongoing supervision and consultation. A client whose problem exceeds a practitioner's professional training or competence should be referred to the appropriate professional.

Innovative or Radical Treatment Approach

Social workers should continually expand their repertoire of tested and reliable methods, relying on professional standards, clinical research literature, supervision, consultation, and continuing education to stay informed of advances in treatment knowledge. Practitioners who consider using a new method should arrange specially focused training, consultation, and supervision and must avoid experimenting on clients or risking a client's well-being by learning a technique at the client's expense.

Watkins and Watkins (1989) encouraged the use of treatment approaches that are accepted and endorsed by the profession as evidenced by those approaches presented at NASW conferences or used in Council on Social Work Education–accredited academic programs. These authors also warned that not all approaches are accepted nationwide.

Nevertheless, as awareness of the biopsychosocial basis of behavior evolves, client problems are being understood in more complex ways. Service innovations have moved beyond previously accepted practice conventions and require the adaptation of non–social work knowledge and the use of new technologies. However, inherent risks exist in recommending radical or nontraditional forms of social work services (Bernstein, 1981). Moreover, new technologies may not be covered under professional liability insurance policies.

The practitioner's departure from traditional practice must be justified based on support from other respected professionals, the literature, and experience. In a malpractice allegation, the use of an innovative treatment may be considered appropriate if the treatment is accepted by a respected minority of practitioners; however, the practitioner must prove that he or she was not negligent in the choice of treatment.

Informed consent can act as a protection in the use of innovative treatment (Bernstein, 1981; Besharov & Besharov, 1987). Practitioners should identify the risks and problems of using a more radical approach, discuss these with the client, document the discussion and the decision to proceed, and secure informed consent to this aspect of treatment by stipulating its use in the service contract.

The use of approaches that emphasize regression, early childhood work, and experiential in vivo activities can be suggestive and has led to lawsuits, for example, from clients' significant others charging evocation of false memories of abuse. The client must have the capacities and strengths to benefit from radical and less-tested forms of treatment without precipitating further crises or regressive states that can lead to emotional or physical harm.

Before using a new modality or technology—whether it is new to the social worker or to the profession—practitioners should

- have adequate training and a thorough understanding of the theory base
- become familiar with well-documented empirical research and evidence of effectiveness and application
- know the contraindications and indications for use
- have the appropriate credentials and licenses
- substantiate and document the rationale for the selected approach or intervention
- practice the techniques under close supervision of experts
- identify and discuss with the client potential risks and benefits
- verify with the insurance carrier coverage under a professional liability policy (Houston & Northen, 1994).

Physical Intervention

Assertions of inappropriate touching can occur and charges of battery may be brought in cases in which the treatment approach involves any physical contact among clients or between clinician and client. In some confrontational approaches, fight techniques, and encounter groups, clients can be exposed to fear arousal and possible objective physical injury. Assault and battery charges can eventuate and heighten the risk of a malpractice suit (Stromberg et al., 1988). When considering radical methods with physical components, practitioners should remember that the social work profession does not endorse or recognize treatment models that inflict excessive emotional suffering or physical harm (Watkins & Watkins, 1989). Also, practitioners should be aware touch can create a potential threat of a lawsuit or action alleging sexual misconduct.

Practitioner Issues

Practitioner issues, including subjective responses, work overload, and professional impairment, can lead to improper service.

Subjective Responses

As social worker and client work together, a stronger attachment evolves and interdependence, acceptance, and mutual trust are reinforced. The client becomes freer to risk disclosure, and the service relationship deepens. Thus, the practitioner may become less objective; more reluctant to change the course of service; more reluctant to address client resistance; or more reluctant to comply with legal requirements to warn and protect others, report abuse, or effect involuntary commitment if doing so threatens to endanger the therapeutic relationship and the continuance of service (Houston & Northen, 1994; Northen, 1995). As issues related to these subjective responses emerge, practitioners may permit themselves to lose sight of the service objectives and move into a pleasant but unfocused relationship with a well-liked, attractive client. In any of these situations, improper and inadequate service can result, exacerbated by the practitioner's unrealistic subjective expectations and reactions.

In some therapeutic relationships, a negative professional–client relationship can prompt clinician responses such as withdrawing from a client by canceling appointments or failing to return telephone calls, making ill-considered referrals to other services, or using inappropriate force in aggression-control techniques when restraining a client.

In both instances of positive and negative responses, practitioners must monitor their feelings and vulnerabilities and seek supervision and consultation. Practitioners who cannot control inappropriate responses to the client must arrange a timely and responsible referral (Schutz, 1982; Simon, 1982).

Work Overload

The current overburdened social services system has resulted in the limited capacity of social workers to respond to the needs of large caseloads, often compounded by severe shortages in affordable adjunct community resources. The inability to secure client housing, substance abuse treatment, caregiver respite, or day care for children and disabled adults can seriously erode the best service plans.

Excess work demands can drain and distract practitioners so they become less objective and less analytical. Work overload can also contribute to relaxation of professional norms, with the consequences of fiscal impropriety or dual relationships. Practitioners who are harried and overworked should be sensitive to their performance and self-monitoring capacity and seek help from a supervisor or consultant for both practice caseload and personal life issues.

Professional Impairment

Professional impairment includes

> interference in professional functioning that is reflected in one or more of the following ways: (1) an inability and/or unwillingness to acquire and integrate professional standards into one's repertoire of professional behavior; (2) an inability to acquire professional skills in order to reach an acceptable level of competency; and (3) an inability to control personal stress, psychological dysfunction, and/or excessive emotional reactions that interfere with professional functioning. (Lamb et al., 1987, p. 598)

Whereas overworked practitioners may miss deadlines, develop a poor service plan because of an incomplete assessment, and not notice subjective cues in a service relationship, impaired professionals may have these problems and also have difficulty seeing their mistakes. Impaired professionals exhibit definable substance abuse or social–psychological clinical symptoms.

Social workers who are impaired are at particular risk of violating the standards of reasonable and prudent practice and of providing inadequate or inappropriate services. Increasingly, professional licensing boards, other professional organizations, and NASW are addressing ways to identify and intervene with impaired professionals. NASW first addressed the issue in a national policy statement on alcohol-related problems approved by the 1979 Delegate Assembly (NASW, 1987). Additional policies and initiatives have been developed to address the needs of impaired professionals (Reamer, 1994, 1995). In 1994 NASW added three sections on the subject to the *Code of Ethics,* which were revised in 1996:

> Social workers should not allow their own personal problems, psychosocial distress, legal problems, substance abuse, or mental health difficulties to interfere with their professional judgment and performance or to jeopardize the best interests of people for whom they have a professional responsibility.

> * * *

> Social workers whose personal problems, psychosocial distress, legal problems, substance abuse, or mental health difficulties interfere with their professional judgment and performance should immediately seek consultation and take appropriate remedial action by seeking professional

help, making adjustments in workload, terminating practice, or taking any other steps necessary to protect clients
and others.

* * *

Social workers who have direct knowledge of a social work
colleague's impairment that is due to personal problems,
psychosocial distress, substance abuse, or mental health difficulties, and which interferes with practice effectiveness,
should consult with that colleague when feasible and assist
the colleague in taking remedial action.

Estimates of the incidence of various types of impairment in the social
work profession are limited. However, studies have reported that from 43
percent to 53 percent of social workers have recognized at least one social
worker with a drug or alcohol problem (Elpers, 1992; Fewell, King, &
Weinstein, 1993; Hiratsuka, 1994).

As help givers, practitioners may not experience reciprocal professional
relationships; client progress may be erratic and slow, leading to the belief
that professional efforts are unsuccessful and do not make a difference. Also,
practitioners may prevent their needs from being met in their personal
relationships by becoming helpers. Being a needy professional can lead to
blurred client–worker boundaries and inappropriate behavior with clients
(Kilburg, Kaslow, & VandenBos, 1988; Reamer, 1994).

In addition, it is unrealistic to expect that because social workers help
others, they know how to deal with all their own problems. Practitioners, too,
may need help with problems related to health, job, marriage, family, social
relationships, finances, substance abuse, and burnout (Reamer, 1994).

Burnout is a state of extreme dissatisfaction with one's work and everyday
living. Characteristics include impairments involving

- thinking—confusion; impaired judgment and decision-making capability; forgetfulness; and decreased ability to identify alternatives, priori-
  tize tasks, and evaluate one's own performance
- mood—emotional exhaustion; loss of a sense of personal accomplish-
  ment and merit; depersonalization and alienation; depression; and
  easy excitability, anger, and irritability
- somatic functioning—lowered energy level, changes in appetite and
  sleeping, gastrointestinal problems, hypochondriacal complaints, and
  exhaustion
- behavioral functioning—increased or decreased activity level; extreme
  fatigue; excessive isolation from coworkers, family, and clients; disor-
  ganization; misplacing items; and impaired competence on the job
  (Institute for the Studies of Destructive Behaviors & Los Angeles
  Suicide Prevention Center, 1988).

Social workers may not be aware of their burnout; instead, colleagues, family,
and friends may indicate the need for a break.

As is the case with burnout, practitioners may have difficulty acknowl-
edging that they have a substance abuse problem. Signs can include using
alcohol or drugs during work; increasing substance use; relying on substances for coping; having impaired professional relationships; having poor

self-esteem; being overinvolved in work; having a family history of abuse; and having concerns about the abuse voiced by family, friends, and colleagues (Reamer, 1994).

To prevent distress from escalating and affecting clients, practitioners should, in addition to listening to the concerns of their colleagues, family, and friends, do periodic self-assessments, knowing their strengths and limitations. It is important to maintain regular supervision and network with colleagues. Practitioners can help take care of emotional needs by taking an occasional "mental health day," going on a vacation, or using stress reduction techniques. Practitioners who find that they are impaired should arrange for a reassignment at work, take time off until they can get their problems under control, and seek appropriate professional help such as psychotherapy or substance abuse treatment.

Resources are available to impaired social workers. NASW chapters have created innovative and responsive programs, including outreach to distressed social workers, prevention and education activities, and monitoring of impaired professionals. Many state professional regulatory boards have implemented programs for impaired professionals. Twelve-step self-help groups, often called "social workers helping social workers," have emerged.

BOUNDARY VIOLATIONS AND DUAL RELATIONSHIPS

RICHARD

Richard, a clinical social worker, had worked for six months with a 42-year-old professional photographer who was HIV positive. The client had no living immediate relatives, and during the previous year his partner had died of AIDS. During a home visit, Richard disclosed that he was a serious amateur photographer and complimented the client on his photographs. Later, issues regarding advanced directives and the client's will were discussed in several interviews. The client expressed his deep gratitude and desire to repay Richard for his help by giving him some of his cameras. Richard, who knew his role was to facilitate the client's autonomous decision making, consciously avoided recommending ways to dispose of the estate, except his suggestion that the cameras should be with "someone who would appreciate them and recognize their value." He also told the client that he was touched by and appreciated the client's wish to remember him in his will. Richard documented in the clinical record discussions with the client about estate disposition.

With the onset of dementia, the client's mental status deteriorated to the point of incompetency. Richard discovered that the client had willed all of his photographic equipment to him, along with many valuable signed prints. While discussing the case during supervision, Richard's supervisor expressed the opinion that Richard may have compromised his client's ability to act independently with respect to the photographic equipment; thus, he may have served his client unethically and heightened his own risk for malpractice.

Boundaries are "limits that allow for a safe connection based on the client's need" (Peterson, 1992, cited in Landers, 1992, p. 3). Any type of interaction outside the therapeutic relationship can lead to client confusion and the erosion of the practitioner's "non-selfish judgment, which is the essence of being a professional" (Zuckerman & Guyett, 1992, p. 50). In addition, boundary violations can jeopardize confidentiality issues. From a risk management perspective, sexual contact with a current or past client is one of the most blatant boundary violations.

A *dual relationship* simultaneously or successively encompasses more than one role, including social or personal, business or financial, religious, and multimethodological interests. As stated in the *NASW Code of Ethics* (1996),

> Social workers should not engage in dual or multiple relationships with clients or former clients in which there is a risk of exploitation of or potential harm to the client. In instances when dual or multiple relationships are unavoidable, social workers should take steps to protect clients and are responsible for setting clear, appropriate, and culturally sensitive boundaries.

> * * *

> Social workers should not take unfair advantage of any professional relationship or exploit others to further their personal, religious, political, or business interests.

Dual relationships often evolve gradually and seemingly harmlessly (Pope, 1988). However, in the past decade, malpractice claims and ethical violations related to the boundaries of the client–clinician relationship and dual relationships, prominently including sexual misconduct lawsuits, have increased dramatically (Landers, 1992). Such trends point to the need for professionals to consider the *NASW Code of Ethics* (NASW, 1996) and be mindful of the potential for and danger of dual relationships (Peterson, 1992). Schoener, Milgrom, Gonsiorek, Luepker, and Conroe (1992) and Peterson (1992) proposed guidelines for preventing boundary violations:

- Notice when rules change for a client, such as loaning money, giving a ride home, or giving out a home telephone number.
- Be alert to feelings of discomfort about any unusual actions, such as feeling victimized by a client, working harder than a client, feeling a client cannot make it without the practitioner, or fantasies of rescuing a client.
- Be attentive to any tendency to use a client for personal needs.
- Be alert to the client who begins to require approval and seek detailed advice, which can lead to client overdependence and exaggerated, unrealistic reactions toward the practitioner.
- Monitor any unavoidable dual relationships; discuss with the client his or her feelings and any responses or encounters that may be influencing the helping process.
- Work out solutions to deal with chance meetings.
- Develop a social support network of people not involved with the client.
- Reduce isolation by consultation, supervision, and continuing education.

- Weigh any potential harm to the client if advice is given.
- Before self-disclosing, determine the disclosure's therapeutic value and how the client could misinterpret it.
- Monitor subjective reactions; if they cannot be controlled, the practitioner may need therapy or to terminate service with the client.
- Appropriately assess and respond to the client's issues related to his or her unrealistic expectations and reactions in the therapeutic relationship; address any client attraction to the practitioner.

Sexual Misconduct

Sexual behavior with clients is the most frequently reported ethical violation in the profession (Kaplan, 1993; "Study Cites Most-Reported Ethics Breaches," 1995). *Sexual misconduct* includes

- verbal and nonverbal behavior such as making seductive and suggestive remarks and gestures
- meeting with the client in a social situation that is construed by the client to indicate sexual interest
- engaging in sexual behaviors such as kissing, stroking, and intercourse.

Much sexual misconduct in service goes unreported. However, malpractice suits for sexual misconduct are increasing despite the prohibition in licensing laws, NASW standards, and the *NASW Code of Ethics*. Studies vary in their findings about the numbers of mental health professionals who have engaged in a sexual relationship with a current or former client. However, researchers have consistently reported that the majority of sexual misconduct cases involve male mental health professionals and female clients (Brodsky, 1986; Pope, 1988; Pope & Vasquez, 1991; Reamer, 1994). However, female clinician–male client and same-sex clinician–client trysts have occurred (Pope, 1988).

Given the closeness of the clinician–client relationship, practitioners may become sexually attracted to a client. The practitioner should personally acknowledge the attraction and take steps to end it, seeking supervision and consultation. The practitioner should determine if the attraction was a fleeting emotion and whether he or she can keep the emotions under control. If, because of the attraction, the practitioner cannot remain objective, the practitioner should terminate service and refer the client to another professional or setting, making sure to do so in a professional manner consistent with the client's needs and interests. Before disclosing the sexual attraction to the client, the practitioner should consider how the disclosure could harm the client (Bennett, Bryant, VandenBos, & Greenwood, 1990).

In addition, it is not unusual for clients to become attracted to the clinician. However, it is the practitioner's responsibility to maintain professionalism. The practitioner should determine if he or she is contributing in any way to the client's response.

If the client openly discusses his or her attraction, the practitioner should deal with it immediately. In a firm, calm, and supportive way, the practitioner should indicate that there is only one relationship—the therapeutic relationship—that the practitioner can now or ever have with the client and he or she should emphasize that sexual contact with a client is unethical and potentially harmful to the client. The practitioner should normalize the experience, letting the client know that strong feelings of attachment and attraction occur in the intensity of a service relationship. The practitioner can use the situation therapeutically, addressing the client's realistic and unrealistic reactions and expectations concerning the practitioner.

If the client's attraction is expressed indirectly, the practitioner may need to initiate a discussion with the client that is based on clinical judgment of the client's ability to handle limit-setting without precipitating a crisis. The practitioner should remember that the client may feel rejected and abandoned and should develop a plan to deal with the client's feelings. If the client's attraction becomes an obstacle to therapy, the practitioner should terminate service or refer the client to another professional or setting (Bennett et al., 1990).

One could reasonably ask why former clients should be off-limits for a relationship after termination of service and the passage of time. From a professional liability perspective, one could say, "once a client, always a client." The nature of the helping relationship and the client's tendency to place on the practitioner unrealistic and intense expectations derived from past experiences with other caregivers create a powerful emotional dependence on the practitioner that extends beyond the end of service. Potential harm to a former client involved in a personal and sexual relationship with a clinician cannot be ruled out. Clients have successfully sued for malpractice even when the professional relationship ended before the sexual contact began. Also, clients who have married their therapists have later filed successful malpractice suits.

The *NASW Code of Ethics*, as revised in 1996, gives the profession's perspective:

> Social workers should not engage in sexual activities or sexual contact with former clients because of the potential for harm to the client. If social workers engage in conduct contrary to this prohibition or claim that an exception to this prohibition is warranted because of extraordinary circumstances, it is social workers—not their clients—who assume the full burden of demonstrating that the former client has not been exploited, coerced, or manipulated, intentionally or unintentionally.

It is clear that practitioners who engage in sexual relationships with former clients run a high risk of professional impropriety.

Nonsexual Physical Contact

Practitioners need to be mindful of the use of touch in the service relationship. Touch is a form of communication, and one touch can have diverse meanings. Touching, even a pat on the hand or shoulder, can be perceived by the client as a sexual advance or a physical threat. Practitioners should be sensitive to situations in which a client is likely to misinterpret touch (for example, if the client is paranoid or acutely hostile or if the client is easily sexually aroused). The practitioner should take into account the client's potentially intense response to the practitioner, fears concerning sexual orientation, identity issues, and culture.

Before using touch with a client, the practitioner should determine whether a client is ready to be touched. The practitioner should ask permission to give the client a hug or hold the client's hand for a moment. These nurturing gestures should be saved for selected, special interventions; practitioners should not make a habit of hugging, patting, or hand-holding with clients (Simon, 1982).

Undue Influence

As the client becomes more dependent on the relationship, the social worker may begin to experience intense subjective feelings and reactions to the client that are not based on the client–professional relationship. The more subjective the responses become, the greater the risk the practitioner will use undue influence on the client. Practitioners must be keenly attuned to issues related to their subjective responses and take care not to use influence or coercion for any reason, especially for their own personal gain. For example, practitioners can personally benefit from encouraging or allowing a client to include the practitioner in the client's will, to bring the practitioner gifts, to do favors for the practitioner, or to use the client's business contacts or professional skills. In addition, practitioners may provide unnecessary services to receive financial gain.

Practitioners who work with diverse populations must understand the nature of the helping relationship from the client's perspective and apply culturally sensitive practice principles in the provision of services and in using professional authority and judgment. Practitioners should be particularly alert to clients in highly vulnerable situations.

Other Dual Relationships

Practitioners can create harmful dual relationships by becoming a friend of a client's family or friends, seeing the client's former spouse in therapy, employing a client, bartering, or accepting gifts. If a dual relationship cannot be avoided, the practitioner should take steps to reduce the potential harm to the client, for example, by setting limits about what will be talked about outside therapy and clarifying that the nature of the relationship to the practitioner will not be revealed to anyone (unless a situation arises in which the law requires confidentiality to be waived).

In a small community the practitioner is likely to meet the client accidentally in public or at social events. Such contacts can evolve into dual relationships without careful management. However, accidental encounters, such as seeing one another at the grocery store, can be handled with planning. Practitioner and client may agree, for example, to ignore each other or exchange only brief pleasantries if the client initiates the interaction.

FRAUDULENT BILLING PRACTICES

MANUEL

Manuel, a clinical social worker in a private, for-profit hospital with both psychiatric and substance abuse service programs, completed an intake form on a patient who presented himself at the emergency room. The chief presenting problem was clearly polydrug abuse, which required hospitalization, and there was indication that the patient may have used drugs in part to cope with situational depression. The patient's insurance did not cover substance abuse service but did provide for inpatient psychiatric care. The patient was very motivated, and payment was the only obstacle. Manuel was faced with a dilemma: He could record drug abuse, knowing that the patient would not be authorized for hospitalization, or he could record a diagnosis emphasizing depression that would lead to an authorized hospitalization. Manuel weighed the benefits of getting the patient into inpatient care as the preferred course of treatment against the risks of misdiagnosis for himself and the client. Manuel recorded a diagnosis of depression, and the patient was hospitalized. Soon after, a chart audit found incongruity between Manuel's intake history and the diagnosis of depression. The patient's health maintenance organization filed a lawsuit against Manuel for deliberately misdiagnosing to secure health benefits.

More than in other service phases, ongoing service exposes practitioners to opportunities for manipulations that constitute fiscal malfeasance. Fiscal wrongdoing in clinical practice includes three types of improper transactions:

1. transactions with third-party payers
2. transactions with colleagues
3. transactions with clients.

Fiscally improper transactions with third-party payers include changing a diagnosis to secure insurance reimbursement, billing for services not actually rendered (for example, billing for individual sessions but providing group counseling), billing for services of people who will not be reimbursed (for example, graduate interns), billing for unnecessary services, and billing more than one payer for the same service so as to receive double payment. Fiscally improper transactions with colleagues include referrals for "kickbacks." Fiscally improper transactions with clients include waiving copayments and deductibles, billing for unnecessary services, and billing for the services of people who will not be reimbursed.

Fiscal impropriety can be well rationalized. For example, practitioners may change a diagnosis because of a strong desire to secure help for a client. Others may reason that the harm is not to an individual but to an antagonistic bureaucracy. Still others may adopt an attitude of "everybody does it" and rationalize that corruption is the norm. Fiscal impropriety can unfold in small steps and may not be recognized as a serious breach of the law and ethics. For example, white-collar criminals may embezzle to address personal financial dilemmas with full intent to pay back what has been stolen after debts or financial stresses have been resolved.

Practitioners should approach the business side of mental health practice with the same thorough awareness of applicable laws and ethical guidelines. Fiscal malfeasance is usually a criminal matter; however, allegations of fiscal malfeasance can come to light as part of a civil malpractice suit as well.

ONGOING SERVICE

The middle phase of service exposes social workers to situations that have much to do with serious errors in judgment that arise from the client's and the practitioner's intense and at times unrealistic expectations of and reactions to one another, the distractions and pressures of work overload, inadequate supervision and training, professional isolation, rationalization, the professional's impairment, and client resistance and noncompliance. A risk management formula for the middle phase of service includes providing proper treatment, avoiding dual relationships, and avoiding fraudulent billing practices.

REFERENCES

Austin, K. M., Moline, M. E., & Williams, G. T. (1990). *Confronting malpractice: Legal and ethical dilemmas in psychotherapy.* Newbury Park, CA: Sage Publications.

Bennett, B. E., Bryant, B. K., VandenBos, G. R., & Greenwood, A. (1990). *Professional liability and risk management.* Washington, DC: American Psychological Association.

Bernstein, B. E. (1981). Malpractice: Future shock of the 1980s. *Social Casework, 62,* 175–181.

Besharov, D. J. (1985). *The vulnerable social worker: Liability for serving children and families.* Silver Spring, MD: National Association of Social Workers.

Besharov, D. J., & Besharov, S. (1987). Teaching about liability. *Social Work, 32,* 517–522.

Brodsky, A. M. (1986). The distressed psychologist: Sexual intimacies and exploitation. In R. R. Kilburg, P. E. Nathan, & R. W. Thoreson (Eds.), *Professionals in distress: Issues, syndromes, and solutions in psychology* (pp. 153–171). Washington, DC: American Psychological Association.

Elpers, K. (1992). *Social work impairment: A statewide survey of the National Association of Social Workers.* Evansville, IN: Author.

Fewell, C. H., King, B. L., & Weinstein, D. L. (1993). Alcohol and other drug abuse among social work colleagues and their families: Impact on practice. *Social Work, 38,* 565–570.

Hiratsuka, J. (1994, June). Aiding colleagues poses unique challenge: When it's a helper who needs help. *NASW News,* p. 3.

Houston, M. K., & Northen, H. (1994, May). *Reducing malpractice risks: A framework for resolving ethical–legal dilemmas and enhancing clinical practice.* Paper presented at the Second National Clinical Social Work Conference for the National Federation of Societies for Clinical Social Work, Washington, DC.

Kaplan, K. O. (1993). *Adjudication trends study.* Washington, DC: National Association of Social Workers, National Center for Policy and Practice.

Kilburg, R. R., Kaslow, F. W., & VandenBos, G. R. (1988). Professionals in distress. *Hospital and Community Psychiatry, 39,* 723–725.

Institute for the Studies of Destructive Behaviors, & Los Angeles Suicide Prevention Center. (1988). *Training manual for human service workers in major disasters* (DHS Publication No. ADM 86-538). Rockville, MD: National Institute of Mental Health.

Lamb, D. H., Presser, N. R., Pfost, K. S., Baum, M. C., Jackson, V. R., & Jarvis, P. A. (1987). Confronting professional impairment during the internship: Identification, due process, and remediation. *Professional Psychology, 18,* 597–603.

Landers, S. (1992, October). Ethical boundaries easily trespassed. *NASW News,* p. 3.

National Association of Social Workers. (1987). *Impaired social worker's program resource book.* Silver Spring, MD: Author.

National Association of Social Workers. (1996). *NASW code of ethics.* Washington, DC: Author.

Northen, H. (1995). *Clinical social work knowledge and skills* (2nd ed.). New York: Columbia University Press.

Peterson, R. (1992). *At personal risk: Boundary violations in professional relationships.* New York: W. W. Norton.

Pope, K. S. (1988). Dual relationships: A source of ethical, legal, and clinical problems. *Independent Practitioner, 8,* 17–25.

Pope, K. S., & Vasquez, M.J.T. (1991). *Ethics in psychotherapy and counseling: A practical guide for psychologists.* San Francisco: Jossey-Bass.

Reamer, F. G. (1994). *Social work malpractice and liability: Strategies for prevention.* New York: Columbia University Press.

Reamer, F. G. (1995). *Social work values and ethics.* New York: Columbia University Press.

Schoener, R., Milgrom, J. H., Gonsiorek, J. C., Luepker, E. T., & Conroe, R. M. (1992). *Psychotherapists' sexual involvement with clients: Intervention and prevention.* Minneapolis: Walk-In Counseling Center.

Schutz, B. M. (1982). *Legal liability in psychotherapy.* San Francisco: Jossey-Bass.

Simon, R. I. (1982). *Psychiatric interventions and malpractice.* Springfield, IL: Charles C Thomas.

Stromberg, C., Haggarty, D. J., Leibenluft, R. F., McMillan, M. H., Mishkin, B., Rubin, B. L., & Trilling, H. R. (1988). *The psychologist's legal handbook.* Washington, DC: Council for National Register of Health Service Providers in Psychology.

Study cites most-reported ethics breaches. (1995, April). *NASW News,* p. 4.

Watkins, S. A., & Watkins, J. C. (1989). Negligent endangerment: Malpractice in the clinical context. *Journal of Independent Social Work, 3*(3), 35–50.

Zuckerman, E. L., & Guyett, I.P.R. (1992). *The paper office 1* (rev.). Pittsburgh: Clinician's Toolbox.

CHAPTER

5

ENDING SERVICE

Malpractice risks during the ending phase of service emerge around lack of preparation for expected and unexpected events, such as a practitioner's change of job or a client's decision to leave service, and insufficient or conflicting evaluation of outcomes (Houston & Northen, 1994; Northen, 1995). Professional liability lawsuits occasioned by termination or transfer are precipitated by perceived or real

- poor results or failure to cure
- unnecessary continuation of service
- inappropriate bill collection
- failure to refer, transfer, or consult when appropriate
- referral to an incompetent service provider
- abandonment or abrupt termination
- improper withdrawal of services
- failure to provide for emergencies
- breach of contract (Cohen & Mariano, 1982; Schutz, 1982).

Malpractice risks associated with termination can be reduced by orienting clients to the probable duration of their service; fees and collection methods; service outcome evaluation; and policies on termination, referral, and follow-up (see Chapters 2 and 3).

The practitioner–client relationship can end in a variety of ways. Ideally, termination should occur based on the joint evaluation of the practitioner and client when the agreed-on goals are achieved (Robertson & Jackson, 1991). Practitioners should be prepared to handle planned and unplanned terminations in a professional manner and consistent with practice guidelines, making certain that the client is not abandoned during a crisis and that there is continuity of care based on client needs.

TERMINATION WITHOUT CLIENT CONSENT

GREG

Greg, an independent practitioner, was providing outpatient treatment for a client who had had several hospitalizations for severe depression and suicide attempts. The client was being maintained on medication prescribed by her family doctor. The client's employer changed benefit plans, and the new managed care entity limited outpatient sessions to 12 per year. Given the client's fragility, Greg saw the client at least weekly, knowing that the session limit would be reached in less than three months. Greg also knew that the client, a building custodian, would not have the means to pay for her own outpatient treatment after the insurance ceased. Faced with the choice of referral to a public mental health center or working on a pro bono basis after the 12th session, Greg decided to initiate the termination process with ample time to deal with ending issues and make referral arrangements.

Greg advised the client that he would be unable to continue treating her past a certain date and discussed other service options. At a later session, Greg asked for and was granted permission to release the client's records to the mental health center to which a referral would be made. At a still later session, Greg proposed a joint meeting with the client, himself, and the intake coordinator at the mental health center. The client did not appear for the joint meeting, nor did she keep her scheduled appointment with Greg the next day. Greg telephoned her home repeatedly but received no response. After two weeks without contact, Greg was notified that the client was again in the hospital, having overdosed on her medication. The client was alleging that Greg "pushed her out of his office and wouldn't see her anymore." The client's son had contacted a lawyer and was urging his mother to sue Greg for malpractice.

In a number of circumstances, practitioners can end the treatment relationship without the client's consent:

- The managed care provider terminates service reimbursement, and the client is unable to pay for continued service.
- The client requires expertise beyond the practitioner's capability.
- The client has achieved planned treatment goals and does not continue to make progress.
- The client does not pay the service fees.
- The client is noncompliant and uncooperative.
- The client files an official complaint against the practitioner or the agency.
- The client threatens or injures the practitioner, his or her family, or his or her colleagues.
- The practitioner moves, retires, sells the practice, becomes ill or incapacitated, or dies (Robertson & Jackson, 1991).

To reduce the risk of malpractice or other adverse actions, termination must always be handled carefully, professionally, and in a manner consistent with the client's needs and interests. It is important to provide adequate referral information.

Managed Care Constraints

In today's world of managed care, working with a client for an extended time is a luxury. In the event that a managed care decision to limit treatment reimbursement is not consistent with the assessment of the client's needs for continued service, the practitioner should ask the care manager to reconsider the decision. The practitioner who does not advocate for the client's service needs, and, therefore, allows the client to be jeopardized by the care manager's decision, may be sued for negligence ("Preventing Liability in the Managed Care Setting," 1994). (See Appendix C for a sample form for filing an appeal with a managed care entity.)

If the care manager does not reconsider, the client has the options of paying the fee or, with the practitioner's assistance, seeking lower-cost services elsewhere. The practitioner who decides to terminate services and refer the client to another provider should obtain the necessary releases of information to expedite the referral and send a registered letter of termination to the client detailing concerns that after termination he or she receive continued service and explaining the rationale for the referral. If the client is a danger to self or others, the social worker must take steps to protect the client and others from harm (see Chapter 6). Regardless of whether the client chooses to continue the existing care or accept a referral, the practitioner should document the termination discussions with the client, related decisions, and reasons for his or her actions.

Lack of Progress

If difficulty arises in achieving the mutually agreed-on service goals in the specified time frame, the practitioner should first discuss the situation with the client, considering whether the service goals need to be modified. With the client's consent, the practitioner also should seek supervision or consultation. During this process, the practitioner should

- Document in the record the discussions with the client and supervisor or consultant, including the supervisor's or consultant's recommendations about how to improve service.
- If the practitioner disagrees with the supervisor or consultant, document the differences of opinions and strive to reach a mutually acceptable compromise.
- If a substantial disagreement occurs between supervisor or consultant and practitioner that cannot be resolved, consider obtaining additional consultation with another professional; transferring the client to another professional; or discussing with the client the supervisor's or consultant's recommendations, the practitioner's opinion, and other options, including continuing with the existing arrangement. Document each step.
- If the client fails to improve or gets worse after a reasonable trial of service based on the supervisor's or consultant's recommendations, terminate service, and if the client consents, arrange for referral and transfer.
- Document in the clinical record the rationale for transferring the client and the discussion about the referral with the client.
- Send a registered letter to the client verifying the termination discussions, decisions, list of referrals, and recommendations (see Appendix C for sample letters addressing termination).

When service is not effective, after reasonable efforts to improve and modify treatment, practitioners have an ethical responsibility to arrange for transfer to another source of services. If the practitioner determines that the client requires expertise beyond his or her capability, the practitioner should explore with the client why he or she is not making progress, discuss the reasons another service approach and clinician are recommended, and document the discussion. The client should have input into the decision to transfer and should be granted a reasonable amount of time to end the professional relationship and follow through with the referral. The practitioner should follow up to ensure the client has sought the recommended help.

Service Goals Achieved

When service goals have been achieved in the opinion of both practitioner and client, the practitioner is obligated to terminate service regardless of the client's preferences. However, some clients may be reluctant to end a satisfying and sustaining relationship. The practitioner should anticipate the client's objections to termination and be prepared to address them therapeutically and in a supportive manner, stating that termination is for the client's well-being. The social worker should take steps to reduce the client's feelings of abandonment and rejection (Barker, 1992).

The practitioner may seek a supervisor's input or ask the client's consent to obtain consultation about the termination and should document the results of supervision or consultation and share this input with the client. Assuming that the supervisor or consultant concurs with the decision to terminate, the practitioner should make efforts to reduce the client's dependence on the existing relationship progressively (for example, by tapering off the frequency or duration of sessions). The practitioner should discuss with the client a referral for appropriate long-term posttreatment services such as a support group.

If, despite the best efforts, the client refuses to accept the termination, the practitioner should

- Make the decision to end service, discuss the decision thoroughly with the client, and make the supervisor aware of the situation. Include in the discussion with the client a review of mutually agreed-on service objectives and outcomes, stating that the gains made in service are the reason for ending.
- Deal with the client's feelings about termination, including his or her dissatisfaction, sense of rejection, and anger toward the social worker.
- Reinforce the client's efforts to be autonomous and independent.
- Identify situations and times when the client may need to contact a service provider or the clinician.
- Clarify how and when follow-up will be provided, and document the discussion.
- Accelerate the process of tapering off sessions, and ultimately, refuse to schedule further appointments. If the client's situation deteriorates and he or she needs services, consider a referral to another clinician.
- Send a registered letter to the client verifying the decision to terminate and the reasons for it, restating the discussions and any recommendations and referrals for alternative services. (Austin, Moline, & Williams, 1990; Bennett, Bryant, VandenBos, & Greenwood, 1990; Woody, 1988).

Sometimes a client who remains unwilling to terminate stops coming to therapy and sues the practitioner for abandonment. The best risk management tactic in this case is in the documentation of the practitioner's professional judgment and the steps taken to effect the termination.

Nonpayment of Fees

A practitioner can end the service relationship for nonpayment of fees if the client's or another's welfare is not jeopardized (see Chapter 6 for how to deal with a client who is a danger to self or others). However, the best practice is not to let the unpaid bills accumulate and to establish a clear financial policy (see Chapter 2).

It is possible that efforts to collect payment will lead to a malpractice suit; therefore, the practitioner should proceed carefully and document all steps (Barker, 1992). The practitioner first should remind the client of the fee agreement and then assess the clinical and situational reasons contributing to the client's lack of payment (some clients may not pay because they are upset or angry at the practitioner or dissatisfied with the service). If the client and practitioner cannot determine a reasonable payment plan, the practitioner should explore with the client sources of no-cost or lower-cost services for which he or she is eligible.

Some state regulatory guidelines and laws prohibit the use of collection agencies. Practitioners who legally use a collection agency should inform the client of the decision, clarify what information will be given to the collection agency, and identify any risks to confidentiality that exist beyond the collection agency (for example, some collection agencies are required by law to report to credit bureaus) (Robertson & Jackson, 1991). If the client does not pay because he or she is dissatisfied with the services provided by the practitioner, the collection efforts might lead to a lawsuit.

If the professional relationship is terminated because of nonpayment of fees, the practitioner should document any efforts to rectify the situation in the client's record, provide two or three referrals, and provide for crises and the client's ongoing needs. Before terminating service the practitioner should give the client reasonable time and assistance to find other affordable and appropriate help and send a registered letter to the client stating the reasons for termination.

Uncooperative and Noncompliant Clients

Occasionally, clients become chronically uncooperative and noncompliant (for example, arriving late or not keeping appointments). Before taking steps to end the professional relationship, the practitioner should make reasonable efforts to explore the conditions contributing to the client's resistance and lack of adherence. If possible, the practitioner should try to remedy the conditions (for example, reducing the fee, arranging for transportation, setting appointments at different times, changing the service approach, renegotiating goals, or sending reminders after failed appointments). If these efforts are unsuccessful, the practitioner should suggest options for other service, explain the conditions under which the client can resume service with the practitioner, and describe any concerns about the client's welfare (Robertson & Jackson, 1991), documenting each step in the termination process. The practitioner should send the client a registered letter explaining the termination decision.

Disgruntled Clients

Disgruntled clients pose a particular risk for litigation (Watkins & Watkins, 1989). "It is worth remembering that an angry client is much more likely to sue. If you sense a client's dissatisfaction, consider talking through the client's feelings" (Besharov & Besharov, 1987, p. 521). Practitioners should try to make peace with disgruntled clients and thoroughly prepare for and document service decisions along with consultation with supervisors or colleagues. If the best efforts to reconcile fail, disgruntled clients should be addressed in the same manner as uncooperative, noncompliant clients.

If a client initiates a formal complaint or lawsuit against a social worker or the agency, the practitioner's responsibility to provide services ends. The practitioner should immediately consult an attorney and not speak with the client without legal counsel (see Chapter 8 for the steps to take when a lawsuit or complaint is filed).

Violent Clients

If the client threatens or injures the practitioner or his or her family or colleagues, the practitioner should initiate action to protect and warn third parties and contact the police (Stromberg et al., 1988). Some agencies have policies concerning filing charges against clients who threaten or harm; practitioners should know the policy and, if they make any exception to the policy, discuss the decision with supervisors and document it carefully. The practitioner should terminate service and document the decision thoroughly in the clinical record and in a registered letter to the client. In addition, the practitioner should make efforts to see that the client receives appropriate help from another source. Alternatives include facilitating voluntary or involuntary psychiatric hospitalization; contacting family or significant others (with the client's informed consent) to help ensure that the client receives additional help; and referring the client to another professional, local mental health clinic, or program that specializes in the treatment of violence. The practitioner should follow the guidelines for termination as mentioned in Chapter 6 and should seek consultation from a qualified expert who can suggest additional alternatives, making certain to document these decisions in the client's record.

Change in Practitioner Life Circumstances

Practitioners who are retiring or moving to another job or community or who are selling an independent practice should give clients notice of their plans by

- announcing plans three to six months in advance (for social workers who can see clients for extended periods of time)
- determining a date after which new clients will not be accepted
- having clients sign appropriate releases of information to expedite referrals, deal with necessary business, and collect fees
- developing procedures to handle telephone inquiries concerning the practitioner's whereabouts (Bennett et al., 1990).

In an independent practice, the reputation and referral sources of the practice—not the clients—are sold. The practitioner should give clients several options, such as continuing service with the person who purchased the practice and at least two other referrals. Similarly, on departure from an agency, the practitioner should apprise clients of alternatives in the agency and referrals in the community.

Practitioners who are leaving a practice setting also have obligations to clients whose cases have been closed. To the extent that former clients can be contacted, the practitioner should advise them of the departure and the whereabouts of their records.

Practitioner death and disability often cannot be anticipated. Agency settings will have mechanisms in place to communicate with clients and arrange for alternative care. However, independent practitioners will need to develop a plan with an attorney providing for a personal representative empowered to handle client matters, referrals, and records. Practitioners should determine appropriate colleagues who could step in during a prolonged emergency, maintain client and setting records, and inform back-up professionals when they are needed to provide service. Practitioners should notify supervisors, support staff, and back-up professionals of emergency plans and coach them in how to respond to client inquiries about the death or incapacitation of the practitioner.

TERMINATION AGAINST PRACTITIONER ADVICE

GLORIA

Gloria, a clinical social worker at a community mental health center, had been providing individual service to a client diagnosed as having a borderline personality disorder. The client had made superficial suicide attempts and was very demanding of Gloria. The client called Gloria four to five times a day, and on weekends she called the clinic's emergency number demanding that the service contact Gloria. In one session, Gloria set limits about how many times a week the client could call and the conditions under which Gloria would respond on weekends. The client became furious and told Gloria that she was cold, uncaring, and incompetent and that she would never see her again. Gloria tried to discuss the client's need for service, but the client stormed out of the clinic. Gloria was secretly relieved and made no effort to contact the client. A week later, the client deteriorated and was admitted to a psychiatric facility for evaluation. The client and her family sued Gloria for not making efforts to provide service and to provide for the client's safety and well-being.

Clients have a right to end the service relationship; however, practitioners have the responsibility to ensure continuity of care and must act with the client's well-being in mind. If a client is not at risk of harm to self or others and insists on prematurely ending service, the practitioner should

- Remain neutral and objective in discussions of the client's decision.
- Objectively explore the reasons why the client wants to terminate.
- Be forthcoming and supportive; in expressing any regrets, do not risk using undue influence.

- Encourage the client to have a final session to process what has and has not worked in service and to say good-bye; consider not charging for this session because it is held at the practitioner's request.
- Explain why further service is recommended or needed.
- Ask the client to sign a form indicating that he or she is terminating against professional advice (see Appendix C for a sample form).
- Provide the client with options and appropriate referrals.
- Send the client a registered letter summarizing concerns and encouraging him or her to continue service; include in the letter a restatement of the list of referrals (see Appendix C for guidelines on preparing a letter) (Bennett et al., 1990).

When a client leaves service without explanation, the practitioner should telephone him or her and send a registered letter summarizing progress, describing issues and concerns yet to be addressed, and identifying the risks of not seeking further service. The practitioner should adopt an open-door policy if the client chooses to return and offer to assist with seeking help elsewhere.

On rare occasions a client may ask to terminate or abruptly end service when he or she is a danger to self or others. The practitioner must act to protect the client and others from harm, including contacting significant others or the authorities or arranging for involuntary commitment. The practitioner should not terminate service to a client who is in crisis.

MUTUALLY PLANNED TERMINATION

PHIL

Phil, a clinical social worker employed in a private outpatient substance abuse program that had just started accepting clients referred by a managed care organization, had been treating a client with a 20-year history of alcoholism and an extensive record for driving under the influence of alcohol. The managed care provider approved only eight visits for the client. The client was aware of the limits of his coverage and agreed to terminate service because he could not afford to pay for individual sessions. Phil was frustrated by the provider's limited coverage and felt the client needed further service. Nevertheless, service was terminated. Two weeks later, the client became intoxicated and had a car accident that caused serious head trauma. The client filed a lawsuit against the managed care company and Phil. The court ruled that Phil and not the managed care company was culpable, because Phil had made no effort to appeal the provider's decision.

In most cases, terminations occur because all or many of the service goals have been achieved and both client and practitioner are satisfied with the progress. Even in planned termination, however, practitioners must be vigilant. When deciding to transfer a client or terminate service, the practitioner should use supervision and seek consultation, engage the client in the evaluation process that leads to transfer or termination, and have clearly delineated referral guidelines. Following Bernstein's (1978) advice, the practitioner should encourage the client to make a definite statement that he or she no longer sees the need to continue service.

In the managed care environment, clients may return for intermittent services. Practitioners should clarify with clients how to identify when they need to be seen again, making certain they understand the care manager's criteria for returning and whether a new referral from a primary care source is required.

When completing the service process, the practitioner should

- Evaluate the outcome of each mutually agreed-on service objective with the client.
- Review the gains made in service, and discuss the areas in which the client needs to make further changes.
- Document that evaluation of service outcomes has taken place and strive for a mutual agreement or compromise about the timing of termination.
- Ensure that abandonment has not taken place by making appropriate referrals.
- Avoid prolonging service unnecessarily.
- Deal with the client's feelings about termination, including any dissatisfaction, sense of rejection, and anger toward the clinician.
- Reinforce the client's efforts to be autonomous and independent.
- Clarify how and when there will be follow-up.
- Send the client a registered letter confirming the termination agreement.
- Document in the clinical record the reason for termination, the client's reaction, details of the termination agreement, provisions for follow-up, and names of referrals.

REFERRAL AND TRANSFER

RUTH

Ruth, a clinical social worker specializing in group treatment of adult survivors of childhood abuse, suspected that a client could have a multiple personality disorder. The client had not improved in group treatment, and she was becoming very upset about her recollections of being abused by her parents, who were members of a cult. Ruth sought professional consultation and decided that the client needed to be in service with a practitioner who specialized in multiple personality disorders and cult abuse. The client agreed to the transfer, and Ruth gave her the name of a local psychiatrist who had represented himself on a television talk show as an expert. The client began service with the psychiatrist, who used hypnotherapy, inner-child work, and past-life regression techniques with the client. Unbeknownst to Ruth, the psychiatrist was not a certified hypnotist and had never treated someone with a multiple personality disorder. The client, who became acutely psychotic and required hospitalization, sued Ruth for referring her to an incompetent professional.

Under any circumstances of termination, appropriate referral and transfer is vital. When referring or transferring cases, practitioners should explain to clients what information will be shared with the other professionals and should seek releases of information and permission to refer. Practitioners should give clients two or three alternative resources and discuss the admission and eligibility criteria for each resource. Practitioners should make certain that referral sources are competent and have the appropriate expertise and credentials to work with clients, have a good reputation, and face no malpractice allegations. Because clients' emotional states at the time of termination may interfere with their ability to comprehend or retain the information conveyed, practitioners may need to provide referral information in written as well as verbal form. Consideration should be given to the client's feelings and response to the transfer (Bennett et al., 1990; Stromberg et al., 1988).

When referring clients, the practitioner should discuss the clients' responsibilities to contact the referrals and help them decide what type of help they want and the expertise and approach they feel most comfortable with (Calfee, 1992). The practitioner and client can rehearse how to interview the referral sources. If possible, the practitioner should plan a joint session with the professionals who assume responsibility for the client. As with all other steps in the termination process, the practitioner should document discussions with clients about referrals, the rationale for referrals, the list of referrals given to clients, and the steps taken to refer and transfer clients (Woody, 1988).

FOLLOW-UP

DIANNE

Dianne, a private practitioner, had been providing services to an 18-year-old depressed client with a history of suicide attempts. The client had made significant progress during the last four months of service, and his depression subsided. The client also had become independent from his parents and recently moved into his own apartment. The client agreed that he was ready to terminate service, and Dianne concurred but provided no plan for follow-up. One month later the client committed suicide. His parents sued Dianne for negligence in failing to provide a reasonable standard of care, which entails following up with suicidal clients.

Systematic client follow-up demonstrates the practitioner's efforts to provide an appropriate standard of care. However, because follow-up happens after service has ended, it occurs outside the contractual service relationship. In the working agreement with clients, practitioners should establish follow-up procedures, taking care to preserve client confidentiality in the procedures (for example, in telephone contact, a letter, or a survey) and making it clear that clients are free to decline a follow-up appointment. At the time of termination, practitioners should review the follow-up procedures with the client (Woody, 1988).

Practitioners should ensure that follow-up procedures are noncoercive and voluntary. Practitioners can develop a consent form that stipulates clients' agreement to follow-up (see Appendix C for a sample follow-up consent form and letter). Practitioners should determine a specific time for follow-up that meets the client's needs and anticipates when he or she may need a "booster shot" appointment to reinforce changes.

ENDING SERVICE

The ending phase of service requires attention to timing and separation issues. On the one hand, practitioners have an obligation not to extend service beyond its objective usefulness in meeting service goals, regardless of client preference. On the other hand, practitioners must continue to offer service as long as a client's needs are being met, goal progress can be seen, a client remains willing, and the professional relationship remains productive.

Practitioners are within their legal rights and meet ethical standards if they terminate service against a client's wishes when the client needs services that the practitioner cannot provide; the client has attained the service goals; the client drops out of service; the client becomes uncooperative, threatens harm, or files an official complaint against the practitioner; and reimbursement of services is no longer possible. If possible, the termination decision should be mutual, and steps must be taken not to abandon the client if other services are needed. Practitioners can reduce malpractice risks related to termination by having a detailed service plan; documenting client progress toward meeting goals; consulting, referring, or transferring a client promptly and with care; providing for interruptions in service; preparing the client for termination; and following up after termination.

REFERENCES

Austin, K. M., Moline, M. E., & Williams, G. T. (1990). *Confronting malpractice: Legal and ethical dilemmas in psychotherapy.* Newbury Park, CA: Sage Publications.

Barker, R. (1992). *Social work in private practice* (2nd ed.). Washington, DC: NASW Press.

Bennett, B. E., Bryant, B. K., VandenBos, G. R., & Greenwood, A. (1990). *Professional liability and risk management.* Washington, DC: American Psychological Association.

Bernstein, B. E. (1978). Malpractice: An ogre on the horizon. *Social Work, 23,* 106–112.

Besharov, D. J., & Besharov, S. (1987). Teaching about liability. *Social Work, 32,* 517–522.

Calfee, B. (1992). *Lawsuit prevention techniques.* Cleveland: ARC.

Cohen, R. J., & Mariano, W. E. (1982). *Legal guidebook in mental health.* New York: Free Press.

Houston, M. K., & Northen, H. (1994, May). *Reducing malpractice risks: A framework for resolving ethical–legal dilemmas and enhancing clinical practice.* Paper presented at the Second National Clinical Social Work Conference for the National Federation of Societies for Clinical Social Work, Washington, DC.

Northen, H. (1995). *Clinical social work knowledge and skills* (2nd ed.). New York: Columbia University Press.

Preventing liability in the managed care setting. (1994, January). *Mental Health Legal Review.* pp 1–3.

Robertson, H. W., & Jackson, V. H. (1991). *NASW guidelines on the private practice of clinical social work*. Silver Spring, MD: National Association of Social Workers.

Schutz, B. M. (1982). *Legal liability in psychotherapy*. San Francisco: Jossey-Bass.

Stromberg, C., Haggarty, D. J., Leibenluft, R. F., McMillan, M. H., Mishkin, B., Rubin, B. L., & Trilling, H. R. (1988). *The psychologist's legal handbook*. Washington, DC: Council for National Register of Health Service Providers in Psychology.

Watkins, S. A., & Watkins, J. C. (1989). Negligent endangerment: Malpractice in the clinical context. *Journal of Independent Social Work, 3*(3), 35–50.

Woody, R. H. (1988). *Fifty ways to avoid malpractice*. Sarasota, FL: Professional Resource Exchange.

6

LIFE-ENDANGERING CRISES

Clients experiencing life-endangering crises present myriad clinical, ethical, and legal challenges. Clients who are potentially dangerous to themselves or others or who are victims or perpetrators of abuse present malpractice risks associated with assessment and prediction. Malpractice claims have been made against social workers alleging

- not identifying or documenting factors that predict risk of danger to self or others (including maltreatment of children, elderly people, and other vulnerable adults)
- failure to warn third parties who have been threatened with harm
- defamation of character
- use of derogatory words
- wrongful reporting
- wrongful commitment
- inappropriate treatment or placement
- abandonment
- breach of confidentiality
- wrongful death of or physical harm to a client
- false imprisonment
- causing or failing to prevent a client's suicide
- negligence in determining foreseeable risk
- liability for the actions of others based on the clinician's negligent or inaccurate assessment.

Practitioners must be equipped with knowledge and skills to identify warning signs, assess degree of risk, intervene appropriately, and follow legal mandates and agency policies. This chapter presents four areas of life-threatening emergencies:

1. potential danger to others
2. suicide
3. child maltreatment
4. adult maltreatment.

Each life-endangering situation poses special malpractice risks and has a specific set of legal and practice parameters.

LAWRENCE

Lawrence worked for a domestic violence program and conducted a group for male batterers. For two weeks, a new
group member, who had a history of battering his wife and
was currently separated from her, had been reluctant to
participate in group activities. In the third week, the client
volunteered to participate in a role play enacting how he
responded aggressively toward his wife. During the role play
the client expressed anger and desire to hurt his wife, saying
"If my wife doesn't shut up, I'm going to strangle the life out
of her." After the enactment, group members gave feedback
to the client and suggested anger management techniques.
Lawrence was very pleased with the client's participation
and felt that he had learned ways to keep from harming his
wife. Lawrence felt that evaluating the client for dangerousness or contacting the wife would jeopardize the helping
relationship and that it was unnecessary to consider treatment alternatives or develop a plan to help the client avoid
risky situations.

After leaving the group, the client visited his wife and told
her of his new insights gained during the group session and
how he was ready to reconcile. The wife became angry and
shouted, "Get out of my house and my life now!" The client
became enraged and attempted to strangle her. The wife
initiated a lawsuit against Lawrence, who was found liable
for failing to take steps to protect the wife. The court found
that Lawrence did not meet the standard of care for working
with a potentially dangerous client.

In the past two decades, extensive research on the prediction of violence
has substantially improved social workers' ability to anticipate individual
acts of violence. Some background and situational variables consistently
correlate with violence; however, past violence is the best predictor of future
violence. Hence, anticipating a person's first violent act is a much greater
gamble than predicting subsequent violence. Moreover, violence in the short
run may be more accurately predicted for most populations than more remote episodes in the future (Buka & Earls, 1993; Chaiken, Chaiken, &
Rhodes, 1994; Fraser, 1995). Nevertheless, it is safest to assume that the
prediction of violence is imprecise and poses a challenge for practitioners
(Hall, 1987; Lidz, Mulvey, & Gardner, 1993; Monahan & Steadman, 1994).

Legal Mandates

During the past 25 years, state laws have expanded the mental health
professional's duties to assess a client's threat to others and self. Practitioners
must endeavor to predict whether a client is likely to lose control and
commit a violent act and to identify individuals who are mentally ill
and dangerous to themselves or others. Practitioners may need to provide

information about a client's demonstrated potential for violence over a long period of time and predict whether he or she may be dangerous in the near future.

Most state laws for responding to potential dangerousness to others are based on the precedent-setting *Tarasoff v. Board of Regents of the University of California* (1976) decision. Prosenjit Poddar, a student at the University of California at Berkeley, was receiving student counseling services from a psychologist. During the course of counseling, Poddar said something that led the psychologist to believe that he would harm his girlfriend Tatiana Tarasoff. At the time of the threat, Tarasoff was in Brazil. The psychologist notified the university police, who interviewed Poddar, decided he was not a genuine threat, and released him. With Tarasoff's brother, Poddar moved into an apartment that was near her apartment. Eight weeks later Poddar murdered Tarasoff, who had returned from Brazil (Reamer, 1994; VandeCreek & Knapp, 1993).

The Tarasoff family filed a lawsuit against the university, alleging that the woman should have been warned. The first court dismissed the case on the basis of sovereign immunity for the defendants and the therapist's need to maintain confidentiality (Reamer, 1994). An appellate court overturned the ruling and ruled that an individual who has information about a threat to others has an obligation to warn. The university was found liable and appealed the appellate court's decision. The state supreme court upheld the ruling and added that mental health professionals have an obligation to take steps to protect the victim. The court ruled, "The protective privilege ends where the public peril begins" (California Supreme Court, cited in Reamer, 1994, p. 31).

Court rulings and state regulations vary in their interpretations of the *Tarasoff* ruling. For some interpretations, the duty to protect potential victims may not necessarily involve warning them. A victim can be protected if, for example, law enforcement is notified or if the dangerous client is hospitalized, medicated, or otherwise treated effectively so that the threat subsides. In other interpretations, victim protection requires specific warning of the possible victim. State laws also may mandate a duty to notify the police. Even if state laws do not include the duty to warn third parties, most courts will consider the *Tarasoff* decision in their rulings. Thus, if a client's potential for dangerousness is predicted and the threat of harm is directed at an identifiable person, there is a duty to warn and protect the potential victim. Also, if it is determined that a bystander may be at risk, that person must be warned and protected as well.

Since the *Tarasoff* decision, the elements for carrying out the duties to predict, warn, and protect have been expanded. Two conditions, if present together, require a practitioner to reveal a client's confidential threat of violence: (1) foreseeable and imminent threat and (2) an identifiable potential victim (Reamer, 1994). State laws differ in how a foreseeable threat must be substantiated. In some states foreseeable threat can include a verbal threat, an overt physically violent act toward property or a person, the use of deadly weapons, behavioral indicators, and documentation of violence in past records. Some states have enacted legislation limiting the professional's duty to protect to only those situations in which the client has specifically and seriously threatened to physically harm an identifiable person. Furthermore, courts have determined that a reasonable and prudent practitioner requests and consults previous records, ruling that absence of a current threat does not eliminate risk. If, from the records, the practitioner can guess who may be a potential victim, the practitioner has a duty to warn him or her (VandeCreek & Knapp, 1993).

Some states do not have specific laws beyond the mandates for involuntary hospitalization. However, in those states case law determines duty. "Courts have generally not found liability when the assessment of dangerousness was carried out with reasonable care, even if, in hindsight, the therapist made an error in judgment" (VandeCreek & Knapp, 1993, p. 58).

The courts are aware that the prediction of violence is imperfect and that statistically predicting violence and clinically assessing potential violence are distinct endeavors (Litwak, 1994; VandeCreek & Knapp, 1993). It is in the assessment arena that liability ensues if due care is not exercised. Practitioners are responsible for asking the right questions and taking the appropriate precautions. Typically, liability has been established based on failure to obtain and consult past records and infer the identity of a potential victim, failure to warn the potential victim, and failure to take appropriate precautions to protect others from harm by, for example, involuntary hospitalization or warning possible bystanders. Malpractice claims related to danger to others have also included failure to comply with mandatory reporting laws, failure to transmit information to appropriate officials, failure in duty to consult or refer, wrongful commitment, malicious prosecution, false imprisonment, and abuse of process.

In a special circumstance involving danger to others, states are struggling with legislation to protect HIV-tested patients' rights to confidentiality as well as to protect others from possible infection. Florida laws reinforce the HIV-positive person's right to privacy. However, more than half of the states have passed laws mandating the warning of partners of HIV-infected people (Landers, 1993). Some states have partner notification programs in which state-trained employees notify partners at the request of the HIV-positive person (VandeCreek & Knapp, 1993). To date, the *Tarasoff* decision has not been applied to HIV/AIDS. However, laws are constantly changing, and professionals do not agree on the best course of action. If a social worker is sued for failing to warn a potential victim about HIV/AIDS, more than likely some expert witnesses will support the duty to warn potential victims and others will refute the decision to violate confidentiality and the right to privacy. Even if the potential victim is warned, unless the client has internalized the need to be responsible and inform and protect others, the client's risky behavior may remain unchanged (Reamer, 1994; VandeCreek & Knapp, 1993).

Overall, state laws vary in their definitions of dangerousness and specification of the practitioner's duty to report and warn. Regardless of a state's laws, practitioners should follow a standard of care in both assessing and in taking additional steps to protect a potential victim by increasing the frequency of sessions with the dangerous client, consulting with other experts, considering other treatment approaches, and referring the client for an additional evaluation (Simon, 1982). Practitioners should know the applicable laws for involuntary commitment and be prepared to follow them.

In many states, estimation of potential dangerousness is a major factor in civil involuntary commitment. The Mental Retardation Facilities and Community Mental Health Centers Construction Act (P.L. 88-164, 1963) and its 1975 amendments (P.L. 94-63) led to significant reforms of state laws and procedures for the commitment of mentally ill people. During the past 25 years, states have revised their mental health laws to emphasize client rights, due process, and the least-restrictive environment. "*Commitment* is any state-imposed compulsory treatment, hospitalization, confinement, or other restriction of liberty premised on mental illness or a mental condition" (Saltzman & Proch, 1990/1994, p. 312, italics added). Determination of commitment is based on the person's inability to care for himself or herself, dangerousness to self or others, or need of psychiatric treatment.

Typically, state involuntary commitment laws provide for emergency and court-ordered commitments. Emergency commitment is based on a professional's determination and does not require a court hearing. However, state laws specify a time period, usually 24 to 72 hours, within which the person must be evaluated, documents must be filed with the court, and a court hearing must be held to continue involuntary hospitalization.

State statutes and rules tend to be vague and general in their definitions of mental illness and dangerousness and in their commitment criteria. Mental health laws are applicable to people who are mentally ill and experiencing consequences of mental illness; therefore, the person's dangerousness to self or others or need for treatment must be secondary to the mental illness and not attributable to other conditions. Definitions of mental illness tend to exclude people exhibiting mental retardation or developmental disabilities, character disorders, and substance abuse. Some states (for example, California and Florida) may have separate commitment statutes for these populations.

Usually, determination of the need for extended nonemergency commitment for dangerousness is based on a person's degree of competence and requires a court judgment. Within the purview of most state laws, guidelines and criteria for incompetence are based on mental illness, mental retardation, age, physical condition, substance abuse, potential for dangerousness, and suicide risk. However, there is little agreement about what constitutes competency and incompetency (Reamer, 1987).

Nonetheless, the assessment of the client's competence is basic to the determination of his or her ability to care for self and to make rational and informed decisions, including informed consent for treatment and voluntary commitment. To achieve a reliable competency evaluation, Reamer (1987) proposed the use of minimal standards such as the mental status examination, as well as the individual's history of mental illness, which could influence current judgment, ability to make reasoned judgments and comprehend abstract ideas, and remote and recent memory. In addition, in the identification of potentially suicidal or dangerous clients, the degree of risk of harm to self or others and the imminence of the risk need to be determined, or one must know where to turn for a skilled assessment of risk.

Assessment

Adequate risk assessment of potentially dangerous clients charges the social worker with three responsibilities (Litwak, 1994):

1. making an exhaustive effort to gather detailed information on the client's history of violence and treatment from all available sources
2. identifying and managing, if it exists, the tendency to avoid or minimize violence-related material. (This includes asking detailed questions of the client and others about the violent episodes and developing a

clear picture of the violence, including frequency, duration, intensity, methods, targets, and precipitants.)

3. determining the degree to which the client fits the profile of people who are statistically likely to be violent.

Assessment of potentially dangerous clients often is complicated by a client's unwillingness to identify violence as a problem and by the unpredictable nature of violence. Typically, violence is egosyntonic and used to protect a person from real or imagined harm. A highly dangerous person is one who is provoked by something that is meaningful coupled with a lack of self-control, morality, or reality testing. Therefore, the violent person sees nothing wrong in the lack of self-control or the violent act. Most people who have resorted to violence have exhibited previously violent behavior (Brizer, 1989; Chaiken et al., 1994).

The majority of people who have been killed, injured, or arrested in connection with violent crimes are male (Krattschnitt, 1993; Reiss & Roth, 1993d; Sampson & Lauritsen, 1993), and most of the violent crimes in the United States are committed by men ages 18 to 30 (Rosenberg & Mercy, 1991; Sampson & Lauritsen, 1993). Many violent individuals have a history of antisocial behavior in childhood and adolescence (Buka & Earls, 1993; Reiss & Roth, 1993e); have a history of self-destructive behavior, including substance abuse (Miczek, Debold, et al., 1993; Rosenberg & Mercy, 1991; Sampson & Lauritsen, 1993); or have histories involving both. Other correlates of violence include lower educational attainment and living in a community characterized by high rates of residential mobility, population density, family disruption, social dislocation, and poverty (Rosenberg & Mercy, 1991; Sampson & Lauritsen, 1993). Youth violence has been commonly linked with family functioning that is characterized by parental neglect, abuse, discord, and criminality (Buka & Earls, 1993; Fraser, 1996; Sampson & Lauritsen, 1993).

One level of assessment is completed after a violent act has already occurred; the other involves assessment of a client who is at risk for dangerousness but who has no known recent occurrence of violence. Practitioners may encounter different types of people with violent tendencies:

- The person fears his or her violent urges and seeks help before a violent episode.
- The person's violent urges are escalating, but he or she has not had a full-blown violent outbreak. The person may or may not be aware of his or her own risk for violence and may or may not be open to help.
- The person has recently acted on violent urges and may or may not be receptive to help.

In each situation, the person has the potential to turn the violence on himself or herself or others.

The assessment and treatment of the dangerous client should follow the steps of crisis intervention. Practitioners should explore the nature of the crisis situation and the meaning of the precipitating event. The following areas should be assessed:

- personal history
- interpersonal relationships and social supports

- psychological factors
- physical conditions
- history of violence
- current threats and plans of violence
- potential crime scene
- current crisis and situation.

Personal History

Recent and remote family histories can serve as predictors of violence. Clients who experience rejection and emotional deprivation in early childhood are more prone to violent behavior during a crisis. Neglectful, brutal, emotionally depriving, and seductive parents can contribute to the development of poor impulse control in children. A personal history that includes incidents of violence and death with little accompanying apprehension or fear about death can predict violence. Typically, violent offenders have a childhood history that includes

- parental absence, rejection, or deprivation
- child abuse
- a violent sibling or parent
- family conflict and frequent disruptions in family life
- an early exposure to violence, including family criminal behavior
- general antisocial behavior
- school problems, including temper tantrums, assaults on teachers, threats, and fights
- problems with authority
- learning disabilities, attention deficit hyperactivity disorder, low IQ, poor motor skills, birth complications, head injury, and other physical anomalies (Buka & Earls, 1993; Fraser, 1996; Reiss & Roth, 1993b; Rosenberg & Mercy, 1991; Sampson & Lauritsen, 1993; Tardiff, 1989b).

Interpersonal Relationships and Social Supports

For youths and adults, lack of or unsuccessful interpersonal relationships and social supports both within and outside the family are predictors of violence (Fraser, 1996). This may be especially true for individuals with psychiatric conditions (Estroff, Zimmer, Lachicotte, & Benoit, 1994). The practitioner may explore

- whether the client has positive feelings about people
- how the client relates to the practitioner
- whether the client has a close friend
- whether the client is self-centered as a defense against feelings of inferiority or inadequacy
- how the client relates to members of the opposite sex. Does he or she need them to sustain dependency needs while feeling angry at them?

The practitioner should assess the client's relationships with family, friends, and coworkers, asking questions such as these:

- Would you describe your family or home as violent?
- Has anything recently changed at your home or with your friends?
- Has an important relationship recently or suddenly been threatened?
- Have you had recent trouble at work?
- Are you the only one among your family, friends, and coworkers who gets into fights?

The practitioner should try to speak with the client's significant others. If the client refuses to grant informed consent to do so, the practitioner should weigh the risks of breaching confidentiality against the benefits of protecting others. If the practitioner decides to breach confidentiality, he or she should advise the client of the decision and rationale and note the decision in the client's record. When speaking with significant others, the practitioner should ask questions about and reveal only necessary information.

Psychological Factors

Some diagnostic categories signal high risk for dangerousness, especially when active symptoms are present (Mulvey, 1994)—for example, individuals with bipolar disorder in the manic phase, substance abuse with active intoxication, and paranoid schizophrenia with acute psychosis. During the mental status examination, the practitioner should look for evidence of delusions (for example, thought control, thought broadcasting), hallucinations (commands or threats from imaginary beings), depersonalization, paranoia, suicidal ideation, and impulsivity (Tardiff, 1989b). Violence also can occur with people who have personality disorders of the explosive, antisocial, paranoid, or borderline types, as well as those with substance abuse disorders and those who are psychotically depressed (American Psychiatric Association [APA], 1994; Gilliand & James, 1993; Tardiff, 1989a). Suicidal clients are potentially violent (Brizer, 1989; Plutchik, vanPraag, & Conte, 1989), as are those who exhibit low empathy, impulsivity, attention deficit, and inability to delay gratification (DeJong, 1994). Some individuals can tolerate introspection, whereas others become enraged at any criticism. The practitioner should evaluate the client's ability to see good and bad and his or her capacity to respond appropriately to challenges to his or her value system. The ability to consider consequences, to fantasize, and to identify anger are important factors in assessing aggressiveness.

Physical Conditions

Organic factors can contribute to behavioral disorders that involve lability of mood and affect, aggressiveness, and impulsivity (Brizer, 1989; Miczek, Mirsky, Carey, DeBold, & Raine, 1993; Mirsky & Siegel, 1993; Reiss & Roth, 1993c; Tardiff, 1989a). For example, intermittent explosive disorder is associated with brain dysfunction and episodes of loss of control over violent impulses (APA, 1994). Alcohol intoxication involves behavioral change (such as aggressiveness, lability, and impaired judgment) caused by the chemical properties of alcohol (APA, 1994; Tardiff, 1989a). Temporal lobe epilepsy has been associated with violence (Tardiff, 1989a), although violence rarely occurs during seizures (Mirsky & Siegel, 1993). Dementia; delirium (APA, 1994); and a variety of neuroanatomical, neurophysiological, neurochemical, and neuroendocrine states and traits may relate to violence (Reiss &

Roth, 1993c). Therefore, practitioners should inquire about a violent client's history of head trauma, convulsions, and periods of unconsciousness. It is important that practitioners determine the potential existence of an underlying organic state that warrants further neurobiological assessment and that may be treatable with medication.

The use of some hallucinogens (such as phencyclidine), inhalants, and amphetamines and withdrawal from opiates also can precipitate violence (Miczek, DeBold, et al., 1993; Reiss & Roth, 1993a; Tardiff, 1989a). For mentally ill clients, drug abuse can also exacerbate violence (Miczek, DeBold, et al., 1993; Mulvey, 1994). Alcohol is the substance most frequently linked with violent outbursts (Fagan, 1993; Miczek, DeBold, et al., 1993; Reiss & Roth, 1993a). Drugs and alcohol can precipitate violence in several ways:

- Substances with disinhibiting effects can take away an individual's self-control, particularly when that control is already tenuous.
- Substances may spark "aggression-specific brain mechanism" (Miczek, DeBold, et al., 1993), or intoxication may result in delirium or toxic psychosis in which confusion, delusions, and hallucinations prompt violent behavior.
- Substance withdrawal may include agitation, confusion, and psychosis.
- Maintenance of a substance habit may lead to involvement in violent crime.

Therefore, practitioners should determine if a client is using drugs or alcohol and closely monitor substance abuse treatment efforts.

History of Violence

The best predictor of future violence is past violence (Brizer, 1989; Chaiken et al., 1994; Tardiff, 1989a). Information from previous records, courts, and significant others can help practitioners determine risk. The practitioner should obtain a detailed picture of previous situations in which the client has acted violently by asking such questions as these:

- How far back does your trouble with violence go (for example, getting into fights)?
- What is the most violent thing you have ever done?
- How badly have you hurt someone?
- What is the closest you have come to killing someone?
- Where do fights usually occur? With whom? What do you usually fight about?
- Do you get into fights more or less often than you used to?
- Are the fights becoming more violent?
- Have you ever been arrested? (Document the dates.)
- Have you been convicted of a crime? (Document the crime, arrest, and sentence.)
- Have you ever been hospitalized because of your violent behavior?
- What weapons have you used in the past? Against whom?
- Do you ever hit your spouse or child?

As the client's history of violence is discussed, the practitioner should evaluate the client's judgment by asking,

- Do you think you will need to behave violently again?
- What do you think will happen to you if you do what you have in mind?

Practitioners who work in settings where a client may arrive in police custody should attempt to get a full description of the event that led to the police intervention and be familiar with the police report. The police report can be compared to the client's account of the precipitating event. Violent offenders often distort their histories of violence by underreporting known significant events and frequently present inconsistent versions of violent incidents (Hall, 1987).

Current Threats and Plans of Violence

All threats of violence must be taken seriously and should be thoroughly explored. The practitioner should ask questions about the method and direction of violence such as, "Because you have not been able to think of any other way to feel better, have you thought about how you would hurt _____?" When the threat is directed at a specific person, the nature of the relationship should be examined (Rosenberg & Mercy, 1991). The social worker should understand the meaning of the person to the client. When violent thoughts are directed at a significant other, that person should be interviewed.

If the client is vague about whom he or she may harm, the practitioner should try to get enough information to identify the potential victim. The practitioner should also try to determine if there is a possibility that other people may be present when the threat is acted on.

The practitioner must determine whether the client has the means to carry out the plan and explore the plan's time frame. A client whose plan is fully developed and who has identified the target has a higher risk for violence (Tardiff, 1989b). The practitioner should carefully explore the precipitating event or cause of the potential violence. If the pattern of the violent impulses is diffuse, the client presents a lower risk. However, a person can be dangerous without explicitly threatening a potential victim. In assessing the current situation, the practitioner should ask such questions as,

- At whom do you feel angry now?
- Is there anyone you would like to hurt or kill?
- Why are you seeking revenge?
- Are you likely to see this person soon?
- How would you carry out your threat?
- How would you protect yourself?
- Do you have a gun, a knife, or other weapon?

Potential Crime Scene

The practitioner should gather information about the whereabouts of the potential victim and the availability to the client of a firearm or weapon. Also, the practitioner should explore provocative environmental stimuli (such as noise, smells, crowdedness), architectural features (such as places to hide and escape routes), location (such as degree of isolation, proximity to an unsafe neighborhood or a police department), and presence of third parties at a potential crime scene (Hall, 1987; Reiss & Roth, 1993c; Rosenberg & Mercy, 1991; Tardiff, 1989b).

Current Crisis and Situation

Examining current crisis factors assists in the prediction of violence. Therefore, the practitioner should explore issues such as current heavy drinking, head injuries, memory difficulty, poor coordination, and poor concentration (Brizer, 1989; Hall, 1987; Reiss & Roth, 1993c; Tardiff, 1989b). Another sign of potential violence is an exaggerated preoccupation with sexual thoughts and fantasies.

Clients whose emotions are not consistent with their thoughts may be planning future action. Clients who are members of a subculture in which violence is acceptable tend to be more violent (Reiss & Roth, 1993c; Rosenberg & Mercy, 1991). Also, psychiatric clients who are noncompliant with taking medication or who were recently released from incarceration in an institution have an increased risk for violence (Torrey, 1994).

Violent behavior can be a response to situations that arouse feelings of fear, weakness, and helplessness (Reiss & Roth, 1993c). For example, a client who is very anxious, has been waiting for a long time, and is underinformed about what is happening or about to happen can become violent. As this client becomes more weary of waiting, he or she may become more violent. Under normal conditions these types of clients might not be dangerous. However, if preceding events have inhibited their coping skills and they later enter a crisis state, these clients are more likely to become violent.

Practice Tips

Regardless of the precipitants of violence, during the clinical interview, clients who are pacing, threatening, resistant to doing what is directed, resistant to talking, shouting, shaking their fists, pushing tables or chairs, or showing a weapon must be regarded as dangerous. The first task in the emergency management of a dangerous person is to ensure the safety of the social worker as well as others. Then a therapeutic relationship with the client can begin. The practitioner should always remind the dangerous client of the limits of confidentiality and should always seek supervision, consultation, and back-up.

Once it is determined that there is an imminent and foreseeable risk of violence, the practitioner must take steps to protect the potential victim by warning him or her directly. Before doing so, the practitioner should try to obtain the client's written consent to do so and make the warning in the client's presence or consider having the client make the warning himself or herself in the social worker's presence.

The practitioner who has difficulty contacting the potential victim should document all efforts to do so and ask the police to make the warning. Because the police response may not be timely enough, the social worker should continue to try to warn the victim (the practitioner might send a registered letter). When communicating with the potential victim, the practitioner should reveal only necessary information and not provide counseling or advice.

For a serious threat of violence, the practitioner should respond at several levels:

- Address the client's anger in treatment.
- Increase the length and frequency of sessions.
- Include significant others in sessions.
- Ask the client to relinquish weapons (if the police are not available, the client should relinquish weapons to any responsible person in the setting).
- Develop a no-violence treatment contract that includes the client's avoiding the potential victim and seeking help when violent impulses increase or intensify (this intervention must be coupled with other efforts).
- Do not abandon the client.
- Use supervision and consultation.
- Refer the client for specialized evaluation.
- If indicated, take steps for voluntary or involuntary hospitalization (VandeCreek & Knapp, 1993).

The practitioner should always document the assessment of a high risk of violence, substantiating it with facts, observations, and direct quotes from the client and others. The practitioner should describe the intervention and precautions, describe how the third party was warned, and include conversations with consultants and supervisors. Also, the practitioner should document if the risk of danger to others was not determined to be present or imminent, noting that imminent risk was not sufficiently established clinically.

To intervene effectively with dangerous clients, a social worker must know the state laws and procedures for commitment as applied to different disability groups, such as mentally ill individuals, mentally retarded people, and substance abusers. States vary in criteria for involuntary commitment.

For a client who is HIV positive and poses a risk to others who are not informed of his or her HIV status, the practitioner can consider a range of steps, including

- making voluntary disclosure of HIV a priority issue in therapy
- addressing in sessions issues related to having a potentially debilitating and terminal disease
- helping the client think through consequences of not informing others and continuing risky behaviors (for example, how his or her actions will influence the relationship, particularly if another person becomes infected)
- assessing why the client is not informing potential victims (for example, denial of the disease, fear of rejection, or an intent to harm)
- seeking supervision, consultation, and legal counsel
- improving his or her knowledge of how people cope with disabling and terminal diseases (for example, attending continuing education workshops and reading professional literature)
- following ethical standards and state statutes
- setting up and following practice guidelines that ensure good professional judgment (Landers, 1993; Reamer, 1991).

A variety of treatment approaches may reduce high-risk behavior of HIV-positive people, including social support interventions, cognitive and behavioral techniques, psychoeducational groups, and communication training (Franzini, Sideman, Dexter, & Elder, 1990; Kelly & Murphy, 1992; Kelly & St. Lawrence, 1988; VandeCreek & Knapp, 1993).

SUICIDE

SHERYL

Sheryl worked as a clinical social worker at a locked forensic unit for mentally ill offenders. Late one afternoon she was assigned a newly admitted 21-year-old male arrested for sexually assaulting a minor. Sheryl interviewed and evaluated the client, finding that he posed a significant risk for attempting suicide. Sheryl was worried that she would have to work overtime because she needed to pick up her children at school that afternoon. Thus, she placed an urgent telephone call to the psychiatrist on duty, emphasizing that she had an emergency case and providing the details of her suicide risk assessment. The psychiatrist immediately came to the unit, determined that the client was acutely suicidal, and ordered suicide watch precautions. Sheryl waited until the psychiatrist completed his evaluation and left without documenting her evaluation, assuming that she could wait until the next day because the psychiatrist would document the risk and precautions.

Immediately after the psychiatrist gave the charge nurse the medical orders to initiate the precautions (that is, medication orders, 24-hour individual supervision, and removal of any items that the client could use to harm himself), he received another emergency call and left without making any notes in the client's record. The charge nurse confused Sheryl's client with another client and did not implement the orders for him. Later that evening, the client committed suicide by cutting his throat with a shard of glass from a mirror in the bathroom. A professional liability suit ensued, and the hospital, the administrators, the charge nurse, the psychiatrist, and Sheryl were found negligent in meeting the commonly accepted standard of care, including taking the necessary steps to prevent a suicide and documenting both suicide risk evaluation and decisions made based on that risk.

One of the most challenging and emotionally charged emergencies is dealing with suicidal intent and behavior. Suicide continues to be one of the top 10 causes of death in the United States (National Center for Health Statistics [NCHS], 1988a, 1988b).

Legal Mandates

In determining malpractice negligence in cases of suicide, courts have tended to review three criteria:

1. foreseeability of or failure to determine the imminence of the suicidal behavior. Courts have found the professional liable if the client had a history of suicide attempts and made observable suicidal actions or verbal threats, and the current treatment was related to the client's suicide potential. Practitioners have not been found liable in situations in which the client was cooperative and did not reveal suicidal intent or threat and then suddenly attempted or committed suicide.
2. reasonableness of professional judgment. Courts look to determine if the clinician identified high-risk suicide factors (for example, depression) and then took the appropriate precautions.
3. thoroughness of the treatment plan and its implementation. Practitioners have been found liable if they neglected evidence and did not take care to ensure that the treatment plan and indicated precautions were executed (for example, not following the advice of a referring or consulting professional) (Reamer, 1994; VandeCreek & Knapp, 1993).

Most state laws impose a duty to predict and prevent suicide. Laws have evolved from ruling suicide as a crime and sole responsibility of the person committing the act to definitions that extend responsibility to others, including professionals (Swenson, 1993). In the case of children, some states have deemed that the ethical and legal responsibility of the social worker is to report to parents the self-destructive tendencies of their children (Besharov, 1985). However, the laws governing practitioner response to suicide are not as precise as those that govern abuse, neglect, exploitation, and danger to others.

Recently, state legislative bodies have addressed issues related to assisted suicide. In 1992, 37 states had laws mandating that actively helping a person die was illegal (Brody, 1992, cited in NASW, 1994). A "Death with Dignity" initiative in Washington State was narrowly defeated in a referendum in 1991. In 1993, assisted-suicide bills were considered in California, Iowa, Maine, Michigan, and New Hampshire. Michigan adopted a bill requiring qualified applicants for assisted suicide to receive social work counseling (Brody, 1992, cited in NASW, 1994). As mandated by the federal Patient Self-Determination Act of 1990 (P.L. 101-508), hospitals accepting Medicaid and Medicare must provide patients with facts about hospital and state policies regarding end-of-life decisions and document discussions with adult inpatients about advance directives. Similar requirements are used in other health care agencies such as hospice and home health (American Hospital Association, 1991, cited in NASW, 1994).

Along with legislative bodies, the helping professions are deliberating end-of-life decisions and rational suicide in the context of terminal illness. The 1993 NASW Delegate Assembly adopted a new policy on end-of-life decisions, which emphasizes the client's right to self-determination. Social workers are encouraged to explore with the client other options when assisted suicide is brought up by the client, including hospice, pain management, advance directives for no life support, and counseling. However, "it is inappropriate for social workers to deliver, supply, or personally participate in the commission of an act of assisted suicide when acting in their professional role. . . . The appropriate role . . . is to help patients express their thoughts and feelings, to facilitate exploration of alternatives, to provide information to make an informed choice, and to deal with grief and loss issues" (NASW, 1994, p. 60).

In cases of suicide, courts have varied in their application of the *Tarasoff* decision and duty to warn. Some courts have not upheld the practitioner's duty to warn others of a client's potential for suicide. Other courts have determined the practitioner should have warned the family of a potentially self-destructive client on his release from an inpatient facility (VandeCreek & Knapp, 1993).

Breach of confidentiality can be established if a practitioner discloses information without the client's consent or without substantiating that the client is at risk of self-harm (Austin, Moline, & Williams, 1990; Kjervik, 1984; Woody, 1988). In outpatient settings, breach-of-confidentiality lawsuits have been filed against practitioners for releasing unnecessary information to third parties without the client's informed consent, not following a systematic or standard protocol for suicide risk assessment, and not taking appropriate precautions. However, in a review of malpractice suits related to breach of confidentiality in cases of suicide, VandeCreek, Knapp, and Herzog (1988) found that there were no successful lawsuits against mental health professionals who breached confidentiality to protect a suicidal client.

Malpractice lawsuits specific to suicide in inpatient settings are common. Social workers, therapists, and physicians who have staff privileges and facility employees can be found liable. Also, the administrators of the facility can be found liable for negligent hiring, inadequate supervision of clients, and operating a hazardous facility. Practitioners who refer clients to inpatient settings can be found negligent for not following up with the client (Woody, 1988). Other lawsuits have included not providing the appropriate level of care (such as providing too much or too little restriction) and abandoning a client or not responding to a client's crisis. Typically, courts have acknowledged that inpatient standards of care have moved from a custodial model to an open-door model (VandeCreek & Knapp, 1993).

Liability for wrongful death can be established if appropriate and sufficient action to prevent suicide is not taken. In addition, failure to follow the rules and procedures of a setting, an acceptable standard of care, or state statutes can substantiate liability. Malpractice may be established when a practitioner errs in judgment about whether to confine a client in conjunction with negligent procedures in assessment and diagnosis (Reamer, 1994).

Assessment

Practitioners have been found liable for failing to follow an appropriate standard of care in the assessment of suicide risk. Principles of crisis theory guide the clinical assessment, which includes an evaluation of

- risk group membership
- current suicide plan and suicidal ideation
- history of attempts
- current situation
- personality factors and mood
- physical conditions
- social supports
- past and current coping skills
- warning signs (Gilliand & James, 1993; Ivanoff, 1991; Ivanoff & Riedel, 1995).

Selected high-risk groups for suicide include

- adolescents. Suicide rates for teenagers have increased markedly since 1960, from 3.6 to 11.3 per 100,000. Suicide is now the third leading cause of death for youths ages 15 to 19 (Ivanoff & Riedel, 1995) and the second leading cause of death if the range is extended to age 24 (Farberow, Heilig, & Parad, 1990).
- substance abusers. Up to 20 percent of suicides are committed by alcoholics. People who commit suicide are more likely to have used alcohol or drugs within 24 hours of their death. Even people who normally do not drink tend to do so shortly before killing themselves (Chiles, Strosahl, Cowden, Graham, & Linehan, 1986; Ivanoff, 1991; Ivanoff & Riedel, 1995; Roy & Linnoila, 1986).
- white people. The suicide rate for white people is about two times greater than that of African Americans and increases with age. Suicide rates for other racial and ethnic groups peak between ages 24 and 35 (Ivanoff & Riedel, 1995; NCHS, 1988b).
- elderly people. The highest suicide rate of any age group is consistently among those older than age 75 (Ivanoff & Riedel, 1995; Maltsberger, 1986; NCHS, 1988b).
- people with serious and persistent mental illness. Adults with an affective disorder have an increased risk of suicide, particularly those with major depression and bipolar diagnoses (Ivanoff, 1991; Ivanoff & Riedel, 1995; O'Carroll, Rosenberg, & Mercy, 1991; Shaffer & Gould, 1987). People with schizophrenia also have an increased risk of suicide, particularly if they are depressed and experiencing a sense of hopelessness related to their mental illness (Ivanoff, 1991).
- single people. A disproportionate percentage of suicides are committed by single individuals, with widows having especially high rates. The lowest rates tend to be among married people, especially those with children (Ivanoff & Riedel, 1995; NCHS, 1988a).
- people with a physical illness. There is a high correlation between physical illness and suicidal behavior. The presence of a painful illness presents a considerable risk. The majority of people who commit suicide have seen a physician within six months of the attempt (Ivanoff, 1991; Linehan, 1988; Maltsberger, 1986).
- men. The risk of suicide is higher among men, although women may make more suicide threats (Ivanoff, 1991; Ivanoff & Riedel, 1995; Maltsberger, 1986; NCHS, 1988b).
- unemployed and retired people. Unemployed and retired people tend to have a higher suicide rate than employed people. However, the suicide rate for young employed professional women is increasing (Ivanoff, 1991; NCHS, 1988a, 1988b).
- people with a family history of suicide. The risk of suicide increases for people with a family history of suicide, especially a parent of the same gender. Environmental, sociocultural, and genetic factors may be involved (Ivanoff & Riedel, 1995; O'Carroll et al., 1991).

Practitioners should develop or adopt a checklist to aid the assessment of suicide and to ensure that a reasonable standard of care is being met. Gilliand and James (1993) offered a list of risk factors to use as a clinical assessment tool. Alternatively, a number of validated measures of suicide potential are available, such as the Reasons for Living Inventory (Linehan, Goldstein, Nielsen, & Chiles, 1983, cited in Fischer & Corcoran, 1994), the Scale for Suicide Ideation (Beck, Kovacs, & Weissman, 1979, cited in Wetzler, 1989), the Scale for Assessment of Suicidal Potentiality (Battle, 1985, cited in Gilliand & James, 1993), or the Risk Estimator for Suicide (Motto, 1985, cited in Maltsberger, 1986). When the results of a standardized instrument and the social worker's clinical assessment differ, the practitioner must document how the discrepancies were reconciled and how a decision was made.

Current Suicide Plan and Ideation

In addition to observing whether the client is among the high-risk groups, the practitioner should use the risk assessment protocol to determine if the client has a current suicide plan and suicidal ideation. With the first interview and at clinically appropriate times during treatment, the practitioner should evaluate and re-evaluate the client's suicidal ideations and plan. The practitioner should explore the seriousness of the client's potential for suicide in the following ways:

- Assess the availability of the proposed method. The client who has a realistic plan for acquiring the method or who has ready access to the method is a higher risk for suicide.
- Determine the lethality of the proposed method. The greater the lethality, the higher the risk for suicide. The practitioner should also determine the client's estimation of the lethality of the method. In some cases, the chosen method may in fact not be lethal; however, the client's belief that it is signals serious intent to commit suicide.
- Assess the proximity of a rescuer or support. If helping resources are not close, the risk for suicide is greater.
- Ascertain the specificity of the plan. The greater the detail the client provides about the suicide plan, the higher the risk.
- Explore the manipulativeness of the suicidal ideation. The more aware the client is of the realistic implications of his or her behavior, the more serious the risk. Conversely, the more the client is aware of and focused on the effect of his or her actions on other people, the more likely it is that the planned behavior would be nonlethal (France, 1990; Hatton & Valente, 1984; Maltsberger, 1986; Schutz, 1982).

History of Attempts

The risk assessment protocol should also include a history of attempts (Farberow et al., 1990; Hatton & Valente, 1984; Maltsberger, 1986). The practitioner should ask questions such as these:

- Have you ever thought of suicide?
- What did you think you might do?
- Did you have the means to carry out the suicide?
- Have you ever attempted suicide?
- What did you wish would happen when you made the attempt?
- How do you feel now?

Four factors must be considered when assessing the current risk of suicide when the client has already made an attempt:

1. timing—the more recent the previous attempt, the higher the risk of another attempt.
2. dangerousness—the greater the dangerousness of the previous attempt, the higher the risk of another attempt.
3. client impression—the person who believed that the previous attempt would be lethal is a higher risk for another attempt.
4. rescue—if the previous attempt was set up in such a way as to increase chances of rescue or if the client helped in his or her rescue, the present risk is lower. The lower the chances of rescue in the previous attempt, the greater the risk of another attempt (Houston & Nuehring, 1988).

Current Situation

The practitioner should determine risk factors in the client's current situation that could lead to a suicide attempt, including

- specific stressors such as the death of a spouse or parent, divorce, separation from family, loss of job, financial problems, and events that have been a blow to the client's self-esteem
- preoccupation with anniversary dates of losses or earlier episodes of abuse or rejection
- degree of destabilization or active crisis state related to the current situation (Gilliand & James, 1993; Maltsberger, 1986).

Social and personal resources—including physical and mental capacities; money; significant others; job and hobbies; daily living necessities such as food, housing, and clothing; health care facilities; and transportation—can facilitate the client's functioning in the current situation. The risk for suicide is lowered by mobilizing these resources and intervening to reduce emotional or physical isolation (Hatton & Valente, 1984; Maltsberger, 1986).

In assessing the client's current circumstances, the practitioner might ask,

- Are you thinking of suicide?
- What happened to make you think of suicide?
- Why do you feel that you would be better off dead?
- How do you see yourself in the future?
- Do you feel that these feelings could go away if you received help?
- What help would you choose if it were available?
- What do you wish could happen now?

Personality Factors and Mood

Clients who pose a high risk for suicide include those who are substance abusers, severely depressed, and diagnosed with borderline personality disorders. Psychotic processes with the loss of reality increase the risk, because the realistic consequences of the behavior are not appreciated. This disturbance becomes even more serious when it is combined with depressed mood, hypochondriacal concerns that reach the delusional stage, or command hallucinations ordering the person to commit suicide (O'Carroll et al., 1991; Maltsberger, 1986; Schutz, 1982).

In addition, the frenetic and unstable search for relationships by the client with a borderline personality disorder increases the risk of suicide. The client's impulsiveness and enraged intolerance for the inevitable imperfections of relationships increase the risk. A client who does not relate to others in a reasonably satisfying manner poses an increased risk (Schutz, 1982).

Suicide risk increases with depressed mood, especially if it is associated with vegetative signs that include loss of appetite, loss of energy, and difficulty falling asleep or staying asleep through the night (chronic or severe insomnia alone indicates an increased suicide risk) or with anxiety, tension, or agitation (Schutz, 1982).

Physical Conditions

The client who has a history of unsuccessful treatment of a chronic physical condition; who has experienced a physical trauma or disability; or who has been recently diagnosed with a terminal, disabling, or chronic medical problem is at increased risk for suicide. The practitioner should evaluate how the client is coping and the person's perceptions of his or her health and prognosis (Gilliand & James, 1993; Ivanoff, 1991; Schutz, 1982).

Social Supports

Social supports include the people on whom the client relies for understanding and support when in distress. The risk of suicide increases if significant others are rejecting the client, daring him or her to attempt suicide, or unavailable to the client or if the client only perceives these behaviors to be true. Isolation from social supports is particularly ominous if the client is also impulsive and has few internal resources to cope with stress (Ivanoff, 1991; Ivanoff & Riedel, 1995; O'Carroll et al., 1991; Maltsberger, 1986; Schutz, 1982).

Past and Current Coping Strategies

The client's past and current coping strategies can determine how he or she will manage the present situation. The more limited or inadequate the client's capacity to cope with stress, the greater the risk of suicide. Coping strategies include adaptive devices such as employment, caring for others, and recreational activities and maladaptive devices such as substance abuse or violence. The use of alcohol or drugs as a strategy for coping with stress is particularly dangerous, because the concomitant loss of impulse control and judgment increases the risk of suicide (Ivanoff & Riedel, 1995; Maltsberger, 1986; Schutz, 1982).

The risk of suicide is reduced by a stable lifestyle. The client who has a chronically unstable lifestyle is more vulnerable and may have difficulty coping with future stressful situations (Schutz, 1982).

Warning Signs

The practitioner should be alert to warning signs such as depressive symptoms, verbal warnings, behavioral warnings, and emergency status. Depressive symptoms include

- insomnia
- eating disorders
- loss of sex drive
- hyperactivity or lack of energy
- apathy
- social withdrawal
- easy discouragement
- dwelling on problems
- low self-esteem
- guilt
- anger, hostility
- helplessness
- hopelessness
- tearfulness
- somatic complaints
- memory impairment (Farberow et al., 1990; Hatton & Valente, 1984; James, 1984; Victoroff, 1983).

Verbal warnings can include statements such as

- I'm going to kill myself.
- I wish I were dead.
- The only way out for me is to die.
- Life has lost its meaning for me.
- It's just too much to put up with.
- Nobody needs me anymore.
- I just can't go on any longer.

A client's behavioral warnings can include actions such as

- previous suicide attempts
- giving away cherished objects in a casual manner
- poor adjustment to the recent loss of a loved one
- composing suicide notes
- writing a will
- asking about donating his or her body to science
- sudden and unexplainable recovery from a severe depression
- purchasing or acquiring a gun or other lethal instrument
- engaging in risk-taking behaviors, such as driving too fast (Farberow et al., 1990).

Assessment of suicidal risk includes determining whether a client is an emergency versus a long-term risk. An *emergency risk* is defined as the estimated potential that the client will commit suicide within the next 24 hours. *Long-term risk* is the likelihood that the client will commit suicide in the next two years (Hatton & Valente, 1984).

Practice Tips

Interventions for suicide should be based on the determination of whether the client poses an emergency or a long-term risk. The client who poses an emergency risk requires treatment such as the application of crisis intervention principles and techniques, referral to appropriate complementary sources of service, family intervention, and voluntary or involuntary hospitalization (see earlier in this chapter). The client who poses a long-term risk requires ongoing treatment and comprehensive services.

In cases in which life-threatening behavior has already occurred and risk has become reality, the practitioner's first aim is the provision of medical assistance to help keep the client alive long enough to achieve stability sufficient to explore alternatives to suicide. This goal may involve involuntary commitment. The next task is to decrease the availability of the lethal means, which may be done by the police, the social worker, the client, or the client's significant other (France, 1990).

After obtaining medical treatment for and ensuring the safety of the client, the practitioner should focus on appropriate problem-solving interventions. The practitioner can do the following:

- Guide the client in an analysis of the pros and cons of death so that the client can become more objective about the desire to die.
- Develop a plan of action that directs the client away from suicide.
- Facilitate the decision-making process and assist in organizing the client's activities.
- Focus on exploring problems that have contributed to the client's suicidal crisis, consider a no-suicide contract to avert harm to self, and implement follow-up (France, 1990; Ivanoff, 1991).

Developing a no-suicide contract includes a series of negotiations. After concluding that the client does not pose a high risk, the practitioner should ask the client, "For what period of time can you, on the basis of your knowledge of yourself, say with confidence that you will not attempt to kill yourself by intent or accident?" If the client cannot commit to a time period of at least several days, the practitioner must continue to take steps to protect the client from harming himself or herself such as hospitalization, partial hospitalization, or the use of a responsible person who can prevent a suicide attempt. For example, a responsible family member or friend could be identified to stay with the client, or the client could agree to talk to a friend, partner, or spouse about his or her feelings.

The no-suicide contract can be used as an assessment technique in the prediction of suicidal behavior. After the client identifies a period of time during which he or she can assure that no suicide attempts will be made, the practitioner can help him or her identify predictors before the client again thinks about suicide and steps the client can take to avert suicidal thoughts, such as talking to a significant other, calling the social worker, calling a crisis telephone helpline, and going to a designated 24-hour emergency mental health service. The plan should state that the client agrees to follow the steps and to seek help before acting on a suicidal impulse. Some practitioners have the client sign such a contract and document the agreement in the clinical record. No-suicide contracts should be time limited and renegotiated and renewed at each session (Jobes & Berman, 1991).

Experts do not agree on the benefits of a no-suicide contract. The "problem with a patient contract against suicide is that it may falsely ease the therapist's concern and lower vigilance without having any appreciable effect on the patient's suicidal intent" (Simon, 1987, pp. 260–261). Also, an attorney may question the practitioner's rationale, that is, if he or she did not think there was a risk of suicide, then why was there a contract to prevent it (Swenson, 1993)? No-suicide contracts alone are not sufficient to protect a client from self-harm and must be used as part of a constellation of therapeutic strategies, including individual and family intervention, referral for medications, support groups, and diligent follow-up.

Some commonly cited tips to help the practitioner deal with a suicidal client include

- trusting his or her own suspicions about suicide
- sharing concerns about suicide with the client
- asking direct questions about the client's suicidal ideations and plans
- focusing directly on problem solving intended to reduce suicidality
- not acting shocked, debating with the client, or promising to keep a secret
- not leaving the client alone during a suicidal crisis
- obtaining back-up, consulting with colleagues, and seeking supervision
- in the case of working with a minor, notifying the appropriate adults and involving them in the situation
- assuring the client that something is being done to keep him or her safe from harm and to combat the suicidal urges
- being active and supportive during the session, understanding the client's ambivalence
- after the suicidal potential is diminished significantly, continuing to monitor the client's progress
- following up after missed appointments and termination (Allberg & Chu, 1990; Berman & Jobes, 1994; Ivanoff, 1991; Jobes & Berman, 1991; Kalafat, 1991).

When assessing and intervening with a potentially suicidal client, the practitioner should use reasonable professional judgment in assessing the risk of the least- and most-restrictive treatment environments. When considering either involuntary or voluntary commitment to a hospital or other institution or treatment regimen, the practitioner should consider

- possible physical causes of the client's condition that warrant a referral for a medical examination
- the least-restrictive environment in which the client would not pose a danger to self or others
- alternatives to confinement
- the client's capability and competence to consent to voluntary treatment or confinement
- procedures and criteria for involuntary commitment, including ex parte orders by the court (in which a mental health professional, family member, or concerned person can present facts and request the court to mandate involuntary commitment) (Bennett, Bryant, VandenBos, & Greenwood, 1990).

If the attempt to have the client involuntarily committed or assigned a guardian or conservator is denied or if the client is released, the practitioner should have a back-up plan. The practitioner should seek an appeal, being prepared to advocate for the welfare of the client and to demonstrate the clinical and legal criteria for commitment and guardianship.

The practitioner should prepare the client for commitment or guardianship by explaining what is happening, including the legal, personal, and family ramifications of any actions. The discussion should be guided by the client's level of comprehension and competence. The practitioner should help prepare significant others for what will occur and involve family along with the client in the choice of an appropriate facility (Bennett et al., 1990). The practitioner should remain involved while the client is in the facility and should assume that he or she will resume care of the client following release from confinement. Following the client's discharge and as treatment is resumed, the practitioner can address issues related to the commitment and develop a treatment plan with a continuum of interventions aimed at preventing further involuntary commitments.

The practitioner should substantiate any decision to reduce suicide precautions, to transfer the client to a less-restrictive setting, or to discharge the client, taking care to follow the formal written policies of the practice setting. In private practice, the practitioner should develop a policy for handling suicidal clients, including whom to contact in case of emergency and procedures for seeking psychiatric consultation and reviewing cases that involve suicide risk. Practice settings without a formal policy have an increased risk of liability (Goldberg, 1987).

CHILD MALTREATMENT

WILLIAM

William, a school social worker, was assigned to work with a 12-year-old girl who had been truant for 30 days. During the home visit, the mother revealed that a year ago her daughter told her that a friend of a neighbor had fondled her and taken pictures of her. The mother refused to give the man's name because he was involved in organized crime, and she thought he might harm them. William inquired about what actions the mother took. She indicated that she had called a "social worker" and reported the sexual abuse. However, by that time, the man reportedly had left the country, and the "social worker" said the report could not be acted on unless the perpetrator could be identified and located. The mother was certain that the man had not returned to the community. Because the incident had occurred a year ago and a report had been made by the mother, William decided not to make a suspected child abuse report. Later, a neighbor reported that the girl was being sexually abused. Child protective services investigated and found that the girl had been the victim of a child pornography ring and that the mother's report had been made to a crisis hotline volunteer and not to a protective services worker. William was sued and found negligent in following the state mandatory child abuse reporting law and in verifying the mother's report.

All 50 states mandate the reporting of child maltreatment—abuse, neglect, and exploitation. Assessment and intervention with children and those suspected of maltreatment requires special knowledge and skill. In addition, practitioners must be able to respond appropriately to state mandates differentiating immediately harmful behavior from cumulatively harmful behavior that poses a continuing threat.

During the past two decades, child maltreatment reports have significantly increased, yet less than half of child maltreatment cases are reported (Kalichman, 1993; National Center on Child Abuse and Neglect, 1988). It is likely that a practitioner will encounter child maltreatment even if he or she does not work in a child welfare setting.

Malpractice risks with child maltreatment are associated with inadequately protecting a child, the reporting of suspected child abuse and neglect, character defamation, and violating parental rights (Reamer, 1994). Other related areas of child welfare liability include

- failure to investigate adequately
- unnecessarily intrusive investigation
- loss of parental rights as a result of the findings of a custody evaluation
- failure to place a child in protective custody
- wrongful removal or withholding of a child
- return of a child to dangerous parents
- failure to provide adequate case monitoring
- malicious prosecution (Besharov, 1985; Reamer, 1994).

Although malpractice suits in child welfare are typically against agencies and less often against individual practitioners, the risk of individual liability remains. For example, in cases that ended in a child's death, individual social workers have been sued, even though they followed agency policies. Furthermore, child abuse reporting laws create malpractice risks because techniques for abuse assessment are poorly developed, determination of potential for abuse or neglect is subjective, and breach of confidentiality can harm the therapeutic relationship (Antler, 1987; Besharov, 1985). Social workers can be held liable for suspected abuse reports that cannot be substantiated, that are not made in good faith, or that cannot be deduced based on sound professional knowledge and reasoning. Social workers can also be held liable for failing to report abuse, even if they were unaware of the abuse (but still should have detected it) (Barker & Branson, 1993; Gothard, 1995).

This section is aimed at helping practitioners who are not specialists in child maltreatment understand reporting laws, legal responsibilities, and key assessment and intervention factors. Practitioners working in a child welfare setting or specializing in child maltreatment need more extensive information and specialized training, which is beyond the scope of this book.

Legal Mandates

Three sets of civil laws address child maltreatment: reporting acts, acts creating public social services, and adoption acts. Reporting acts (the focus of this discussion) fulfill three purposes:

1. They encourage the identification of children who are at risk of being maltreated.
2. They designate the agencies that receive and investigate reports.
3. They specify procedures for filing, investigating, and reporting suspected child maltreatment (Saltzman & Proch, 1990/1994).

Although state child maltreatment laws vary greatly, all state laws address four areas:

1. They define reportable child maltreatment.
2. They set criteria and guidelines for mandatory reporting, such as age of children; professionals and others who are mandated to report; and when, where, and how to report.
3. They provide for incentives to report, such as immunity from prosecution for reports made in good faith.
4. They stipulate penalties for failure to report, such as criminal prosecution, fines, jail sentences, civil lawsuits, and professional disciplinary actions (Kalichman, 1993; VandeCreek & Knapp, 1993).

Typically, state laws are based on the 1974 Child Abuse Prevention and Treatment Act (P.L. 93-247) and the 1984 amendments to that act (P.L. 98-457). This act requires states receiving federal funding to include in child maltreatment laws provisions for immunity for reporting suspected child maltreatment.

Definitions

State laws vary in their definitions of maltreatment. In general, state laws define *abuse* as an act of commission that includes physical pain and injury; mental anguish and psychological injury; unreasonable confinement; failure to care for and treat physical conditions; or failure to prevent physical or psychological pain or injury, intimidation, and self-abuse. These laws define *neglect* as an act of omission that includes deprivation of basic services, absence of responsible care, and failure to protect and provide for. *Exploitation* usually refers to an illegal or improper use of an individual's property, resources, or person to take advantage of that individual. This includes sexual abuse. The majority of maltreatment definitions include an identifiable incident of adult misbehavior toward a child, psychological or physical harm or endangerment caused by the adult's behavior, and a causal connection between the adult's behavior and the harm to the child (Faller & Russo, 1981; Kalichman, 1993).

Most state laws delineate four categories of child maltreatment: physical abuse, neglect, sexual abuse, and emotional abuse (Kalichman, 1993). Videka-Sherman (1991) summarized the definitions set forth by the National Center on Child Abuse and Neglect:

> [Physical] abuse connotes an act of commission that results in harm to the child. It includes intentional injury such as burns, bruises, fractures, contusions, lacerations, or other injuries resulting from physical assault. *Emotional abuse* results from verbal assault or chronic scapegoating by the parenting person. Verbal assaults include conveying to the child that he or she is no good, worthless, evil, or hated. Emotional abuse also includes confinement, threats, and withholding [of] life necessities such as sleep or food.
>
> *Sexual abuse* is a specific form of physical abuse. In this form of abuse, injury to the child results from sexual contact by a

caretaking person. Sexual contact includes intercourse, touching, and fondling. Other acts that use children as sexual objects are also included in the definition of child sexual abuse, such as child pornography and subjecting children to viewing sexual acts committed by adults.

Physical child neglect usually results from a parental act of omission; the parent fails to provide for a child's basic needs, making that child actually suffer or be susceptible to harm or injury. The most common types of child neglect include . . . failing to provide basic physical needs such as shelter, clothing, health care, and food; abandonment; and expulsion of the child from the home. *Educational neglect* includes failing to enroll the child in school, permitting chronic truancy, or not attending to special educational needs of the child. *Emotional neglect* includes inadequate nurturance or affection, chronic domestic violence, and permitting alcohol or substance abuse by a child. (p. 346, italics added)

Beyond the number of categories of maltreatment, state definitions of child maltreatment vary along a number of additional lines, including specificity of definitions and types of evidence needed to require reporting (Howing & Wodarski, 1992; Kalichman, 1993). Child maltreatment may be defined in general or specific terms. For example, California law differentiates among degrees of severity of neglect:

Neglect means the negligent treatment or the maltreatment of a child by a person responsible for the child's welfare under circumstances indicating harm or threatened harm to the child's health or welfare. . . . *Severe neglect* includes . . . severe malnutrition, medically diagnosed nonorganic failure to thrive . . . intentional failure to provide adequate food, clothing, shelter, or medical care. . . . *Willful cruelty or unjustifiable punishment* of a child means a situation where any person willfully causes or permits any child to suffer, or inflicts thereon, unjustifiable physical pain or suffering. (California Penal Code, Section 1165, cited in Kalichman, 1993, p. 14, italics added)

Colorado law specifies the types of evidence that indicate reportable child maltreatment:

An act or omission in one of the following categories which threatens the health or welfare of a child . . . evidence of skin bruising, bleeding, malnutrition, failure to thrive, burns, fracture of any bone, subdural hematoma, soft tissue swelling, or death and either the history given concerning such condition is at variance with the degree or type of such condition or death or circumstances indicate that such a condition may not be the product of an accidental occurrence. (Kalichman, 1993, p. 15)

Some states set forth broader definitions. For example, Maine's statutes define *child maltreatment* as a "threat to a child's health or welfare by physical or emotional injury or impairment, sexual exploitation, deprivation of essential needs or lack of protection from these" (Kalichman, 1993, p. 17). If child maltreatment is defined in broad terms, there may be less clarity about what to report and therefore an increased necessity to rely more on professional judgment. On the other hand, specific definitions may not take into account all the dimensions of child maltreatment.

There are many problems in defining child maltreatment, including how to differentiate excessive from acceptable discipline and appropriate from inappropriate treatment. Creating legal and clinical definitions of child maltreatment that take into account parental rights, cultural differences, and children's rights is a very complex process.

Statutes differ in their specifications of who may be a victim or a perpetrator. The Child Abuse Prevention and Treatment Act (P.L. 93-247, 1974) specified that anyone responsible for a child's welfare or health can be a perpetrator of abuse, including parents, other relatives, legal guardians, babysitters, teachers, youth group directors, day care workers, and other institutional staff. However, some states have declared certain classes of individuals as immune from child maltreatment prosecution, such as school personnel (Davidson, 1988). Also, some state statutes limit child protective services to children younger than 17 and limit the ability of child protective services to petition the court for custody and impose court-ordered conditions.

Mandatory Reporting

The type of evidence required to warrant making a report varies among states as well. Most child maltreatment laws do not specify a requisite degree of certainty that abuse has occurred or will occur. Some state laws specify that a report is warranted on the basis of observable parental or child behavior. Other states mandate reporting when the signs, symptoms, and effects of possible child maltreatment are present. Still other states mandate reporting based on hearsay or reasonable suspicion. The more objective the language used in the statute, the easier it is to enforce penalties for failure to report (Kalichman, 1993).

Statutes specify who is mandated to report. In all 50 states, social workers are among those required to report suspected child maltreatment (Reamer, 1994). Even if a case has been previously reported, the professional has a legal responsibility to report it when child abuse is again suspected. Some states require any person suspecting abuse to make a report (Hutchison, 1993; National Center on Child Abuse and Neglect, 1988). State laws tend not to address the professional's responsibility to report cases where an adult client experienced abuse as a child. States differ in the format of reporting required, such as written, oral, or both; what agency is required to receive the report; and who investigates the report.

Incentives to Report

State laws provide immunity from civil and criminal liability for those who report in good faith. If child maltreatment is observed or suspected, confidentiality related to reporting is waived by law, and practitioners are immune from prosecution for good-faith reporting (Alexander & Alexander, 1995; Reamer, 1994; Saltzman & Proch, 1990/1994; Swenson, 1993). However, whether or not and how much immunity exists for actions beyond reporting is ambiguous.

Failure to Report

All states provide penalties for failure to report, and most stipulate that failure to report must be knowing and willful. Criminal penalties range from fines to jail (Kalichman, 1993). Professional regulatory laws may also provide for disciplinary action (for example, license revocation for failure to fulfill statutory requirements). Failure to follow a statute also establishes the grounds for not providing a reasonable standard of care and may constitute malpractice (Alexander & Alexander, 1995; Reamer, 1994). If laws and professional ethics conflict with agency child abuse reporting policies, the practitioner must first abide by laws and professional ethics and standards and then by agency policies.

Assessment

The interviewing of children, parents, and family members about suspected maltreatment requires specialized knowledge and skill because of the unique characteristics of the families involved. Maltreating families may be involuntary participants in service, may not directly show the actions that caused service, and may represent complex and multiproblem households (Hansen & Warner, 1992). Differentiation must be made between immediately harmful behavior and cumulatively harmful behavior that poses a continuing threat. Maltreatment tends to be a family secret. The child may be unable to respond to questions directly and may be fearful of the parents' retribution, therefore limiting the information that can be directly collected. Hence, practitioners must be alert to the "soft signs" of abuse and neglect, which may include physical, emotional, and family interaction cues indicating potential for maltreatment. In general, the assessment should therefore include consideration of

- the child's behavior and symptoms
- parental, marital, and family functioning.

Child's Behavior and Symptoms

The characteristics of the maltreated child vary greatly. Children who are most frequently abused tend to be younger (average age 7.1 years) and to exhibit a variety of symptoms including lower IQ, poor school performance, poor peer relationships, behavior problems, developmental deficits, health problems, delinquent and acting-out behaviors, and depression (Hegar, Zuravin, & Orme, 1993; Kanda, Orr, Brissett-Chapman, & Lawson, 1993, cited in Brissett-Chapman, 1995; Videka-Sherman, 1991). Children may exhibit fear of their parents or reluctance to discuss the alleged maltreatment. The practitioner's assessment of the child should include

- physical functioning and evidence of maltreatment
- cognitive, intellectual, and psychosocial development.

Physical functioning and evidence of maltreatment
Evidence in the child's physical condition can substantiate the presence of abuse or neglect (Videka-Sherman, 1991). Also, children with physical impairments, needs, and illnesses are at an increased risk (Brissett-Chapman, 1995) because of the stresses generated for their parents and caregivers. For example, a colicky newborn can be difficult to care for and can trigger an abusive response in a parent with poor impulse control and few resources. Personal observations, past and current medical records, and a medical evaluation are basic to the assessment of physical functioning.

Practitioners should look for indications of normative growth in such areas as height and weight (Videka-Sherman, 1991). Maltreated children may have physical developmental delays (Herring, 1992, cited in Brissett-Chapman, 1995; Kanda et al., 1993, cited in Brissett-Chapman, 1995; Thornburg & Mumford, 1994) and, in extreme cases, fail to thrive. Also, a child's physical condition may reveal evidence of both past and present abuse. Practitioners should consider evidence such as scars, healed broken bones, bruises, burns, or physical deprivation.

Practitioners should look for both direct and circumstantial physical evidence of maltreatment, including

- reports of eyewitnesses to the maltreatment
- the child's description of the maltreatment
- medical findings of maltreatment
- the congruence of the child's injuries or neglect with the parent's explanation of them.

The practitioner can ask the child questions such as those set forth by Ansell and Breckman (1988, cited in Breckman & Adelman, 1992):

- Has anyone ever hurt you?
- Has anyone ever touched you when [or where] you did not want to be touched?
- Has anyone ever forced you to do something against your will?
- Has anyone ever taken anything that was yours without your permission?
- Have you ever given anything away even though you really did not want to? Why?
- Does anyone ever talk [to] or yell at you in a way that makes you feel lousy or bad about yourself?
- Are you afraid of anyone?
- Has anyone ever threatened you?
- Has anyone ever refused to help you take care of yourself when you needed help? (pp. 244–245)

Practitioners should always consult with a physician and refer for a medical evaluation of the child's health, development, and evidence of abuse and neglect.

Cognitive, intellectual, and psychosocial development
Maltreated children may have developmental delays in their cognitive, intellectual, and social functioning. In addition to gathering information from interviews with the child, the school, and significant people, practitioners

should consider referring children for a specialized assessment of cognitive and intellectual functioning. Also, social workers can use a number of clinical assessment tools that measure infant and child development. The Bayley (1969) Scale of Infant Development and the Minnesota Child Development Inventories (Ireton & Thwing, 1974) are among those noted by Videka-Sherman (1991). Practitioners should also consider the child's peer relationships (Kanda et al., 1993, cited in Brissett-Chapman, 1995; Thornburg & Mumford, 1994), including the ability to get along with others and the capacity to maintain intimacy and develop friendships (Videka-Sherman, 1991). The lack of mastery of basic life skills such as dressing, toileting, and self-grooming (Videka-Sherman, 1991), as well as poor academic performance and school attendance, can be both predictors and indicators of maltreatment.

Parental, Marital, and Family Functioning

Parents who abuse their children come from many ethnic, racial, and economic backgrounds. Typically, the primary caretaker is the perpetrator of the maltreatment. In comparison with nonabusive parents, a number of demographic and biopsychosocial factors can increase the potential for maltreatment, including

- spousal abuse
- a history of abuse in the family of origin
- a personal history of violence
- childbearing at a young age
- a complicated pregnancy
- lower socioeconomic status and educational attainment, poverty
- unemployment
- social isolation
- health, mental health, and substance abuse problems
- high levels of anger
- poor frustration tolerance
- perception of parenting as stressful
- many stressors in conjunction with limited resources and coping skills (Reiss & Roth, 1993f; Thornburg & Mumford, 1994; Videka-Sherman, 1991).

Assessment of the parents should include sources of stress and coping skills, environment, parent–child interaction, and family functioning.

Sources of stress and coping skills
Parents pose a greater risk for maltreatment when they are or perceive themselves to be under stress and lacking in coping resources (Milner, 1993). The practitioner should identify the sources of stress, including the family's financial situation, housing needs, employment status, neighborhood conditions, and lack of social supports. Parents of a difficult child or one with special health or emotional needs may be at greater risk for maltreatment (Herring, 1992, cited in Brissett-Chapman, 1995). Social isolation and inadequate knowledge of child development exacerbates abuse potential among parents (Milner, 1993). In addition, families may experience stress because of divorce, separation, or removal of a member.

Parents with substance abuse problems or a psychiatric illness are at risk of resorting to abuse or neglect (Milner, 1993; Hansen & Warner, 1992; Thornburg & Mumford, 1994). Parents with limited coping skills may resort to maltreatment of their child. The practitioner should assess the parents' capacity to think before acting, ability to control anger, ways of managing the child's behavior, and capacity to maintain relationships. At-risk parents may also lack basic life skills, such as financial management, household management, and self-care (Hansen & Warner, 1992; Videka-Sherman, 1991).

Environment
Assessment of the family's environment should include the safety of the living conditions, the family's physical resources, the amount of living space, the availability of community resources, and the availability of social supports and natural helping systems (Ayoub, Jacewitz, Gold, & Milner, 1983, cited in Chaiken et al., 1994; Hansen & Warner, 1992; Milner, 1993).

Parent–child interaction
The nature of the parent–child interaction is central to determining the risk of child maltreatment (Ayoub et al., 1983, cited in Chaiken et al., 1994; Hansen & Warner, 1992; Milner, 1993; Videka-Sherman, 1991). The practitioner should observe how parents deal with differences, conflict, and the child's noncompliance and should determine the amount, nature, and quality of parent–child interaction, including the level of nurturance and stimulation. The parents should have a repertoire of child management skills beyond the use of corporal punishment. In addition, the practitioner should gather information about the parents' relationship and evaluate their capacities for intimacy and tolerance for autonomy and independence, both of which can predict maltreatment.

Family functioning
Assessment of the family's level of functioning should include consideration of the family's willingness and capacity to nurture and protect, to express needs, to elicit caregiving, and to foster individuality. Nonabusive families tend to have flexible roles and nonrigid forms of thinking and behaving, skills in problem solving and shared or participatory decision making, and a capacity to respond to crisis situations by relying on the family. Abusive families are characterized by negative affect, interactions, and problem solving (Milner, 1993), and they use coercion, force, and violence to resolve conflicts. They tend to have constricted verbal communication and blurred or confused boundaries. Autonomy is discouraged by symbiotic ties of dependency. Discipline is harsh, and parenting is aimed at controlling the child (Milner, 1993). The child may be expected to nurture the parents, and the parents may place excessive expectations on the child.

Based on the predictors and indicators of abuse identified in the literature (Herring, 1992, cited in Brissett-Chapman, 1995; Kanda et al., 1993, cited in Brissett-Chapman, 1995; Milner, 1993; Reiss & Roth, 1993f;Thornburg & Mumford, 1994; Videka-Sherman, 1991), the practitioner's assessment of the family should address

- family composition and chronology (that is, early marriage or child-birth)

- a history of family violence in the childhood or background of adults in the family
- the overreliance on physical punishment or belief that increasing the severity of corporal punishment increases the effectiveness of learning
- the degree to which the family is socially isolated and lacking in social supports
- the quality of communication, affect, and cohesion that characterizes the family
- the forms of violence currently experienced in the family
- child protective services or legal system involvement with the family
- the family's strengths
- the degree to which the family is willing to accept and respond to help and outside assistance.

Practice Tips

The practitioner's first and foremost concern in cases of child maltreatment is the safety of the child. The practitioner must report the suspected maltreatment verbally and in writing to appropriate authorities. If there is concern that there will not be a timely response, the practitioner should also contact the police. Once the report is made, the risk for the child may increase. The practitioner should take precautions to protect against this risk by informing child protective services of and giving evidence for his or her concerns. The practitioner should document in the clinical record any efforts to intervene and the response of child protective services. In some cases child protective services may not decide to investigate the case because the report does not meet their criteria for mandatory child maltreatment investigation. The social worker who believes that the child is still at risk should seek consultation, take steps to better substantiate concerns, and make the report again. The practitioner must continue to assess for risk if the maltreated child remains in or returns to the home.

Once the child's safety is assured, the practitioner can implement an appropriate continuum of interventions. Paralleling Videka-Sherman's (1991) recommendations, the practitioner should

- Set clear and realistic intervention goals, keeping the client informed about the intervention process and expectations.
- Develop a no-abuse contract similar to a no-suicide contract (discussed earlier in this chapter).
- Develop a treatment plan that includes effective case management; ensures regular monitoring of the continued risk of maltreatment; stipulates the steps parents should take before they act, such as contacting the practitioner, Parents Anonymous, or another support system; and provides for the development of parenting and coping skills.
- Consider providing services on a more frequent and intensive basis.
- Arrange for provision of a continuum of services, such as job finding, money management, prenatal care, family leisure time activity training, home safety training, and substance abuse treatment.

Practitioners working with families suspected of child maltreatment should discuss their legal responsibility to report child maltreatment and explain the penalty for failure to report. The practitioner should consider having the parents present when the report is made and, if possible, having the parents make the report themselves (however, the social worker is still legally bound to make his or her own report). The practitioner should be prepared to deal with the parents' feeling of betrayal.

ADULT MALTREATMENT

VERONICA

Veronica, a clinical social worker who was employed at an outreach program for the family caregivers of people with Alzheimer's disease, had worked with an elderly couple for the past six months. The husband, who had been his wife's sole caretaker for many years, was adamant that he would not place her in a nursing home. However, recently the husband was hospitalized for a stroke that left him with a slight short-term memory impairment and dependent on a walker to get around. Since his hospital discharge, a home health agency had provided a visiting nurse two times a week, a home health aide and homemaker services three times a week, and Meals on Wheels.

For more than a month after his discharge, the conditions of both the husband and wife deteriorated. On several occasions Veronica observed that the husband had bruises and seemed confused, and during one visit she noticed that he had a black eye and multiple bruises on his body. The husband explained that his wife had become disoriented during the night and hit him while he was sleeping. As Veronica once again explored nursing home placement for the wife, the husband opposed any suggestions of placement and begged Veronica to let him care for his wife until she died. He also begged Veronica not to tell anyone about his condition, saying he "couldn't face it if people saw him like this . . . beaten by his own wife."

Although Veronica was concerned about the wife's aggressive behavior and the husband's ability to protect himself, she felt he had a right to decide how he wanted to live and that the couple were receiving adequate services through the home health agency. Veronica decided to intensify her work on helping the husband overcome his resistance to placing his wife. One morning, the visiting nurse discovered the husband unconscious with multiple injuries to his head and body and reported the maltreatment to elder protective services, which determined both husband and wife were at risk of harm. Veronica was sued for failing to follow the state's law for the mandatory reporting of elder maltreatment, failing to determine the husband's competence and ability for self-care and protection, and failing to take steps to protect him from harm.

Legal Mandates

Laws addressing abuse, neglect, and exploitation of older and disabled or other vulnerable adults have been modeled after child maltreatment laws, with the exception that adult maltreatment includes financial exploitation or material abuse (Blunt, 1993; Tatara, 1995; Williams, 1992), as well as physical, sexual, and psychological abuse and willful and nonwillful neglect. All states and U.S. territories except Puerto Rico have legislation that includes mandatory reporting requirements for domestic elder and adult maltreatment (Pillemer & Frankel, 1991; Salend, Kane, Satz, & Pynoos, 1984; Tatara, 1995; Wolf, 1988). However, not all states penalize the failure to report, not all states provide specialized adult protective services, and not all states have laws that speak to institutional elder maltreatment (Kosberg, 1990; Saltzman & Proch, 1990/1994; Tatara, 1995). Ideally, adult protective services include legal intervention and authority to remove the maltreated adult without consent. However, this can be a problem if the adult is competent and chooses to stay in the abusive situation. Typically, the laws apply to those adults who are unable to care for themselves because of a mental or physical incapacity or incompetence.

All states provide immunity from liability for good-faith reporting. In other respects, laws governing reporting of adult maltreatment are significantly more variable and often have been enacted more frequently than child maltreatment laws. All states consider violence or threat of violence against anyone a crime. In some instances, states have enacted separate criminal offenses for maltreatment of older and disabled people; in other states this type of violence is considered a more serious offense (Saltzman & Proch, 1990/1994).

Relevant legislation may reside in adult protective services laws, in domestic violence statutes, or in specific adult abuse laws. If domestic violence statutes protect disabled and older adults, an order of protection can be issued to prevent further harm. In states that have adult protective services legislation, additional services can be provided.

As with child maltreatment laws, state adult protective services laws vary in generality and specificity of criteria and procedures. However, common components include

- defining abuse, neglect, or exploitation
- designating adults who are provided services
- recommending or mandating reporting to appropriate authorities
- providing immunity for good-faith reporting
- setting penalties for failure to report
- stipulating investigative procedures
- delineating criteria for when intervention and services can be provided without informed consent of the adult served (Saltzman & Proch, 1990/1994).

Definitions

States vary greatly in their definitions of adult maltreatment and adult protective services. As with child maltreatment, federal and state legal definitions may differ from definitions used in research and those specified in clinical sources (Tatara, 1995). Kosberg (1990) proposed a comprehensive clinical definition of *adult maltreatment* encompassing both elderly and disabled adults that included

- *passive neglect,* which is characterized by a situation in which the person is left alone, isolated, or forgotten. Because of the abuser's lack of intelligence or lack of experience as a caregiver, he or she is often unaware of the neglect or consequences of the neglect.
- *active neglect,* which is characterized as the intentional withholding of items necessary for daily living such as food, medicine, companionship, and bathroom assistance.
- *verbal, emotional, or psychological abuse,* which is characterized by situations in which the person is insulted, infantalized, frightened, intimidated, humiliated, or threatened.
- *physical abuse,* which is characterized by the person being hit, slapped, bruised, sexually molested, cut, burned, or physically restrained.
- *material or financial misappropriation,* which is characterized by actions including monetary or material theft or misuse.
- *violation of rights,* which is characterized by efforts to force a person from his or her dwelling or to force him or her into another setting without any warning, explanation, or opportunity for input.

A definition of adult maltreatment set forth by the National Aging Resource Center on Elder Abuse also included *self-abuse and neglect* sufficient to threaten the health and safety of the elderly person (Tatara, 1995).

Adult protective services are defined in a variety of ways from state to state (Saltzman & Proch, 1990/1994; Tatara, 1995). In Florida, the definition specifies services:

> *Protective services* means those services, the objective of which is to protect an aged or disabled adult from abuse, neglect, or exploitation. Such protective services include, but are not limited to, evaluation of the need for protective services; casework for the purpose of planning and providing needed services; obtaining financial benefits to which the aged person or disabled adult is entitled; securing medical and legal services; maintenance of the aged person or disabled adult in his own home through the provision of protective services; assistance in obtaining out-of-home services, including respite care, emergency housing, and placement settings, as necessary; and seeking protective placement, as necessary. (14 Florida Stat. Ann. 415.102, cited in Saltzman & Proch, 1990/1994, italics added)

In California, the definition specifies the conditions requiring intervention:

> *Adult protective services* means those preventive and remedial activities performed on behalf of elders and dependent adults who are unable to protect their own interests; [are] harmed or threatened with harm; [are] caused physical or

mental injury due to the action or inaction of another person or their own action due to ignorance, illiteracy, incompetence, mental limitation, or poor health; [are] lacking in adequate food, shelter, or clothing; [are] exploited of their income and resources; or [are] deprived of entitlement due them. (California Welfare and Institution Code 15610, cited in Saltzman & Proch, 1990/1994, italics added)

Adult protective services statutes uniformly include vulnerable adults living at home, and most extend to those in institutions or community-based facilities. In cases in which an adult chooses to live in his or her home in spite of unsanitary and unsafe conditions, the difficult decision to determine the person incompetent and eligible for placement out of the home must be considered. If active maltreatment is involved, the decision to relocate the individual may be simpler. However, adult protective services interventions are often reactive to the availability of service alternatives in the community. The situation is further complicated when the reporting and protective services intervention is done by law enforcement instead of social services. A report of maltreatment may result in the arrest of the caregiver; may intrude on the maltreated adult's freedom, privacy, and rights; and may result in placement against the adult's wishes (Saltzman & Proch, 1990/1994).

There is limited information on the rate and types of malpractice suits for maltreated adults who live at home; more lawsuits tend to be filed for vulnerable adults placed in long-term care facilities. Recently, lawsuits and criminal charges have been filed against court-appointed guardians and conservators who financially exploit or neglect the person appointed to their care (VandeCreek & Knapp, 1993).

Assessment

Given limited data on the rate of reported cases of adult maltreatment, there is no clearly agreed-on profile of the victim or abuser. However, in general, the maltreatment tends to be recurring, and the maltreated vulnerable adult tends to be older, frail, and multiply dependent with care needs related to hygiene, nutrition, safety, and toileting (Fulmer, 1988; Kosberg, 1990). Abusers are more likely to be men; victims are more likely to be women (Tatara, 1995). Little empirical work has been done with respect to race and ethnicity (Tatara, 1995), but there are indications that white elders are more likely to be self-neglectful, black elders are more likely to be neglected by others, and both races are equally likely to be physically abused or materially exploited (Longres, 1992). The major factors cited as exacerbating the risk of domestic adult maltreatment include

- a caregiver who has a mental illness, substance abuse, or other disabling condition
- a financially dependent caregiver
- a family history of violence
- the presence of multiple stressors and personal problems of the caregiver, including financial problems, unemployment, divorce, and other life crises
- social isolation of the family

- impairment of the dependent elder (Fulmer, 1991; Lacks, Berkman, Fulmer, & Horowitz, 1994; Phillips, 1983; Pillemer, 1986; Pillemer & Frankel, 1991; Strauss, Gelles, & Steinmetz, 1980; Tatara, 1995).

The assessment of vulnerable adults should include detailing the concrete circumstances of the maltreatment and examining possible evidence of maltreatment such as cognitive functioning, functional status, health and physical conditions, living arrangements, financial support, social support, stressors, and emotional or psychological factors (Breckman & Adelman, 1988, cited in Breckman & Adelman, 1992; Fulmer, 1988).

Concrete Circumstances of the Maltreatment

The practitioner should gather information about the nature and extent of the suspected maltreatment, including

- the frequency, duration, severity, and type of maltreatment
- the time and place of events leading to the maltreatment
- the abusers and their motives
- whether the harm is intentional or unintentional
- the client's and abuser's acknowledgment of and explanations for the maltreatment
- the history of past maltreatment and interventions attempted (Breckman & Adelman, 1992).

Cognitive Functioning

The practitioner should consider the client's level of cognitive functioning and its reversibility, especially if it has recently changed. The practitioner should determine if the client is taking medications that may affect his or her cognitive functioning or if the cognitive impairment is related to possible victimization. Determining the degree to which the cognitive impairment has affected social relationships and the caregiver's understanding of and responses to the client's cognitive capacities is important (Breckman & Adelman, 1988, cited in Breckman & Adelman, 1992).

Functional Status

In assessing the client's and caregiver's functional statuses, the practitioner should consider

- the client's competency
- the client's ability to perform activities of daily living
- the frequency, quality, and adequacy of help provided to the client by the caregiver
- the degree of risk if the client does not receive necessary help
- the caregiver's competency
- the client's and caregiver's expectations of one another
- the caregiver's negative and positive feelings about the caregiving responsibilities
- informal social supports available to the caregiver

- formal supportive services being used (Breckman & Adelman, 1988, cited in Breckman & Adelman, 1992).

Health and Physical Conditions

Depending on the nature of the maltreatment, maltreated adults can be in relatively good physical health. In addition, many elders tend to downplay physical injuries, which may be caused by accidents. Nevertheless, the practitioner should identify any medical problems, such as problems with hearing or vision, that could interfere with the adult's self-protection, as well as conditions that could be manifestations of abuse or neglect. If the client has evidence of an injury, the practitioner should obtain explanations from both client and possible abuser and also look for past history of unexplained or accidental injuries and past assessments of suspicious signs and symptoms of abuse, neglect, or exploitation. The practitioner should determine the adequacy of the caregiver's response to the client's medical problems and the client's understanding of the need for medical treatment (Breckman & Adelman, 1988, cited in Breckman & Adelman, 1992).

Living Arrangements

In domestic maltreatment situations, either the perpetrator or the victim typically depends on the other for housing. The practitioner should explore the history of and rationale for the client's living arrangements, who owns the home, and its accessibility to outsiders (Breckman & Adelman, 1988, cited in Breckman & Adelman, 1992). Conditions such as overcrowding should be noted.

Financial Resources

The practitioner should examine the amount and source of the client's assets, who manages the money, the degree to which the caregiver contributes to the financial costs of the client's care, and the degree to which the caregiver is financially dependent on the client. With respect to financial dependency, "a serious imbalance of dependency in either direction . . . [is] a potential risk factor" (Pillemer & Frankel, 1991, p. 170). The practitioner should determine whether the financial arrangements are informal or a formal legal agreement and why and how long they have been in effect, looking for evidence of possible financial exploitation (Breckman & Adelman, 1988, cited in Breckman & Adelman, 1992).

Social Support

The social isolation of both victims and abusers presents a risk factor for maltreatment (Pillemer & Frankel, 1991). The practitioner should consider the nature and frequency of and satisfaction with family and other social contacts and whether the caregiver prevents the client from having contact with others. In addition, the practitioner should explore the ways the caregiver and client spend time together and the quality of their relationship. Finally, the nature, quality, and frequency of formal social supports used by the client and caregiver should be thoroughly explored (Breckman & Adelman, 1988, cited in Breckman & Adelman, 1992; Dane, 1990).

Stressors

The practitioner should assess the degree to which caregivers are equipped to function in their roles. Does the caregiver understand the elderly client and the reasons for his or her behavior and condition? Does the caregiver know about and use formal and informal resources and supports? Does the caregiver attend to his or her own needs and balance these with the demands of others? How well does the caregiver cope, maintain the home, and manage the behavior of the elderly client (Toseland & Smith, 1991)? In addition, the practitioner should determine external stressors that may be contributing to the maltreatment, such as unemployment, marriage, divorce, changes in residence, death of a significant other, substance abuse, arrest, or other major life events. Further, the practitioner should determine any other stressors that may be causing conflict between the client and the caregiver and should be especially attuned to caregiver burden (Bendick, 1992; Breckman & Adelman, 1988, cited in Breckman & Adelman, 1992; Tatara, 1995).

Emotional and Psychological Factors

The practitioner should look for emotional and psychological symptoms of victimization on the part of the client, such as depression, withdrawal, confusion, fear, guilt, anxiety, lowered self-esteem, shame, and helplessness. In addition, the practitioner should determine if the mood of the client or caregiver has changed recently and if there is a history of mental illness, developmental disability, substance abuse, or violence on the part of either abuser or victim (Breckman & Adelman, 1988, cited in Breckman & Adelman, 1992).

Practice Tips

The practitioner's first and foremost responsibility is to the vulnerable adult. The practitioner should report the maltreatment appropriately and immediately. The report to the appropriate authorities must present facts, behavioral observations, and victim and abuser quotes and must emphasize the risk factors. The clinical record must accurately and precisely document the rationale for the actions, the data to confirm the conclusion, the actions taken, the person contacted and consulted, the precautions taken, and the client's response. While interviewing vulnerable adults, the practitioner should assume competence and pose direct questions, keeping in mind that the adults might be fearful of the consequences of revealing information.

For the client who is in jeopardy, the practitioner should seek crisis intervention alternatives that provide adequate protection, such as a restraining order; out-of-home placement; or, in the case of a client in an institutional or community-based residential setting, relocation. The practitioner should seek medical help if the client has been harmed and should not leave the client or family alone.

The practitioner can consider helping obtain respite for caregivers. If the client is separated from his or her primary caregiver, treatment efforts should be aimed at fostering a sense of control over his or her environment and coping with losses. The practitioner can consider a range of institutional, congregate, community-based and home-based replacement caregiving services such as long-term care placement, hospitalization, outpatient medical treatment, rehabilitation, sheltered residential facilities, adult day care, home health care, homemaker services, and use of informal supports such as neighbors and family. If the client is not separated from the caregiver or is placed in the care of another family member, the practitioner should provide resources and help the family understand the client's limitations, learn to respond appropriately, adapt to the caregiver role, and make adjustments in their lifestyle (Toseland & Smith, 1991).

Therapeutic interventions may include anger management, substance abuse counseling, new coping skills, and caregiver education programs and support groups. The practitioner can provide help such as modifications in the physical environment of the home or can help the elderly client and his or her family consider service alternatives such as those noted earlier. If the vulnerable adult remains with the caregiver, the practitioner should develop a plan to protect the client from further harm and to aid the caregiver in using additional supports (Kosberg, 1990).

REFERENCES

Alexander, R., & Alexander, C. L. (1995). Criminal prosecution of child protection workers. *Social Work, 40,* 809–814.

Allberg, W. R., & Chu, L. (1990). Understanding adolescent suicide: Correlates in a developmental perspective. *School Counselor, 37,* 343–350.

American Psychiatric Association. (1994). *Diagnostic and statistical manual of mental disorders* (4th ed.). Washington, DC: Author.

Antler, S. (1987). Professional liability and malpractice. In A. Minahan (Ed.-in-Chief), *Encyclopedia of social work* (18th ed., Vol. 2, pp. 346–351). Silver Spring, MD: National Association of Social Workers.

Austin, K. M., Moline, M. E., & Williams, G. T. (1990). *Confronting malpractice: Legal and ethical dilemmas in psychotherapy.* Newbury Park, CA: Sage Publications.

Barker, R., & Branson, D. (1993). When laws and ethics collide. In C. Munson (Ed.), *Forensic social work* (pp. 43–53). New York: Haworth Press.

Bayley, N. (1969). *The Bayley Scale of Infant Development.* Palo Alto, CA: Psychological Corporation.

Bendick, M. F. (1992). Reaching the breaking point: Dangers of mistreatment in elder caregiving situations. *Journal of Elder Abuse and Neglect, 4*(3), 39–59.

Bennett, B. E., Bryant, B. K., VandenBos, G. R., & Greenwood, A. (1990). *Professional liability and risk management.* Washington, DC: American Psychological Association.

Berman, A. L., & Jobes, D. A. (1994). Treatment of suicidal adolescents. *Death Studies, 18,* 375–389.

Besharov, D. J. (1985). *The vulnerable social worker: Liability for serving children and families.* Silver Spring, MD: National Association of Social Workers.

Blunt, P. A. (1993). Financial exploitation of the incapacitated: Investigation and remedies. *Journal of Elder Abuse and Neglect, 5*(1), 19–32.

Breckman, R. S., & Adelman, R. D. (1992). Elder abuse and neglect. In R. T. Ammerman & M. Hersen (Eds.), *Assessment of family violence: A clinical and legal sourcebook* (pp. 236–252). New York: John Wiley & Sons.

Brissett-Chapman, S. (1995). Child abuse and neglect: Direct practice. In R. L. Edwards (Ed.-in-Chief), *Encyclopedia of social work* (19th ed., Vol. 1, pp. 353–366). Washington, DC: NASW Press.

Brizer, D. A. (1989). Introduction: Overview of current approaches to the prediction of violence. In D. A. Brizer & M. Crowner (Eds.), *Current approaches to the prediction of violence* (pp. xi–xxx). Washington, DC: American Psychiatric Press.

Buka, S., & Earls, F. (1993). Early determinants of delinquency and violence. *Health Affairs, 12*(4), 46–64.

Chaiken, J., Chaiken, M., & Rhodes, W. (1994). Predicting violent behavior and classifying violent offenders. In A. J. Reiss, Jr., & J. A. Roth (Eds.), *Consequences and control: Understanding and preventing violence* (pp. 217–295). Washington, DC: National Academy Press.

Child Abuse Prevention and Treatment Act, P.L. 93-247, 88 Stat. 4 (1974).

Child Abuse Prevention and Treatment Act, P.L. 98-457, 42 U.S.C., S101, Sec. 3(1) (1984).

Chiles, J. A., Strosahl, K., Cowden, L., Graham, R., & Linehan, M. (1986). The 24 hours before hospitalization: Factors related to suicide attempting. *Suicide and Life-Threatening Behavior, 16,* 335–342.

Dane, A. (1990). Services to families of the elderly. In A. Monk (Ed.), *Handbook of gerontological services* (2nd ed., pp. 297–325). New York: Columbia University Press.

Davidson, H. (1988). Failure to report child abuse: Legal penalties and emerging issues. In A. Manez & S. Wells (Eds.), *Professional responsibilities in protecting children* (pp. 93–102). New York: Praeger.

DeJong, W. (1994). *Preventing interpersonal violence among youth.* Washington, DC: U.S. Department of Justice, National Institute of Justice.

Estroff, S. E., Zimmer, C., Lachicotte, W. S., & Benoit, J. (1994). The influence of social networks and social support on violence by persons with serious mental illness. *Hospital and Community Psychiatry, 45,* 669–679.

Fagan, J. (1993). Interactions among drugs, alcohol and violence. *Health Affairs, 12*(4), 65–79.

Faller, K., & Russo, S. (1981). Definition and scope of the problem of child maltreatment. In K. Faller (Ed.), *Social work with abused and neglected children* (pp. 3–10). New York: Free Press.

Farberow, N. L., Heilig, S. M., & Parad, H. J. (1990). The suicide prevention center: Concepts and clinical functions. In H. J. Parad & L. G. Parad (Eds.), *Crisis intervention* (Vol. 2, pp. 251–274). Milwaukee, WI: Family Service America.

Fischer, J., & Corcoran, K. (1994). *Measures for clinical practice: Volume 2: Adults* (2nd ed.). New York: Free Press.

France, K. (1990). *Crisis intervention: A handbook of immediate person-to-person help* (2nd ed.). Springfield, IL: Charles C Thomas.

Franzini, J., Sideman, L., Dexter, K., & Elder, J. (1990). Promoting AIDS risk reduction via behavioral training. *AIDS Education and Prevention, 2,* 313–321.

Fraser, M. W. (1995). Violence. In R. L. Edwards (Ed.-in-Chief), *Encyclopedia of social work* (19th ed., Vol. 3, pp. 2453–2460). Washington, DC: NASW Press.

Fraser, M. W. (1996). Aggressive behavior in childhood and early adolescence: An ecological–developmental perspective on youth violence. *Social Work, 41,* 347–363.

Fulmer, T. (1988). Elder abuse. In M. B. Strauss (Ed.), *Abuse and victimization across the life span* (pp. 188–199). Baltimore: Johns Hopkins University Press.

Fulmer, T. (1991). Elder mistreatment: Progress in community detection and intervention. *Family and Community Health, 14*(2), 26–34.

Gilliand, B. E., & James, R. K. (1993). *Crisis intervention strategies* (2nd ed.). Pacific Grove, CA: Brooks/Cole.

Goldberg, R. (1987). Use of constant observation with potentially suicidal patients in general hospitals. *Hospital and Community Psychiatry, 38,* 303–305.

Gothard, S. (1995). Legal issues: Confidentiality and privileged communication. In R. L. Edwards (Ed.-in-Chief), *Encyclopedia of social work* (19th ed., Vol. 2, pp. 1579–1583). Washington, DC: NASW Press.

Hall, H. V. (1987). *Violence prediction: Guidelines for the forensic practitioner.* Springfield, IL: Charles C Thomas.

Hansen, D. J., & Warner, J. E. (1992). Child physical abuse and neglect. In R. T. Ammerman & M. Hersen (Eds.), *Assessment of family violence: A clinical and legal handbook* (pp. 123–147). New York: John Wiley & Sons.

Hatton, C. L., & Valente, S. M. (1984). Assessment of suicidal risk. In C. L. Hatton & S. M. Valente (Eds.), *Suicide: Assessment and intervention* (pp. 61–82). New York: Appleton-Century-Crofts.

Hegar, R. L., Zuravin, S. J., & Orme, J. G. (1993). Can we predict severe child abuse? *Violence Update, 4*(1), 1–2, 4.

Houston, M. K., & Nuehring, E. M. (1988). *The mental health emergency screener's handbook* (Florida Department of Health & Rehabilitation Services Contract No. LCH-11). Miami: Barry University School of Social Work.

Howing, P. T., & Wodarski, J. (1992). Legal requisites for social work in child abuse and neglect. *Social Work, 37,* 330–336.

Hutchison, E. D. (1993). Mandatory reporting laws: Child protective case finding gone awry? *Social Work, 38,* 56–63.

Ireton, H., & Thwing, E. (1974). *Manual for the Minnesota Child Development Inventory.* Minneapolis: Behavioral Science Systems.

Ivanoff, A. (1991). Suicide and suicidal behavior. In A. Gitterman (Ed.), *Handbook of social work practice with vulnerable populations* (pp. 677–709). New York: Columbia University Press.

Ivanoff, A., & Riedel, M. (1995). Suicide. In R. L. Edwards, (Ed.-in-Chief), *Encyclopedia of social work* (19th ed., Vol. 3, pp. 2348–2371). Washington, DC: NASW Press.

James, N. (1984). Psychology of suicide. In C. L. Hatton & S. M. Valente (Eds.), *Suicide: Assessment and intervention* (2nd ed., pp. 34–59). Norwalk, CT: Appleton-Century-Crofts.

Jobes, D. A., & Berman, A. L. (1991). Crisis intervention and brief treatment for suicidal youth. In A. R. Roberts (Ed.), *Contemporary perspectives on crisis intervention and prevention* (pp. 53–69). Englewood Cliffs, NJ: Prentice Hall.

Kalafat, J. (1991). Suicide intervention in the schools. In A. R. Roberts (Ed.), *Contemporary perspectives on crisis intervention and prevention* (pp. 218–239). Englewood Cliffs, NJ: Prentice Hall.

Kalichman, S. E. (1993). *Mandated reporting of suspected child abuse: Ethics, law, and policy.* Washington, DC: American Psychological Association.

Kelly, J., & Murphy, D. (1992). Psychological interventions with AIDS and HIV: Prevention and treatment. *Journal of Consulting and Clinical Psychology, 60,* 576–585.

Kelly, J., & St. Lawrence, J. (1988). *The AIDS health crisis.* New York: Plenum Press.

Kjervik, D. K. (1984). The psychotherapist's duty to act reasonably to prevent suicide: A proposal to allow rational suicide. *Behavioral Sciences and the Law, 2,* 207–218.

Kosberg, J. I. (1990). Assistance to victims of crime and abuse. In A. Monk (Ed.), *Handbook of gerontological services* (2nd ed., pp. 450–473). New York: Columbia University Press.

Krattschnitt, C. (1993). Gender and interpersonal violence. In A. J. Reiss, Jr., & J. A. Roth (Eds.), *Understanding and preventing violence* (Vol. 3, pp. 293–376). Washington, DC: National Academy Press.

Lacks, M. S., Berkman, L. F., Fulmer, T., & Horowitz, R. I. (1994). A prospective community-based pilot study of risk factors for the investigation of elder mistreatment. *Journal of the American Geriatric Society, 42,* 169–173.

Landers, S. (1993, January). AIDS deepens duty to warn dilemma. *NASW News,* p. 3.

Lidz, C. W., Mulvey, E. P., & Gardner, W. (1993). The accuracy of predictions of violence to others. *Journal of the American Medical Association, 269,* 1007–1011.

Linehan, M. M. (1988). Dialectical behavior therapy: A treatment for the chronic parasuicidal client. *Journal of Personality Disorders, 1,* 328–333.

Litwak, T. R. (1994). Assessment of dangerousness. Legal, research, and clinical developments. *Administration and Policy in Mental Health, 21,* 361–377.

Longres, J. F. (1992). Race and type of maltreatment in an elder abuse system. *Journal of Elder Abuse and Neglect, 4*(3), 61–83.

Maltsberger, J. T. (1986). *Suicide risk: The formulation of clinical judgment.* New York: New York University Press.

Mental Retardation Facilities and Community Mental Health Centers Construction Act, P.L. 88-164, 77 Stat. 290 (1963).

Mental Retardation Facilities and Community Mental Health Centers Construction Act, P.L. 94-63, 89 Stat. 309, 352 (1975).

Miczek, K. A., DeBold, J. F., Haney, M., Tidey, J., Vivian, J., & Weerts, E. M. (1993). Alcohol, drugs of abuse, aggression and violence. In A. J. Reiss, Jr., & J. A. Roth (Eds.), *Understanding and preventing violence* (Vol. 3, pp. 377–570). Washington, DC: National Academy Press.

Miczek, K. A., Mirsky, A., Carey, G., DeBold, J., & Raine, A. (1993). An overview of biological influences on violent behavior. In A. J. Reiss, Jr., & J. A. Roth (Eds.), *Understanding and preventing violence* (Vol. 2, pp. 1–20). Washington, DC: National Academy Press.

Milner, J. S. (1993). Assessing physical child abuse risk: The child abuse potential inventory. *Clinical Psychology Review, 14,* 547–583.

Mirsky, A. F., & Siegel, A. (1993). The neurobiology of violence and aggression. In A. J. Reiss, Jr., & J. A. Roth (Eds.), *Understanding and preventing violence* (Vol. 2, pp. 59–172). Washington, DC: National Academy Press.

Monahan, J., & Steadman, H. J. (1994). Toward a rejuvenation of risk assessment research. In J. Monahan & H. J. Steadman (Eds.), *Violence and mental disorder: Developments in risk assessment* (pp. 1–17). Chicago: University of Chicago Press.

Mulvey, E. P. (1994). Assessing the evidence of a link between mental illness and violence. *Hospital and Community Psychiatry, 45,* 663–668.

National Association of Social Workers. (1994). Client self-determination in end-of-life decisions. In *Social work speaks: NASW policy statements* (3rd ed., pp. 58–61). Washington, DC: NASW Press.

National Center for Health Statistics. (1988a). Annual summary of births, marriages, divorces, and deaths, United States 1987. *Monthly Vital Statistics Report, 36*(13) (DHHS Pub. No. PHS 88-1120). Hyattsville, MD: U.S. Public Health Service.

National Center for Health Statistics. (1988b). *Vital statistics of the United States, 1986, Volume 2: Mortality, Part A* (DHSS No. PHS 88-1122). Washington, DC: U.S. Government Printing Office.

National Center on Child Abuse and Neglect. (1988). *National study of the incidence and severity of child abuse and neglect*. Washington, DC: U.S. Department of Health and Human Services.

O'Carroll, P. W., Rosenberg, M. C., & Mercy, J. A. (1991). Suicide. In M. L. Rosenberg & M. A. Fanley (Eds.), *Violence in America* (pp. 184–196). New York: Oxford University Press.

Patient Self-Determination Act of 1990, P.L. 101-508, 104 Stat. 1388 et seq.

Phillips, L. R. (1983). Abuse and neglect of the frail elderly at home: An exploration of theoretical relationships. *Journal of Advanced Nursing, 3*, 379–392.

Pillemer, K. A. (1986). Risk factors in elder abuse: Results from a case-control study. In K. A. Pillemer & R. Wolf (Eds.), *Elder abuse: Conflict in the family* (pp. 239–263). Dover, DE: Auburn House.

Pillemer, K., & Frankel, S. (1991). Violence against the elderly. In M. L. Rosenberg & M. A. Fanley (Eds.), *Violence in America* (pp. 158–183). New York: Oxford University Press.

Plutchik, R., vanPraag, H. M., & Conte, H. R. (1989). Correlates of suicide and violence risk, III: A two-stage model of countervailing forces. *Psychiatric Research, 28*, 215–225.

Reamer, F. G. (1987). Informed consent in social work. *Social Work, 32*, 425–429.

Reamer, F. G. (1991). AIDS, social work, and the duty to warn. *Social Work, 36*, 56–60.

Reamer, F. G. (1994). *Social work malpractice and liability: Strategies for prevention*. New York: Columbia University Press.

Reiss, A. J., Jr., & Roth, J. A. (1993a). Alcohol, other psychoactive drugs, and violence. In A. J. Reiss, Jr., & J. A. Roth (Eds.), *Understanding and preventing violence* (Vol. 1, pp. 182–220). Washington, DC: National Academy Press.

Reiss, A. J., Jr., & Roth, J. A. (1993b). The development of an individual's potential for violence. In A. J. Reiss, Jr., & J. A. Roth (Eds.), *Understanding and preventing violence* (Vol. 1, pp. 357–403). Washington, DC: National Academy Press.

Reiss, A. J., Jr., & Roth, J. A. (1993c). Expanding the limits of understanding and control. In A. J. Reiss, Jr., & J. A. Roth (Eds.), *Understanding and preventing violence* (Vol. 1, pp. 291–326). Washington, DC: National Academy Press.

Reiss, A. J., Jr., & Roth, J. A. (1993d). Patterns of violence in American society. In A. J. Reiss, Jr., & J. A. Roth (Eds.), *Understanding and preventing violence* (Vol. 1, pp. 42–97). Washington, DC: National Academy Press.

Reiss, A. J., Jr., & Roth, J. A. (1993e). Summary. In A. J. Reiss, Jr., & J. A. Roth (Eds.), *Understanding and preventing violence* (Vol. 1, pp. 1–30). Washington, DC: National Academy Press.

Reiss, A. J., Jr., & Roth, J. A. (1993f). Violence in families. In A. J. Reiss, Jr., & J. A. Roth (Eds.), *Understanding and preventing violence* (Vol. 1, pp. 221–254). Washington, DC: National Academy Press.

Rosenberg, M. L., & Mercy, J. A. (1991). Assaultive violence. In M. L. Rosenberg & M. A. Feeny (Eds.), *Violence in America: A public health approach* (pp. 14–50). New York: Oxford University Press.

Roy, A., & Linnoila, M. (1986). Alcoholism and suicide. *Suicide and Life-Threatening Behavior, 16*, 244–273.

Salend, E., Kane, R., Satz, M., & Pynoos, J. (1984). Elder abuse reporting: Limitations of statutes. *Gerontologist, 24*, 61–69.

Saltzman, A., & Proch, K. (1994). *Law and social work practice*. Chicago: Nelson-Hall. (Originally published in 1990)

Sampson, R. J., & Lauritsen, L. J. (1993). Violent victimization and offending: Individual-, situational-, and community-level risk factors. In A. J. Reiss, Jr.,

& J. A. Roth (Eds.), *Understanding and preventing violence* (Vol. 3, pp. 1–114). Washington, DC: National Academy Press.

Schutz, B. M. (1982). *Legal liability in psychotherapy.* San Francisco: Jossey-Bass.

Shaffer, D., & Gould, M. (1987). *Study of completed and attempted suicides in adolescents.* Unpublished progress report, National Institute of Mental Health, Bethesda, MD.

Simon, R. I. (1982). *Psychiatric interventions and malpractice.* Springfield, IL: Charles C Thomas.

Simon, R. I. (1987). *Clinical psychiatry and the law.* Washington, DC: American Psychiatric Press.

Strauss, M. A., Gelles, R., & Steinmetz, S. K. (1980). *Behind closed doors: Violence in the family.* Garden City, NY: Anchor/Doubleday.

Swenson, L. C. (1993). *Psychology and law for the helping professions.* Belmont, CA: Brooks/Cole.

Tarasoff v. Board of Regents of the University of California, 551 P.2d 334 (1976).

Tardiff, K. (1989a). *Assessment and management of violent patients.* Washington, DC: American Psychiatric Press.

Tardiff, K. (1989b). A model for the short-term prediction of violence potential. In D. A. Brizer & M. Crowner (Eds.), *Current approaches to the prediction of violence* (pp. 1–12). Washington, DC: American Psychiatric Press.

Tatara, T. (1995). Elder abuse. In R. L. Edwards (Ed.-in-Chief), *Encyclopedia of social work* (19th ed., Vol. 1, pp. 834–841). Washington, DC: NASW Press.

Thornburg, K. R., & Mumford, J. A. (1994). Physical abuse of children: A synthesis of the research. *Violence Update, 4*(11), 1–2, 4, 10.

Torrey, E. F. (1994). Violent behavior by individuals with serious mental illness. *Hospital and Community Psychiatry, 45,* 653–662.

Toseland, R. W., & Smith, G. (1991). Family caregivers of the frail elderly. In A. Gitterman (Ed.), *Handbook of social work practice and vulnerable populations* (pp. 549–583). New York: Columbia University Press.

VandeCreek, L., & Knapp, S. (1993). *Tarasoff and beyond.* Sarasota, FL: Professional Resource Press.

VandeCreek, L., Knapp, S., & Herzog, C. (1988). Privileged communication for social workers. *Social Casework, 69,* 28–34.

Victoroff, V. M. (1983). *The suicidal patient: Recognition, intervention, and management.* Oradell, NJ: Medical Economics Books.

Videka-Sherman, L. (1991). Child abuse and neglect. In A. Gitterman (Ed.), *Handbook of social work practice with vulnerable populations* (pp. 345–381). New York: Columbia University Press.

Wetzler, S. (1989). *Measuring mental illness: Psychometric assessment for clinicians.* Washington, DC: American Psychiatric Press.

Williams, O. J. (1992). Elder maltreatment: Cultural diversity and violence. *Violence Update, 3*(4), 1, 4, 6.

Wolf, R. S. (1988). Elder abuse: Ten years later. *Journal of the American Geriatrics Society, 36,* 758–762.

Woody, R. H. (1988). *Fifty ways to avoid malpractice.* Sarasota, FL: Professional Resource Exchange.

CHAPTER

7

VICARIOUS LIABILITY

Courts recognize a theory of vicarious liability, also known as "imputed negligence" or the "doctrine of *respondeat superior*," by which anyone can be held accountable for the malfeasance, misfeasance, or nonfeasance of subordinates and assistants, supervisees, or colleagues. The logic of vicarious liability posits that because the employer, consultant, supervisor, teacher, other authority figure, or colleague was in a position of strong influence and responsibility and could in some way gain from the actions of the subordinate or colleague, then he or she can be held responsible.

> Clinicians should not only conform their own practices to appropriate standards of care but should also strive to assure similar conformity by team members, supervisees, partners, and others for whose malpractice they may be held to answer. In this regard, it is most prudent for clinicians to assume that they *will* be liable for the negligent acts of their team colleagues, supervisees, and partners. Such an assumption, while not always valid, will lead to the exercise of greater care by clinicians in their professional relationships [and other actions] and, therefore, to the minimization of the potential for malpractice claims. (Woody, 1985, p. 522)

Attorneys are bound by the legal profession's standard of care to file a lawsuit against anyone potentially and reasonably implicated in their clients' harm. Hence, responsible lawyers may design all-encompassing lawsuits naming many parties who have direct or indirect (vicarious) relationships to the client. The central question is whether the social worker was closely enough connected to the situation to know about or to be responsible for knowing about the harmful acts of others in the work context. Several professional roles and work arrangements can heighten social workers' vulnerability:

- employing or supervising paraprofessionals (Reamer, 1994)
- independently contracting to supervise other social workers preparing for their license ("Q & A," 1993; Reamer, 1994)
- supervising professional coworkers in an agency setting (Bullis, 1995; Reamer, 1994; Robke, 1993)
- supervising student interns (Reamer, 1994; Smith, 1994)
- arranging internships and field placements (Kurzman, 1995; Smith, 1994; Zakutansky & Sirles, 1993)

- serving as a case consultant (Reamer, 1994)
- teaching or training (Kurzman, 1995)
- referring clients to other professionals (Reamer, 1994)
- serving on boards of directors (Siciliano & Spiro, 1992)
- serving in an executive or administrative capacity in an agency or group practice (Bullis, 1995; Kurzman, 1995; Reamer, 1993)
- affiliating with others in a group practice (Robertson & Jackson, 1991)
- associating with impaired colleagues (NASW, 1996; see Appendix A).

This chapter discusses vicarious liability as it relates to

- supervision
- consultation
- teaching and training
- referrals
- board membership
- administration
- impaired colleagues
- affiliations.

SUPERVISION

ELENITA

Elenita was a supervisor at a family and marriage counseling agency where she had supervised Lori for the past two years. Elenita had been Lori's field instructor 10 years ago and had maintained a friendship with her and her family. Elenita and Lori met weekly for supervision and discussed Lori's cases. Their supervisory relationship was casual and friendly.

Lori had worked with a married couple in counseling for six months until they decided to divorce. Following the divorce, Lori continued to treat the husband. Supervisory sessions between Elenita and Lori focused on issues related to the client's adjustment to the divorce. At one point, Lori indicated to Elenita that treatment was a financial burden for her client, even with his six-figure salary, and asked for and received an approval to reduce the client's fee. Frequently, Lori discussed her concerns about her client's depression and his need to begin dating. Elenita was aware that Lori had given the client her home telephone number and that he called her at home almost daily. In one supervisory session, Elenita documented that they had discussed Lori's self-disclosure to the client that she also was divorced. However, unknown to Elenita, Lori and her client were having a sexual relationship.

The client stopped seeing Lori personally and professionally after he began dating a legal secretary. The client's attorney filed a lawsuit against Lori for sexual misconduct and against Elenita for failing to detect the misconduct of her supervisee.

The court found Elenita negligent in her supervision and in failing to ask Lori about sexual feelings and personal, nonprofessional involvement with her clients.

In the *Guidelines for Clinical Social Work Supervision* (NASW, National Council on the Practice of Clinical Social Work, 1994), *supervision* is defined as

> the relationship between supervisor and supervisee that promotes the development of responsibility, skill, knowledge, attitudes, and ethical standards in the practice of clinical social work. . . . During supervision, the supervisee provides information to the supervisor regarding the assessment, diagnosis, and treatment of each client. In a reciprocal dialogue, the supervisor provides oversight, guidance, and direction in assessing, diagnosing, and treating clients, and evaluates the supervisee's performance. (p. 2)

Supervisors have experienced an increase in liability actions. Reamer (1989) noted that court cases against supervisors have found them liable for the "actions of supervisees who ordinarily are directly under their supervision, actions of supervisees who ordinarily are not under the social worker's supervision, [and] delegations of responsibility by the social worker to a paraprofessional or unlicensed assistants" (p. 446).

Vicarious liability does not free the supervisee from responsibility; rather, it also allocates the responsibility to the supervisor. Vicarious liability in supervision requires three elements:

1. The supervisee agrees to work under the direction and control of the supervisor in ways that benefit the supervisor, whether or not financial gain occurs.
2. The supervisor has the authority to control the supervisee.
3. The supervisee's activities fall within the scope of agreed-on training objectives (Robke, 1993).

It is not always apparent whether a supervisor's liability is *vicarious* (indirect and related to the errors and omissions of a subordinate) or *direct* (related to the supervisor's own errors and omissions), or a combination of both. Nonetheless, supervisors can be held directly liable for a wide range of commissions and omissions (Besharov, 1985; Bullis, 1995; Cohen & Mariano, 1982; Hogan, 1979; NASW, National Council on the Practice of Clinical Social Work, 1994; Reamer 1994) such as failure to

- provide adequate information to a supervisee to permit proper practice
- review a supervisee's work
- correctly assess a supervisee's capacity and skill level
- detect a supervisee's error in any aspect of service
- determine that a specialist is needed in a particular situation
- detect or stop a negligent service plan or service that is being continued beyond its effectiveness
- identify that a supervisee is sexually involved with a client or exerting unnecessary influence on a client, even if the supervisee conceals it from the supervisor

- meet regularly with a supervisee
- review and approve a supervisee's decisions
- provide adequate coverage when a supervisee is unavailable
- note that a client's record is not adequate
- supervise within the parameters of state laws and professional regulations
- detect and act on a supervisee's impairment.

Clearly, the line between vicarious liability in supervision and direct liability for supervisory omissions is often indistinct, and both allegations could easily be made in one set of circumstances.

Paraprofessionals and Unlicensed Professionals

Settings may employ paraprofessionals or unlicensed professionals who by plan or evolution perform tasks beyond their legal qualifications. The practitioner who employs or supervises paraprofessionals and unlicensed professionals should take special care that their duties do not exceed their capabilities and that they cannot be misconstrued as professionals (Reamer, 1994). Even if no harm is determined, if a paraprofessional or unlicensed professional is found performing beyond his or her recognized limit, the social worker may be found to have violated ethical norms by providing substandard care, which puts the client at risk. If the paraprofessional's actions or omissions do result in harm to the client, the practitioner is at serious risk of being held liable for knowing about and failing to avert the client's jeopardy. In addition, the practitioner could be charged with permitting an unqualified person to perform functions reserved for a licensed professional (Swenson, 1993).

Student Interns

In the case of social work student interns, vicarious liability can be extended beyond the field instructor to agency administration, school or university administration, field staff, or anyone else involved in the decision to place the student in the internship (Zakutansky & Sirles, 1993). However, the field instructor or supervisor has the central responsibility to know the student's caseload and activities well enough to anticipate and prevent problems. This knowledge requires intensive involvement and close communication with students, a problem in a busy, underresourced agency. Therefore, social workers should not accept student interns if they lack the time and resources to supervise them correctly.

Other Professional Coworkers

It is generally understood that the supervisor has the right and ability to control a supervisee's work, and if the supervisee is discharging agreed-on responsibilities, he or she is considered an extension of the supervisor. Hence, it is presumed that a close, attentive, communicative supervisory process is provided and the supervisor is responsible for knowing a supervisee's clients and actions. In addition, the supervisor is responsible for participating in and approving service plans. Failure to supervise meticulously can result in a charge of negligent supervision (Bullis, 1995) or can incur vicarious liability (Kurzman, 1995; Reamer, 1993, 1994).

Increasingly, social workers are called on to supervise other social workers who are not located in the same work setting. These arrangements may exist in the context of licensure and credentialing requirements, third-party reimbursement requirements, and regulatory and accreditation requirements ("Q & A," 1993). However, the supervisor is still responsible for the same supervisory duties mentioned earlier.

Supervision of a prospective social work licensee must conform to standards ordinarily specified by state statutes or regulations. Care must be taken to meet and engage in formal supervision within the parameters specified by the state licensure laws for social work.

Supervision Tips

Whether supervising paraprofessionals, unlicensed professionals, student interns, or other professional colleagues, the social work supervisor's best safeguards against a malpractice suit include principles set forth in the *Guidelines for Clinical Social Work Supervision* (NASW, National Council on the Practice of Clinical Social Work, 1994) and emphasized by Reamer (1994):

- having a written agreement with the supervisee that clarifies the context or purpose of the supervision; stipulates the intent to follow applicable regulations; sets forth a detailed plan of supervision, including a learning plan with clear objectives; sets the frequency, duration, structure, and format of supervision sessions; discusses supervision methods; determines client information and formats to be used; delineates the responsibilities of the supervisor and supervisee; discusses practice evaluation methods; discusses the relationship of supervision to personnel evaluations; delineates a conflict resolution plan; explains the termination process; and states any applicable fees
- documenting the supervisory sessions, including dates of contacts, goal progress, and recommendations for the supervisee or client
- having proper qualifications to supervise, including following the *Guidelines for Clinical Social Work Supervision* (NASW, National Council on the Practice of Clinical Social Work, 1994), having an MSW degree from an accredited graduate program, being state licensed or certified at the highest level for social work, having substantial post-master's direct practice experience in an organized setting and with the supervisee's client population and practice methods, maintaining active affiliations with professional social work organizations, having formalized supervision training, knowing the community and its resources, and keeping clinical knowledge current through professional development activities
- supervising with an eye toward ethics—including referring frequently in supervision to the *NASW Code of Ethics* (NASW, 1996), asking supervisees directly about specific breaches of ethics and regulations, and investigating and taking action in cases of supervisee impairment—boundary issues; violations of professional standards and regulations; and malfeasance, misfeasance, and nonfeasance
- ensuring that services provided by a supervisee are above minimal standards
- obtaining consultation whenever the supervisee's needs or client issues are beyond the supervisor's capacity

- ensuring that the supervisee's clients have properly and specifically agreed to the release of information required for supervision and that clients know the supervisor and how to contact him or her
- treating the supervisee with respect, conducting evaluations fairly, maintaining confidentiality about supervisory material, and not exploiting the supervisee or supervising anyone with whom a dual relationship exists.

CONSULTATION

TIM

Tim had a contract to provide regular case consultation one day a week to the counselors at a shelter for homeless families. On his consultation day, Tim met with individual counselors to discuss their questions about cases. One case Tim consulted on involved a homeless woman with two young daughters in her care. In her service, the client's counselor focused her intervention on job training and securing the family a place to live. The counselor failed to address the client's history of substance abuse and never mentioned it to Tim. One night the woman and her children failed to return to the shelter. Tim later learned that a lawsuit had been filed against the shelter, the counselor, and himself. Allegations against Tim included the statement that the client lost custody of her children because her substance abuse problem was not adequately addressed in therapy.

Consultation is a voluntary relationship in which the consultee can accept or reject information and advice. Unlike a supervisor, a consultant is not understood to have the right and ability to control a consultee's work, and the consultee is not considered an extension of the consultant. The consultant has no legal authority over the consultee; only ethical standards govern the relationship (Shulman, 1995). However, in an agreement to provide consultation to another service provider concerning a case, it is assumed the consultant will learn the details of the case and the actions taken and contemplated by the consultee. The consultant is expected to possess verifiable expertise consistent with the client's needs. If the consultee is alleged to have harmed a client, the practitioner may be held accountable for negligence if the quality or content of the consultation is shown to be a proximate cause of the harm. A practitioner who consults with agencies and organizations about macropractice domains (administration, program planning, and evaluation) is at risk of liability if the consultation is judged harmful to the consultee or client (Reamer, 1995).

The social worker should protect himself or herself by documenting the role he or she agrees to play as a consultant, the scope and limits of the involvement, and the content of the consultation sessions. The consultant should ensure that clients about whom he or she consults have agreed to the releases of information necessary for consultation. The social worker should forcefully advise against actions or omissions that could breach ethics or harm clients and should take action, as discussed later in this chapter, against an impaired consultee.

MICHELLE AND BEVERLY

Michelle and Beverly, professors of social work, conferred with their employer and concluded that they were covered by the university's protection in the event that a student sued them because of a grade, advisement, or classroom issue. Accordingly, both decided not to purchase malpractice insurance. A client in an agency found fault with services delivered by a student intern who was Michelle's advisee and Beverly's student in the practice class that was required concurrent with field work. A subsequent malpractice suit implicated the agency for accepting the student, the school for placing the student, the student's agency-based field instructor for failing to ensure proper treatment by a subordinate, Michelle for failing to recognize the student's limitations and preventing the placement, and Beverly for failing to educate the student sufficiently to avoid the mistake. Eventually, a judge declared the lawsuit frivolous. However, Michelle and Beverly had incurred substantial legal fees in their defense, and the university's liability insurance did not cover faculty in the event of a student error.

Social work educators are at risk of vicarious liability (Kurzman, 1995; Smith, 1994). Social workers who are members of a social work faculty may encounter occasions when class assignments involve field placements and client information. Students may be asked to make case presentations in class or conduct research projects with client participation. Although it is a field instructor's responsibility to ensure that clients have provided informed consent to agency procedures and that client information is released only with client permission, it is also the university-based field liaison's and classroom instructor's mutual obligation to reinforce these principles and to ensure the client's well-being. For example, classroom instructors involved with student research projects should be apprised of the codes that articulate the protection of human study participants and determine if the university requires formal institutional review for student projects (see Chapter 2). If so, instructors should acquaint themselves with the procedures and act accordingly.

The field liaison must ensure that all steps provided for by the agency and the university have been taken to protect the client's privacy and the right to informed consent. If a client were to file a lawsuit because of a student's action, it is possible for the litigation to extend to faculty for failing to teach related ethical principles and legal regulations and for failing to comply with university and agency policies governing client confidentiality and informed consent (Zakutansky & Sirles, 1993).

In addition, sometimes social workers are asked to teach an in-service session for staff, a workshop in the community, or a course in a school of social work. In any of these roles, professionals run the risk of conveying information that is in itself unsound or that is misinterpreted by a trainee. Perhaps the social worker did not have time to prepare well or to update his or her knowledge, perhaps he or she gave an "off-the-cuff" answer to a question, or perhaps he or she simply did not think the situation through and failed to recognize potential ethical or legal breaches. The trainee, relying on presumed expertise, acts on the information and is later charged with, for example, failure to avert a suicide or with misdiagnosis, improper treatment, or a violation of confidentiality. In these situations, the professional social worker also can be implicated. Therefore, the best protections are

- keeping knowledge and skills current
- being aware of the layers of liability in malpractice
- thoughtfully considering the ethical and legal implications of the role of a teacher or trainer.

REFERRALS

LYDIA

Lydia, who worked as a clinical social worker for a home health agency, was assigned to help a client who recently had a severe heart attack. The client and his wife were also caring for their 40-year-old mentally retarded son at home. After several sessions, the couple voiced their concerns about who would care for their son in the event that they were unable to do so. The mother had become progressively more impaired due to her arthritis and found it increasingly difficult to care for her son and husband. The couple had no other living relatives.

Lydia suggested that a vocational day program for developmentally disabled people might ease some of the daily burden of caring for the son and prepare him for when they could not care for him. The couple was optimistic about the program. Lydia looked in her resource manual and identified a program. A month later, the son returned from the facility with bruises and cuts, stating that one of the staff had hit him repeatedly. During the process of filing a lawsuit against the program, the couple's attorney discovered that the program had been under investigation for abuse and had its license suspended three months before the son's admission. The attorney filed a professional liability lawsuit against Lydia, who was found negligent in referring the family to an unlicensed program that was under investigation.

On the one hand, practitioners are responsible for making appropriate referrals when clients need resources beyond their capacity; failing to do so could involve them in charges of improper service and termination. On the other hand, practitioners are responsible for selecting competent and properly credentialed referral sources known to practice ethically and legally. Because a referral implies a professional sanction, a practitioner could be implicated in a malpractice suit as a proximate cause of the harm that a client sustained because of actions or omissions of the referral provider. Referrals made without attention to standard procedures create a risk for a claim of negligent referral (Reamer, 1994).

Practitioners can guard against malpractice claims for referrals by

- being very familiar with providers to whom clients are referred
- avoiding providers with a history of regulations violation, ethical breaches, criminal convictions, or malpractice litigation
- following up with referrals with the client's consent.

An effort by practitioners to ensure that the referral proceeded as intended and that the client was served as expected could be evidence of a sincere effort to refer in a conscientious manner and with the client's best interests in mind. It is generally good practice to provide clients with more than one referral; this avoids the appearance of steering the client toward a particular referral, perhaps with some benefit to be derived by the practitioner.

BOARD MEMBERSHIP

MIGUEL

Miguel served on the board of a day treatment program for severely emotionally disturbed adolescents. A referring agency that contracted for service had raised a concern that clinical staff were enmeshed in administrative activity and did not spend time in direct service, made cursory assessments, made diagnoses that often appeared to be reimbursement driven, and developed treatment plans that lacked individuality. As part of the corrective measures devised by the board, the agency hired an external consultant to analyze clinical staff activity.

Following the study, the agency administrator reported to the board that the consultant had found that 80 percent of clinical time was devoted to direct client services and that the problem was not staff time allocation but staff motivation and skills in assessment and service planning. The administrator indicated these issues would be addressed through training and supervision. Board members raised several questions about how the consultant had defined direct client services, how in-service training would be enhanced, what the motivation problems were attributed to, and why the consultant was not present to help interpret the findings. On all points the administrator seemed to hedge and, indicating that time was up, moved on to another agenda item.

The board did not know and did not investigate the reality that the clinical staff was swamped with paperwork, exhibited poor morale, and needed significant skills building in service delivery strategies for the managed care environment. The board members did not ask for a copy of the consultant's original report and thus did not know that the administrator's report had reinterpreted the data with a very broad definition of direct client service. In addition, the members did not inform themselves of the nature and progress of the training and supervision efforts promised by the administrator to alleviate skill and morale problems.

Several months later, following a suicide attempt by a teenager in the program, the youth's parents filed a lawsuit alleging that their son's level of depression had not been recognized by the program. Details included statements that his assigned clinician had in the prior six months seen the youth only in group therapy, met with him individually only on a brief and ad hoc basis, and had been available to meet with the parents only one time. Documentation included reports of many unanswered telephone calls from the parents to the counselor and evidence of charges to the parents' insurance for individual treatment sessions. Miguel and the other board members were cited in the lawsuit for failing to investigate thoroughly and follow up on the problems with service delivery identified formally by the contractor, failing to pursue their own concerns recorded in the minutes of their meeting, failing to obtain the consultant's report, and failing to inform themselves of the progress of corrective measures. In addition, the board members were considered responsible for fiscal procedures that allowed for fraudulent billing for individual treatment sessions that did not occur.

At the top level of many social services agencies' decision-making and policy-setting structures is a board of directors that likely includes social work practitioners. In their capacity as board members, social workers should keep themselves apprised of court rulings related to nonprofit boards and of standards of conduct applied to directors. Board members can be implicated in lawsuits that allege that they as directors should have known about and halted unethical or illegal practices occurring in the agency at any level. They can also be at risk for conflict-of-interest issues such as encouraging the agency to enter business arrangements that serve their personal financial interests. In addition, if the agency's funds are not well invested, board members can share in the responsibility for fiduciary liability (Siciliano & Spiro, 1992). If fiscal errors or omissions are linked with inadequate services to clients or client harm, malpractice could be claimed.

To offset the risk of vicarious liability, social workers should

- know the agency's activities and procedures
- urge that situations such as insufficient supervision, lack of staff development and training, and inattention to client rights and codes of ethics be corrected
- document efforts to correct potentially harmful situations and vote against actions that may place the agency in financial or legal jeopardy
- obtain specific directors and officers liability coverage for board members, because professional liability coverage relates only to social work actions.

LEONARD

Leonard was the newly appointed and very harried director of a satellite outpatient program operated by a large county general hospital in a multiethnic community. This was his first large-scale administrative job. The hospital had been cutting positions; Leonard had two vacant clinical social work positions and major unmet client demands and needs and was also worried about losing the positions if they remained unfilled. The hospital was having difficulty recruiting candidates who were bilingual and willing to work for the relatively low salary scale. When Luis's resume was forwarded, Leonard was eager to interview him; Luis had both clinical and administrative experience, was bilingual, held an MSW degree from a well-respected program, and was eligible to apply for the social work license (licensure of social workers remained technically optional because the program was a public service system).

During the interview, Leonard and Luis "clicked." Leonard was interrupted several times during the interview but explored most of the areas he judged important. Leonard felt confident in Luis's skill and suitability for the position and also sensed that Luis would be an experienced colleague, even mentor, as Leonard learned the ropes of his administrative role.

Leonard, who asked for an expedited personnel decision, was able to hire Luis the following week by giving assurance that he had telephoned references and prior employers. However, with the hectic pace of his job, Leonard was unable to do so. Some time later, a client accused Luis of making sexual advances. In the licensing board review that followed, Leonard was implicated for being instrumental in hiring Luis without having conducted a careful background investigation. Had Leonard more carefully interviewed Luis and contacted his prior employers, he likely would have been alerted to Luis's previous sexual impropriety with clients.

The agency as an entity and administrators as individuals may be at risk of vicarious liability when staff actions harm clients. Reamer (1993) cautioned about two categories of administrative liability risks:

1. management of client information
2. treatment and service delivery.

Management of Client Information

Lawsuits related to management of client information may be filed against primary practitioners, supervisors, administrators, and directors under a variety of circumstances that seem to embody the adage, "You're damned if you do, and you're damned if you don't." For example, if staff fail in their legal duty to report maltreatment of children and protected groups of adults or fail to protect and warn potential victims of client violence, agency administrators may be implicated in a lawsuit. However, even if confidential client information is legally and intentionally disclosed, a lawsuit may still be filed for breach of confidentiality, and administrators may again be liable. Moreover, if confidential information is inadvertently and unlawfully or unethically disclosed, administrators may be held accountable for failing to exercise effective controls on information.

Social work administrators should consider the following precautions for the handling of client information:

- Stay current on state laws, state professional regulations, and case law concerning the duty to protect and warn, and convey this information to supervisors and staff (see Chapters 2 and 6).
- Be aware of and convey to supervisors and staff the state's parameters of privileged communication and the proper way to deal with subpoenas and other court requests for confidential information (see Chapter 2).
- Establish policies and procedures that prevent the inadvertent revelation of confidential client information in the course of day-to-day activity in the workplace, and convey this information to supervisors and staff (see Chapters 2 and 3).
- Establish procedures in which every employee, intern, volunteer, and board member, regardless of function or position, signs an agreement to preserve client confidentiality (see Appendix C).
- Establish policies and procedures for the proper maintenance of, protection of, and client and court access to clinical records (see Chapters 2 and 3).

Treatment and Service Delivery

Malpractice litigation for treatment and service delivery involves either

- omission or *nonfeasance* (the failure to perform a duty such as making a needed referral, properly supervising residential clients, discouraging an intoxicated client from driving home, and providing an emergency weekend or vacation contact for clients)
- commission in the form of *malfeasance* (an illegal act such as sexual battery or furnishing medication to a client) or *misfeasance* (improper execution of a lawful act such as prolonging a client's service to generate revenue or discharging an inpatient without an adequate discharge plan) (Reamer, 1993, 1994, 1995).

Similar to the risks of liability that supervisors face, the vicarious liability of an administrator for omissions and commissions of direct services staff members rests on the administrator's assumed ability to control staff in the conduct of activities that are within the scope of their assigned duties. However, institutions and administrators could also be at risk for direct liability for omissions such as

- failure to provide for sufficient staff supervision
- failure to select and screen staff with reasonable care
- failure to provide sufficient training and staff development
- lack of clear policies and procedures for client care and client relations
- lack of a clear risk management policy with well-articulated procedures
- breaches of client confidentiality owing to inadequate controls over clinical records and information systems
- deficient mechanisms to identify and assist impaired employees (Reamer, 1993; Smith, 1994).

Sexual impropriety is one of the most common types of professional liability cases (NASW Insurance Trust & American Professional Agency, 1996; Wimpfheimer, Klein, & Kramer, 1993). Kaufman (1993) highlighted three areas of administrative responsibility:

1. identifying and taking action in situations in which a human services professional has had sexual contact with a current or former client. The administrator should know the clues to exploitative behavior (for example, retaining the client in treatment for too long, resisting supervision or consultation, conducting sessions at unusual times or places, not collecting fees); provide an easy-to-use, nonthreatening client feedback system that facilitates and encourages candid complaints; investigate the situation and document the process; if warranted, terminate the employee and report the disciplinary action to the state professional regulation authority; and without compromising client confidentiality, apprise staff of the situation to control rumors and highlight the agency's commitment to ethical standards and client safety.
2. screening new staff for possible sexual exploitation of clients. The administrator should obtain a detailed professional employment history (for example, by contacting all former employers of the past five years, identifying the states in which the applicant has been licensed or registered to deliver human services, and requesting a search for ethical or legal violations and disciplinary actions); check the applicant in public civil and criminal court records and the files of malpractice insurance carriers; advise the applicant that the screening will occur; and obtain releases of information specific to each previous employer and each insurance carrier. The administrator should use certified mail to send requests for information.
3. disclosing known occurrences of sexual contact with current or former clients by clinicians when this information is sought by employers or prospective employers. The administrator should require a signed release of information from the former employee and honor only written requests for information.

Kaufman (1993) offered the following tools that can assist in the prevention of client exploitation:

- a clearly stated agency mission that stresses client rights, dignity, and respect
- an agency policy manual that explicitly prohibits sexual harassment under any circumstances with clients, student interns, and coworkers; that identifies disciplinary actions that will be taken for violations; and

that describes procedures for investigating complaints of exploitation and harassment

- a client's bill of rights that is disseminated widely to staff and clients
- staff training that addresses ethical practice and highlights the prevention of client exploitation
- volunteer screening and training for ethical and nonexploitative behavior of the same standard as that for paid staff
- an ethics committee that is useful for airing conflicts about values and ethics
- clinical supervision used as the first line of defense against boundary violations
- consultation from external management consultants who are experts in therapeutic relationships and sexual exploitation dynamics in the event that sexual exploitation is a problem.

In addition, when possible, licensed professionals should be hired. The blend of professional education in an accredited graduate program along with licensure preparation and maintenance ensures exposure to ethical practice principles, a measure of professional experience, and a history of supervision, which all operate to reduce the risk of boundary violations and client exploitation. However, there is no perfect prevention mechanism; therefore, administrators should be vigilant.

Kurzman (1995) recommended a risk management audit as a means of reducing exposure to malpractice. Administrators should verify that

- the agency's government licenses (such as those with the department of mental health, division of substance abuse services, or board of social welfare) are current and sufficient
- the agency's papers of incorporation and current bylaws fully authorize the current scope of practice and service
- the state licenses and the current registrations of all professional practitioners are active
- protocols for emergency actions (for example, fire drills, involuntary client hospitalization, staff safety, and accident reporting) are well known and updated
- premiums for all forms of casualty insurance are paid and current, and they cover new programs, staff, and settings
- procedures for the maintenance and safeguarding of client records are clear and respected
- staff evaluations are conducted and reviewed on a scheduled basis
- vouchers and records for fiscal disbursements are properly authorized and filed
- insurance reimbursement forms are completed in a timely fashion and are authenticated in accordance with contractual requirements. (p. 1925)

IMPAIRED COLLEAGUES

BOB

For the past five years, Bob worked as a substance abuse specialist for a home-based substance abuse program. Since

Bob's wife died a year ago, his colleagues, who were also substance abuse specialists and social workers, had noticed that he had become more withdrawn and forgetful and was frequently absent from work. The coworkers were aware that Bob was not completing his records and that he failed to follow up on telephone calls and referrals and frequently canceled his appointments. On a number of occasions, staff had smelled alcohol on his breath and observed that his speech was slurred. Regularly during lunch, Bob's coworkers discussed his deteriorating behavior.

Bob was assigned a family who needed help with their 15-year-old daughter, who was addicted to crack cocaine. Bob made an initial home visit and completed the demographic information on the intake form but did not complete the psychosocial assessment or other forms. Over the course of four weeks, Bob scheduled and canceled appointments with the family. The parents left several messages a week asking for his help and describing the daughter's aggressive behavior and persistent substance use, but Bob did not return their calls. One day the daughter, in a state of toxic psychosis, stabbed her mother. The family filed a malpractice suit against the agency, Bob's supervisor, and Bob. The attorney submitted breach of ethics complaints against Bob's coworkers for failing to take appropriate measures to intervene with an impaired colleague as directed in the NASW Code of Ethics.

As discussed in Chapter 4, NASW charges social workers with responsibility for protecting clients from impaired professionals and taking measures to assist ill colleagues. Since the earliest policy statement in 1979 (NASW, 1987), the definition of the impaired professional has been elaborated upon to include sources of impairment such as life stress, emotional or mental illness, substance abuse, and physical illness. In addition, the meaning of *impairment* has been clarified as the

> interference in professional functioning that is reflected in one or more of the following ways: (a) an inability and/or unwillingness to acquire and integrate professional standards into one's repertoire of professional behavior; (b) an inability to acquire professional skills in order to reach an acceptable level of competency; and (c) an inability to control personal stress, psychological dysfunction, and/or excessive emotional reactions that interfere with professional functioning. (Lamb et al., 1987, p. 598)

Social work practitioners work with severely disabled clients and profoundly complicated situations, with homelessness, and with violence and abuse, often in agencies with inadequate resources. Therefore, it should be no surprise that practitioners are vulnerable to stress-generated burnout, substance abuse, and emotional distress.

Regardless of the cause or manifestation, when a colleague's practice deteriorates to the point that clients are jeopardized and another practitioner recognizes or should be able to recognize the predicament, then failure to intervene could be found to be vicarious liability in the event of a lawsuit by a client of the impaired practitioner. Social workers are responsible to report the impairment in such a way that a colleague's confidentiality is protected to the fullest extent possible, that actions taken will be as nonpunitive as possible, and that the *NASW Code of Ethics* (NASW, 1996) provisions for dealing with impaired colleagues are upheld.

Reamer's (1992) model assessment and action plan suggested a procedure for direct intervention with an impaired colleague:

- Identify and collect data on the impairment.
- Determine the causes of the impairment.
- Determine the best person to approach the professional and arrange to confront the professional constructively with evidence of the impairment.
- Urge the professional to seek help and review options.
- Emphasize to the professional the consequences of failing to address the problem.
- If necessary and if not done in an earlier step, notify a local regulatory body or NASW committee on inquiry.
- If the social worker is in a supervisory or administrative relationship with the impaired professional, arrange for the formulation of a rehabilitation plan or impose sanctions as appropriate following standard due-process proceedings, monitor and evaluate the professional's progress, and review and modify as appropriate the professional's standing in the profession (such as licensure and employment status).

Sources of help for an impaired colleague may include the organization's employee assistance program, the NASW chapter's Colleague Assistance Program (consistent with the NASW Delegate Assembly's 1987 policy statement), the state professional regulatory body's impaired professional program, and 12-step–based self-help programs such as Social Workers Helping Social Workers and Psychologists Helping Psychologists.

AFFILIATIONS

CARRIE

Carrie joined a group of clinical social workers in a shared office arrangement in which the waiting room was common. The group called themselves "Social Work Affiliates" (SWA) and printed individual business cards and letterhead with the SWA logo. The social workers were, however, unincorporated, and each made and kept his or her own appointments, recorded messages on individual voice mail, and was available by individual beeper. If one of the group needed back-up, it was customary to make an arrangement with one of the other social workers and give clients the colleague's telephone and beeper numbers.

One Saturday, Betty, one of Carrie's affiliate colleagues, was out of town for the day. Because Betty planned to be out of beeper range for only a few hours, she had made no back-up arrangements. Unfortunately, a client of Betty's with a borderline personality disorder had a crisis. The client had over time collected business cards from all the affiliates from the dispensers in the waiting room, and she called the numbers. However, no one was available throughout the afternoon. By the time the client reached Betty on Saturday evening, the client had overdosed with an over-the-counter medication, causing permanent liver damage. The client later initiated a complaint with the licensing board charging all the affiliate practitioners, including Carrie, with abandonment.

As a response to managed care, many social workers are joining group practices that may be incorporated arrangements or groups of independent contractors or colleagues sharing only the cost of office space. Although there are means for minimizing the risk of judgments of vicarious liability through contractual arrangements, it is the appearance of the group that can foster malpractice suits, extending associates' liability to individual practitioners. A litigator could reasonably assume that each practitioner had the responsibility to protect the interests of any client seen in the group because of shared space and the benefits of reduced overhead costs, mutual referrals, and shared consultation. Hence, each social worker could be vicariously liable for any of the others' negligence.

For these reasons, when constituting a group practice, social workers should

- investigate the state's contractual and incorporation options
- seek specific legal advice
- carefully select associates with proper and professional credentials, reputations, attitudes toward client services and care, and attitudes toward relationships with clients and a lack of ethical and legal problems
- review this book, and evaluate the capacity of prospective associates to prevent malpractice suits and complaints to regulatory bodies.

AVOIDING VICARIOUS LIABILITY

Social workers can manage the risks of vicarious liability in many ways. Supervisors should be knowledgeable about supervisees' cases, strengths and weaknesses as practitioners, and capacity for disciplined professional conduct; should develop a minimum standard for information received from supervisees; and should know their own responsibilities such as providing back-up. Consultants should document their role and the scope and limits of their involvement. Social work educators should make certain that research projects implemented by students conform to study participants' protection standards. Administrators should pay close attention to the security of client records and information systems. Practitioners should make responsible referrals, accept appointments to boards only if they are prepared to commit the time to fulfill the role responsibly, deal unflinchingly with impaired colleagues, and affiliate only with competent and professional colleagues.

References

Besharov, D. J. (1985). *The vulnerable social worker: Liability for serving children and families.* Silver Spring, MD: National Association of Social Workers.

Bullis, R. K. (1995). *Clinical social worker misconduct.* Chicago: Nelson-Hall.

Cohen, R. J., & Mariano, W. E. (1982). *Legal guidebook in mental health.* New York: Free Press.

Hogan, D. B. (1979). *The regulation of psychotherapists: Volume I-A: Study in the philosophy and practice of professional regulation.* Cambridge, MA: Ballinger.

Kaufman, B. L. (1993). Agency responsibility in client exploitation. *Journal of Law and Social Work, 2,* 21–32.

Kurzman, P. A. (1995). Professional liability and malpractice. In R. L. Edwards (Ed.-in-Chief), *Encyclopedia of social work* (19th ed., Vol. 3, pp. 1921–1927). Washington, DC: NASW Press.

Lamb, D. H., Presser, N. R., Pfost, K. S., Baum, M. C., Jackson, V. R., & Jarvis, P. A. (1987). Confronting professional impairment during the internship: Identification, due process, and remediation. *Professional Psychology: Research and Practice, 18,* 597–603.

NASW Insurance Trust, & American Professional Agency. (1996). *NASW Insurance Trust Professional Liability Insurance Program: Claims experience—Individual policies. Occurrence form, 1969–1995.* Unpublished manuscript, Washington, DC.

National Association of Social Workers. (1987). *Impaired social worker's program resource book.* Silver Spring, MD: Author.

National Association of Social Workers, National Council on the Practice of Clinical Social Work. (1994). *Guidelines for clinical social work supervision.* Washington, DC: Author.

National Association of Social Workers. (1996). *NASW code of ethics.* Washington, DC: Author.

Q & A. (1993, July). *Mental Health Legal Review,* p. 4.

Reamer, F. G. (1989). Liability issues in social work supervision. *Social Work, 34,* 445–448.

Reamer, F. G. (1992). The impaired social worker. *Social Work, 37,* 165–170.

Reamer, F. G. (1993). Liability issues in social work administration. *Administration in Social Work, 17,* 11–26.

Reamer, F. G. (1994). *Social work malpractice and liability: Strategies for prevention.* New York: Columbia University Press.

Reamer, F. G. (1995). *Social work values and ethics.* New York: Columbia University Press.

Robertson, H. W., & Jackson, V. H. (1991). *NASW guidelines on the private practice of clinical social work.* Washington, DC: National Association of Social Workers.

Robke, D. O. (1993, June). Supervisory liability: The buck stops here. *Progress Report,* pp. 14–15.

Shulman, L. (1995). Supervision and consultation. In R. L. Edwards (Ed.-in-Chief), *Encyclopedia of social work* (19th ed., Vol. 3, pp. 2373–2379). Washington, DC: NASW Press.

Siciliano, J., & Spiro, G. (1992). The unclear status of nonprofit directors: An empirical survey of director liability. *Administration in Social Work, 16,* 69–80.

Smith, S. R. (1994). The legal liabilities of mental health institutions. *Administration and Policy in Mental Health, 21,* 379–394.

Swenson, L. C. (1993). *Psychology and law for the helping professions.* Belmont, CA: Brooks/Cole.

Wimpfheimer, F., Klein, M., & Kramer, M. (1993). The impact of liability concerns on intraorganizational relationships. *Administration in Social Work, 17,* 41–56.

Woody, R. H. (1985). Public policy, malpractice law, and the mental health professional: Some legal and clinical guidelines. In C. P. Ewing (Ed.), *Psychology, psychiatry, and the law: A clinical and forensic handbook* (pp. 509–525). Sarasota, FL: Professional Resource Exchange.

Zakutansky, T. J., & Sirles, E. A. (1993). Ethical and legal issues in field education: Shared responsibilities and risk. *Journal of Social Work Education, 29,* 338–347.

CHAPTER

$$8$$

LOOKING FORWARD AND BEING PREPARED

By looking forward and being prepared, social workers can mitigate many malpractice risks. As emphasized throughout this book, practitioners should be engaged in ongoing supervision, consultation, and continuing education. Practitioners should understand professional liability coverage, be adequately insured, and know how to respond to allegations of misconduct. In addition, by anticipating and keeping up to date about emerging areas of liability, social workers will be able to reduce their professional risks.

OBTAINING CONTINUING EDUCATION, SUPERVISION, AND CONSULTATION

AARON

After working for 15 years as a social worker in a nursing home, Aaron began a part-time private practice, specializing in cases involving children with developmental disabilities and attention deficit hyperactivity disorder. Aaron had always liked children, but his only professional experience with them was 20 years ago at his first MSW practicum in a school setting. Although Aaron was busy with his full-time job and new private practice, he knew that he needed continuing education, so he had taken several workshops about repressed memories of childhood sexual abuse. Also, Aaron was trying to find an affordable clinical consultant who was available on weekends and planned to find one within the year.

During play therapy with a developmentally disabled six-year-old girl, Aaron observed what he determined to be signs of sexual abuse by her father, and he made a report. Child protective services determined the sexual abuse allegations were unfounded. The client's father filed a malpractice suit against Aaron, who was found liable for breach of confidentiality, defamation of character, and inappropriate treatment because of lack of established competence. The court determined that Aaron had not followed the standards for receiving ongoing consultation and supervision or continuing education sufficient to enable him to work with children.

State professional regulations, NASW's *Standards for the Practice of Clinical Social Work* (NASW, 1989), and other professional organizations set forth minimal standards for the independent practice of clinical social work. NASW (1989) requires

- a graduate degree from a social work program accredited by the Council on Social Work Education
- two years of full-time (or equivalent part-time) clinical social work experience supervised by a clinical social worker
- current membership in the Academy of Certified Social Workers or a state license or certification at the appropriate level. (p. 12)

In addition, state professional regulations, accrediting bodies, and the *NASW Code of Ethics* (1996; see Appendix A) and other professional practice standards mandate continuing education and ongoing case consultation and supervision.

These measures assist the practitioner in preventing flawed or inappropriate service, in remaining knowledgeable about current standards of care, and in supporting professional judgment in the event of a lawsuit. Social workers have been sued for failing to practice within their area of expertise and at their skill level. In a malpractice suit, the social worker's practice will be judged based on the standard of care established for the profession.

Social workers can advance their competence as well as document their accountability by developing a specific written plan for their professional development, including learning objectives and education activities and supervision and consultation. In formulating the plan, practitioners can consider both familiar and new areas of practice in which their knowledge needs to be enhanced, updated, or expanded. Practitioners who encounter new settings and clients with special needs should update the written professional development plan accordingly. Practitioners learning a new approach must keep up-to-date on literature and research, seek appropriate training, and undergo ongoing supervision until they have achieved mastery.

Continuing Education

Robertson and Jackson (1991) specified several forms of continuing education:

- reading current professional literature
- attending professional clinical social work workshops or seminars
- participating in advanced practice training seminars
- participating in peer education or supervision groups
- providing instruction for clinical continuing education training programs
- using supervision and consultation. (p. 3)

No matter what the type of practice, the social worker should develop a logical personal curriculum by choosing quality programs that demonstrate linkages to specific practice emphases.

The NASW Insurance Trust advises that social workers in nearly all disciplines, even nonclinical and nondirect practices, face some risk of professional liability. Therefore, the continuing education pursued can be of an administrative or supervisory nature as well as specifically for the reduction of personal malpractice risk. The practitioner should maintain good records of continuing education activities for licensure as well as for risk management purposes.

Supervision and Consultation

When a difficult case or risky situation such as a suicidal client is encountered, consulting with colleagues and seeking supervision may help substantiate that there was no negligence involved in practice. A supervisor or consultant can offer an unbiased opinion about the practitioner's work, provide expertise in new or difficult situations, help in a diagnostic understanding of a client and in the selection of interventions, and enrich practice skills. As discussed by Robertson and Jackson (1991):

> Supervision/consultation takes place when one professional seeks direction from another concerning any aspect of practice, including managing individual cases, upgrading the clinician's skills (new techniques or new client group), managing medical issues, monitoring the effects of prescription drugs, managing the business, or dealing with legal and financial issues. (p. 9)

Supervision and consultation are commonly differentiated based on differences in authority. Unlike a supervisor, a consultant does not have authority to act in the event of a problem with the consultee. Supervision is more specifically defined by professional credentialing and regulatory boards (Robertson & Jackson, 1991). Practitioners can refer to the NASW *Guidelines for Clinical Social Work Supervision* (NASW, National Council on the Practice of Clinical Social Work, 1994) and state professional regulations for definitive descriptions of the role of the supervisor.

The *NASW Guidelines on the Private Practice of Clinical Social Work* (Robertson & Jackson, 1991) identified questions that practitioners can consider when selecting a supervisor or consultant:

- Is peer consultation available?
- What type and how much supervision or consultation is needed?
- How frequently is supervision or consultation required?
- What theoretical orientation is desired?
- What is the supervisor's or consultant's fee?

Legal Consequences

State licensure laws set forth minimum continuing education and supervision requirements; these stipulations are typically consistent with the *NASW Code of Ethics* (NASW, 1996) and social work practice standards. Practitioners who are remiss in fulfilling these obligations may face the loss of licenses and malpractice insurance coverage as well as ethical sanctions. A malpractice allegation that occurs at the same time that a practitioner's license is in jeopardy for inattention to continuing education and supervision will be significantly strengthened. Securing case consultation is much more discretionary and case oriented; failure to obtain it ordinarily will be raised as a point of argument only in a malpractice case.

OBTAINING MALPRACTICE LIABILITY PROTECTION

GLORIA

Gloria worked at an inpatient psychiatric unit as a discharge planner on a contract, part-time basis. Several months after Gloria began working, a client made sexual abuse allegations against the staff and filed a lawsuit against the hospital, the administrators, the supervisors, and anyone with whom she had contact, including Gloria. Gloria, who had met the client only once in a family meeting to discuss discharge plans and who was innocent of any misconduct, had let her personal malpractice insurance lapse when she began employment, assuming that the hospital provided coverage. However, she discovered that the hospital's coverage did not include contract employees. With no professional liability coverage, Gloria had to hire an attorney to represent her. Nearly a year and $25,000 later, the allegations against Gloria were dropped. Gloria had followed every standard of care but neglected to examine her employer's professional liability insurance and maintain her own personal insurance.

Who needs malpractice liability protection? Social workers with any client-related responsibilities—no matter how indirect and regardless of role and position—who do not maintain malpractice liability coverage expose themselves to tremendous risk. The insurance or indemnification coverage selected should protect practitioners from the expensive process of presenting a defense against a malpractice claim and, in the event that a court finds in favor of the plaintiff or the case is settled, should cover damages.

Without question, social workers in independent practice need coverage. However, it has often been assumed that agency-based social workers did not need individual malpractice policies and that lawsuits are filed only against agencies and those with "deep pockets." However, this is no longer the case. Both the individual social worker and agency can be affected by malpractice allegations. Social workers should be responsible for securing their own malpractice coverage, even if they practice in a setting that is indemnified.

In addition, social workers employed by agencies should know the exclusions or limits of the agency's policy, including the definitions of employment, the covered job functions, and the time period of coverage. Also, agency policies may have discretionary indemnification programs; social workers should know how the decision to cover an employee is made and by whom (Besharov, 1985). Some policies do not cover or have limits when sexual impropriety is alleged. Most cannot cover violations of civil rights and criminal offenses (Saltzman & Proch, 1990/1994; Watkins & Watkins, 1989). In addition, the agency may alter or cancel provisions of a policy without warning.

Types of Coverage

There are two types of malpractice insurance policy forms:

1. occurrence policies
2. claims-made policies.

Occurrence policies cover wrongful acts that take place when the policy is in effect, even if the claim is reported later. Occurrence policies are not readily available and are expensive. In the more widely available claims-made policies, both the wrongful act and the reporting of the claim or lawsuit to the insurance agency must occur while the policy is still in force. Claims-made insurance policies are typically much less expensive and, coupled with an "extended reporting period endorsement," are considered equally as valuable as occurrence policies to social workers. Because most claims are made years after the alleged negligent act occurred, social workers with this type of insurance must be certain to obtain an extended reporting period endorsement to an expiring policy. This endorsement provides extended protection, or a "tail," which covers incidents that occurred during the time the policy was in effect but that are reported after the policy was terminated. The time period for coverage is set by the insurance carrier. The NASW-sponsored malpractice policy offers an unlimited time period in its tail coverage and is free to those insured on their permanent retirement, permanent disability, or death or is available for a nominal fee to those whose policies are terminated for other reasons.

The more common indemnity plus costs and fees coverage pays costs and fees for the legal defense and monetary damages awarded to a plaintiff if a practitioner is found legally liable. Costs and fees only coverage is unusual and pays only for costs related to defense and not for damages.

Social workers are at times asked to sign "hold harmless" service contracts. Managed care firms, employee assistance programs, and preferred provider organizations ask contract social workers to absolve contractors of liability, or hold them harmless, in events that may arise from the social workers' actions. Therefore, practitioners' omissions and commissions are totally their responsibility and cannot be attributed to the contractor. Firms also require that providers indemnify the contractor. Therefore, even if social workers are covered for damages assessed against themselves, they are also liable for damages assessed against the agency owing to their actions. Practitioners should determine if their insurance policy covers this type of exposure. One feature of the NASW-sponsored malpractice policy protects policyholders at no additional charge for the professional social work liability they assume under contracts.

Nearly all professional liability insurance policies do not extend coverage beyond the profession's social work functions and services. The definition of social work for insurance purposes is negotiated between the profession and the insurance carrier. For example, the definition does not extend to activities associated with another professional occupational group, even though performed by a social worker, such as massage or nutritional consultation, and it excludes many generic administrative functions that could be performed by variously trained and credentialed people without accredited social work degrees. Tasks such as hiring and firing staff, selecting office equipment, budgeting, and evaluating the program, therefore, are not covered by a social work professional liability insurance policy. Furthermore, the coverage does not extend to disputes between the social worker and agency (Hiratsuka, 1993).

Social workers who have been sued previously or who are under investigation by a professional regulatory body may be denied malpractice insurance coverage. The NASW-sponsored program does not automatically deny coverage in such instances. The renewal of the policy largely depends on the nature of the social worker's infraction. However, if a social worker is still involved in an unresolved investigation or lawsuit, a new application for coverage may be denied until after the case is resolved.

Most insurance companies omit coverage or limit the amount for punitive damages. Punitive damages are awarded by civil courts when there has been gross misconduct on the part of the practitioner. Punitive damages are a more severe penalty than mere damages, which are intended to punish the guilty party. Like some other policies, the NASW-sponsored policy has an aggregate insurance sublimit of $25,000 for sexual misconduct allegations, which means the insurance company will pay this maximum in damages during any given policy year. However, the limit does not apply to legal defense costs.

Obtaining Coverage

Selecting the right insurance coverage requires an examination of individual needs, the nature of the practice, and the availability of appropriate insurance policies in the marketplace. For example, does the practitioner need malpractice coverage for specialized interventions such as biofeedback or psychoanalysis? Also, does the practice involve a group of professionals, a partnership, or independent contractors? To cover these risks, an additional premium is usually required, particularly if the group includes psychologists and psychiatrists, who pose higher risks for malpractice and have higher insurance rates.

While selecting professional liability insurance, practitioners should compare coverage, costs, carriers, program longevity, and endorsements. Premiums may vary as much as 150 percent. Typically, the lowest premiums are attained through group insurance arrangements made by major professional organizations.

Role of the NASW Insurance Trust

The NASW Insurance Trust was established in 1967 as a subsidiary of the National Association of Social Workers. The Trust, which is administered by five social work volunteers who are appointed by the NASW president, is committed to offering to NASW members the best available professional liability coverage at the most affordable cost.

Recently, the Trust has sponsored and conducted numerous risk management activities and educational workshops about social work liability. These activities strengthen NASW's malpractice program, keep premiums low, reduce the number of lawsuits against members, and can increase the chances of a successful defense for those insured, if they are sued.

RESPONDING TO ALLEGATIONS

ANDY

Andy worked as a family practitioner at a children's and family agency. He had been seeing a 14-year-old adolescent in weekly individual treatment and seeing the youth's family biweekly. During the course of treatment, the youth began missing school and having hostile confrontations with his parents and siblings. The family voiced concerns that the services were not helpful. Andy reassured the family that many times things get worse before they get better. After several months and without explanation, the adolescent and the family dropped out of treatment. Andy made a follow-up telephone call and discovered that the teenager had run away and had not been located. Andy told the family that any time they wanted counseling, his door was open.

Several months later, Andy received a written complaint from the family's attorney. Andy felt very guilty and did not respond to it for several weeks. When he did call the family and their attorney, Andy stated that he felt very responsible for what had happened to the youth and that he may have erred in his judgment. He acknowledged that he should have referred the youth for additional services. After speaking with them, Andy assumed that their concerns were assuaged. When he received a summons two weeks later, Andy contacted his professional liability insurance agency and sent a letter outlining the details of the complaint.

Lawsuits against professionals arise frequently, and many lawsuits are frivolous. A client's single complaint can emerge into a series of complaints. In addition, the client's attorney may make multiple allegations so as to maximize the chances that the client's case will be founded and that damage settlements will reach the maximum allowed (Calfee, 1992; Helliczer, Lorenzen, & Lambert, 1993).

Malpractice Complaint

Practitioners who suspect the possibility of a malpractice complaint should contact an attorney if they are not insured. If they are insured, they should contact their malpractice insurance agency, or in the case of NASW members, the Managing General Agent, the American Professional Agency (NY). In fact, many policies obligate the insured to alert the agency. If a client is dissatisfied with the help provided, the practitioner should first institute appropriate therapeutic measures to address the client's concerns, including re-evaluating the service goals and plan; seeking a better approach to helping the client; and making a referral if warranted. During the process, the practitioner should seek consultation and supervision and fully document all actions and substantiate the basis for any professional judgment. The practitioner should discuss with legal counsel the steps that should be taken at once and any actions that should be anticipated.

If therapeutic measures are not successful or if the client's threat becomes an official, formal complaint, the practitioner must prepare a written statement to the insurance company including all relevant materials such as the client's name, the reason the client was seen, the dates of service, a summary of the allegations, an explanation of how the allegations fit with the practitioner's judgment, and a copy of the court summons. Once a report is submitted, a claims examiner will determine what the policy will cover. If a practitioner is served with an official complaint and summons, the insurance company will assign him or her a local attorney. The attorney assigned by the insurance company will work with the social worker until the lawsuit is resolved (Calfee, 1992; Helliczer et al., 1993). Most cases take one to two years to settle.

If sued by a client or a client's significant other, the social worker must end all contact with the client; the professional relationship has ceased. Attorney–client privilege is waived if the social worker speaks to someone else about the case. The social worker should not make any admissions of guilt or incriminating statements. The social worker should not communicate with the client or the client's attorney without the social worker's attorney present, should not talk about the case with anyone but his or her attorney, and should not keep secrets from his or her attorney. Calfee (1992) suggested that practitioners should keep personal files of court documents and should assert themselves if they feel uninformed by or dissatisfied with their legal counsel.

The practitioner should respond immediately to his or her attorney's requests for information and materials. The practitioner should not alter clinical records; if additional information needs to be added, he or she should ask the attorney how to do so. Altered records are illegal and give the appearance of guilt.

The social worker will be required to give depositions, submit client records, and meet with attorneys (Calfee, 1992; Helliczer et al., 1993). During a deposition, which can be used in the trial to discredit testimony, the client's attorney will ask questions of the social worker. The practitioner should prepare for the deposition by reviewing all records. Calfee (1992) proposed some tips on testifying at trial or in a deposition:

- Do not respond to leading questions in which the answer is in the question—for example, Isn't it true that since January 1, 1994, a social and sexual relationship has developed with the client?—or to multiple questions—for example, Is it true that your first field placement was at the Veterans Hospital and ever since then you have regularly engaged in sexual relationships with your clients? Instead, ask the attorney to clarify or restate the question.
- Take time answering questions, and if the answer is not known or remembered, say so.
- Respond in brief and uncomplicated terms. If there is a jury, use nontechnical language.
- Respond only to the questions asked.
- Keep calm.

The hearing of a lawsuit or complaint will be a stressful time. The social worker should continue to practice, meeting the standard of care, and might want to see a therapist for support. The sessions would be protected by legal privilege when personal concerns related to the claim are discussed.

Professional Regulatory Complaint

It is more likely that a complaint will be filed with the licensing board than that a lawsuit will be filed against an individual practitioner. State laws and licensing boards vary in how they handle complaints. Although some policies have coverage for legal defense in a licensing board complaint, many do not.

Complaint procedures vary by state. Generally, following receipt of the complaint, the licensing board will review the allegations and notify the licensee. An investigator may call, write, or visit unannounced to request an appointment. At this point, the practitioner should remain silent and call an attorney. Typically, a panel of several board members will review the evidence and determine whether there is probable cause to pursue a formal complaint procedure. In lieu of the formal procedure, the board may send a letter of guidance rather than pursue the violation.

Once a formal complaint is filed, the practitioner has a limited time to respond to and dispute the charges. If the social worker is found in violation, the board will determine the penalty and stipulations for remedial or corrective action, which can be appealed. During an appeal there may be formal and informal hearings in which a hearing officer examines the evidence and hears testimony of witnesses. The hearing officer may make a recommendation to the board. Typically, the attorney has the right to submit exceptions for consideration by the hearing officer. The board then makes its recommendations based on the ruling of the hearing officer's consideration of the facts. A final order is then issued. The social worker may have the right to appeal the final order.

If the complaint is related to impairment, the social worker will need to describe recovery efforts, nature and length of the impairment, and current condition. Many state regulatory boards have procedures for dealing with impaired professionals (Calfee, 1992). Disciplinary actions can include denying, suspending, or revoking a license; requiring the professional to retake the licensure examination; requiring the professional to receive supervision or treatment; or restricting practice. If the professional is found guilty and does not comply with the disciplinary action, he or she can be fined or jailed.

Charge of Ethical Violations

A complaint of an ethical violation, which can be made by anyone with knowledge of the situation, may be made to the state professional regulatory agency or to one or more professional associations espousing the code of ethics that is believed to have been breached. NASW has set forth procedures and criteria for addressing grievances and determining ethical violations. Each NASW chapter and the national organization (which reviews appeals) have committees on inquiry for the purpose of resolving professional disputes outside civil court. These committees operate based on the NASW *Procedures for the Adjudication of Grievances* (NASW, 1994), guidelines for the composition and operation of these committees, and conventions concerning types of sanctions made.

If a social worker is found in violation of the *NASW Code of Ethics* (NASW, 1996), NASW can make one of three recommendations:

1. corrective actions, which are aimed at restoring or bringing a social worker to an appropriate level of competence and ethical functioning (for example, the social worker may be required to seek supervision or consultation; follow a course of study; apologize to the injured party; or rectify a wrong by, for example, giving a client access to records or correcting a biased letter, evaluation, or report)
2. sanctions, which can include suspension or expulsion from NASW and notification of the state regulatory board, publication in the

NASW News or chapter newsletter, and notification of the social worker's employer and credentialing bodies

3. a combination of both.

Typically, corrective actions are requested first. Maximum sanctions are determined in grievous cases or when the social worker does not comply with the remedial measures.

ANTICIPATING TRENDS

BRIDGETTE

Bridgette worked as a clinical social worker at a for-profit outpatient counseling program. A client was referred by her physician for treatment of depression and had been taking an antidepressant for six months. Two years ago, the client's father died, leaving her stepmother as her only living relative. Last year after breaking up with her boyfriend of two years and also completing her teaching degree, the client moved 500 miles away from home to teach third grade at a local private school. However, her teaching contract recently was not renewed, and although the client had responded to Bridgette's interventions, she became more despondent after losing her job.

The client's health maintenance organization (HMO) informed Bridgette that it would cover only one more session. Bridgette was very concerned about the client's well-being and felt that she needed more sessions. In the last session, Bridgette explored with the client the implications of not having insurance coverage for mental health services, including her inability to pay the fee. Bridgette was very uneasy about terminating services, but the for-profit agency did not allow sliding-scale fees. Bridgette referred the client to a mental health clinic with a sliding fee. Bridgette also conducted a suicide risk evaluation, finding that the client did not pose an acute risk.

Several days after termination, the client was hospitalized for depression and filed a lawsuit against her HMO for failing to provide medically necessary services. In addition, the attorney initiated a lawsuit against Bridgette for inappropriate termination and failing to provide appropriate care. The courts found that the HMO was not liable because it was not informed of the necessity of continued services by Bridgette, who was found negligent for failing to advocate for the client's treatment needs and for inappropriate termination of services. Bridgette had failed to anticipate how her social work role and responsibilities would be interpreted in the managed care environment.

Professional liability is changing as practice arenas expand, as the knowledge base and technology evolves, and as new court rulings are made. Social workers must keep informed of these changes.

New Roles and Areas of Social Work Practice

Increasingly, social work practitioners are assuming roles as expert witnesses and evaluators using new practice approaches. As new roles are assumed and methodologies applied, social workers will encounter additional malpractice risks. A social worker who integrates methods or introduces adjunct information or treatments must have appropriate skills based on education or training and verifiable by credentials or certification. A social worker who includes nontraditional approaches to treatment or service such as nutrition information, massage, virtual reality methods, and hypnosis must demonstrate competence by having acceptable levels of education, training, and supervision. The use of such alternatives should be explained fully to clients and be acceptable to them before service is initiated. Before starting a service plan using a nontraditional approach, the social worker should contact the insurance company to obtain written confirmation that the modality is covered.

Specialty practice areas such as divorce mediation, child custody, or determination of personal injury benefits (for example, worker's compensation) have additional malpractice risks, including losses due to the outcomes of evaluations, negligent assessment, and defamation of character. In such services, clients may assume that the practitioner's conclusions will be favorable; when they are not, the client may sue. In addition, the practitioner may be called on to provide expert testimony and must be sufficiently trained in and knowledgeable about legal requirements and giving expert testimony. Also, the practitioner must set role parameters so that he or she does not go beyond the role of evaluator and provide counseling, which may place him or her in conflict with the client's interests.

Also, with new communication technologies adapted to meet clients' needs, new risks of malpractice liability emerge. For example, in 1995, the American Psychological Association's (APA's) Ethics Committee adopted a statement on telephone therapy that highlighted the pitfalls of using the Internet to deliver therapy. Telephone and teleconferencing psychotherapy and counseling services also portend a variety of risks. Hiratsuka (1993) described social workers' concerns about obtaining informed consent from telephone clients, the expertise of counselors, and the service fees. Telephone counselors are limited in their capacity to ensure continuity of care, successful referral procedures, and follow-up. In addition, counselors may respond to clients in other states, leading to questions of whether the counselor has the appropriate credentials and which state's laws take precedence. Moreover, clients who are addicted to the telephone could be taken advantage of, harmed financially, and diverted from more effective treatment.

Recently, there has been a debate in both the courts and practice arenas about repressed versus false memories. In May 1994, a landmark case in California (*Ramona v. Isabella*) awarded a plaintiff $500,000 in a lawsuit that involved recovered memories. Gary Ramona filed a lawsuit against his daughter's therapists based on loss of his job, reputation, and wife caused by allegations of incest made by his 23-year-old daughter. It was found that one of the two counselors, in the course of treating the daughter's bulimia, mentioned that the majority of women with eating disorders have experienced sexual abuse. The counselor later administered sodium amorbarbital (used to induce hypnosis) to the daughter, emphasizing to her that any recollections that arose during this induced state were the truth. Experts testified that these procedures were not reliable or trustworthy and that gross negligence was involved in treating the daughter. Presently, there is no scientifically agreed-on theory of memory, and it is difficult to determine the accuracy of induced recollections. This case showed practitioners' potential liability to others who are close to the client and are harmed because of the practitioner's negligence (Ewing, 1994) and also demonstrates the need to use sound theories and not make misleading statements.

Managed Care

Managed care has influenced and is likely to continue to influence social work practice standards in many ways. Because of managed care's emphasis on efficient, effective, and affordable services, social workers must be able to achieve and substantiate service outcomes and link client assessment with preferred treatment. Both practitioners and managed care systems are struggling with ways to determine the preferred treatment for specific diagnoses. Practitioners should not relegate their professional decision making to third-party payers but should instead collaborate to develop guidelines that support clinical decision making ("Managed-Care Dilemmas," 1994).

Managed care requires substantiating effectiveness based on client outcomes. Practitioners must remain up-to-date with empirical evidence substantiating their selection of service approaches and be able to document client outcomes. Measurable outcomes can be stated based on the client's symptoms, functional status, satisfaction, health, social functioning, employment, sobriety, or quality of life. An outcome orientation not only helps qualify clients for third-party benefits, but also provides a means of ensuring a reasonable standard of care and preventing professional negligence.

As practitioners adapt their practice to the realities of managed care, new forms of liability may occur. For example, one health care professional was found liable for not appealing the third-party payer's decision to deny coverage for further hospitalization of a depressed client ("Preventing Liability in the Managed Care Setting," 1994). Practitioners in managed care should know the appeal procedures and provide the reviewer with complete information documenting the need for continued benefits, further evidence of the necessity of keeping exemplary records and maintaining good communication.

* * *

CONCLUSION

Social workers will encounter many challenges, opportunities, and risks in practice. To apply the information provided in this handbook, practitioners will need to adapt the tips and tools to fit a specific practice, clientele, and personal style. The challenge is to be innovative in using the suggested forms and protocols in a user friendly manner.

This book has highlighted a range of strategies to mitigate malpractice risks:

- Be aware of potential liability risks and know how to respond to related allegations.
- Keep informed about the laws affecting social work practice and be aware of the changes and emerging trends in case and civil law.

- Use regular case consultation and supervision.
- Adhere to one's professional code of ethics.
- Obtain legal counsel.
- Keep up-to-date about the social work profession and maintain competence and expertise through continuing education.
- Maintain accurate, current, and timely documentation of practice and professional decisions.
- Obtain and understand professional liability insurance.

Facing the challenges of preventing a malpractice suit affords social workers and the profession abundant opportunities to refine skills, provide better services, become more exact in professional standards, and clarify roles. Most of all, social workers' best safeguard against malpractice is to think ahead and practice ethically, competently, and legally.

REFERENCES

APA's Ethics Committee adopts statement on telephone therapy. (1995, October). *APA Monitor*, p. 15.

Besharov, D. J. (1985). *The vulnerable social worker: Liability for serving children and families*. Silver Spring, MD: National Association of Social Workers.

Calfee, B. (1992). *Lawsuit prevention techniques*. Cleveland: ARC.

Ewing, C. (1994, July). Plaintiff awarded $500,000 in landmark "recovered memories lawsuit" [Judicial Notebook]. *APA Monitor*, p. 22.

Helliczer, J. R., Lorenzen, D., & Lambert, P. W. (1993). *Legal risk management for counseling and mental health professionals in Florida*. Eau Claire, WI: Professional Education Systems.

Hiratsuka, J. (1993, March). Dialing for answers: 900-Therapy. NASW News, p. 3.

Managed-care dilemmas cited for media. (1994, November). NASW News, p. 6.

National Association of Social Workers. (1989). *Standards for the practice of clinical social work* (rev. ed). Silver Spring, MD: Author.

National Association of Social Workers, National Council on the Practice of Clinical Social Work. (1994). *Guidelines for clinical social work supervision*. Washington, DC: Author.

National Association of Social Workers. (1994). *NASW procedures for the adjudication of grievances* (3rd ed.). Washington, DC: Author.

National Association of Social Workers. (1996). *NASW code of ethics*. Washington, DC: Author.

Preventing liability in the managed care setting. (1994, January). *Mental Health Legal Review*, pp. 1–3.

Ramona v. Isabella, No. 61898, Cal. Sup. Ct. Napa (May 13, 1994).

Robertson, H. W., & Jackson, V. H. (1991). *NASW guidelines on the private practice of clinical social work*. Silver Spring, MD: National Association of Social Workers.

Saltzman, A., & Proch, K. (1994). *Law and social work practice*. Chicago: Nelson-Hall. (Originally published in 1990)

Watkins, S. A., & Watkins, J. C. (1989). Negligent endangerment: Malpractice in the clinical context. *Journal of Independent Social Work, 3,* 35–50.

APPENDIX

A

NASW CODE OF ETHICS

OVERVIEW

The NASW *Code of Ethics* is intended to serve as a guide to the everyday professional conduct of social workers. This *Code* includes four sections. The first section, "Preamble," summarizes the social work profession's mission and core values. The second section, "Purpose of the *NASW Code of Ethics*," provides an overview of the *Code*'s main functions and a brief guide for dealing with ethical issues or dilemmas in social work practice. The third section, "Ethical Principles," presents broad ethical principles, based on social work's core values, that inform social work practice. The final section, "Ethical Standards," includes specific ethical standards to guide social workers' conduct and to provide a basis for adjudication.

PREAMBLE

The primary mission of the social work profession is to enhance human well-being and help meet the basic human needs of all people, with particular attention to the needs and empowerment of people who are vulnerable, oppressed, and living in poverty. A historic and defining feature of social work is the profession's focus on individual well-being in a social context and the well-being of society. Fundamental to social work is attention to the environmental forces that create, contribute to, and address problems in living.

Social workers promote social justice and social change with and on behalf of clients. "Clients" is used inclusively to refer to individuals, families, groups, organizations, and communities. Social workers are sensitive to cultural and ethnic diversity and strive to end discrimination, oppression, poverty, and other forms of social injustice. These activities may be in the form of direct practice, community organizing, supervision, consultation, administration, advocacy, social and political action, policy development and implementation, education, and research and evaluation. Social workers seek to enhance the capacity of people to address their own needs. Social workers also seek to promote the responsiveness of organizations, communities, and other social institutions to individuals' needs and social problems.

The mission of the social work profession is rooted in a set of core values. These core values, embraced by social workers throughout the profession's history, are the foundation of social work's unique purpose and perspective:

Adopted by the NASW Delegate Assembly, August 1996.

- service
- social justice
- dignity and worth of the person
- importance of human relationships
- integrity
- competence.

This constellation of core values reflects what is unique to the social work profession. Core values, and the principles that flow from them, must be balanced within the context and complexity of the human experience.

PURPOSE OF THE NASW CODE OF ETHICS

Professional ethics are at the core of social work. The profession has an obligation to articulate its basic values, ethical principles, and ethical standards. The *NASW Code of Ethics* sets forth these values, principles, and standards to guide social workers' conduct. The *Code* is relevant to all social workers and social work students, regardless of their professional functions, the settings in which they work, or the populations they serve.

The *NASW Code of Ethics* serves six purposes:

1. The *Code* identifies core values on which social work's mission is based.
2. The *Code* summarizes broad ethical principles that reflect the profession's core values and establishes a set of specific ethical standards that should be used to guide social work practice.
3. The *Code* is designed to help social workers identify relevant considerations when professional obligations conflict or ethical uncertainties arise.
4. The *Code* provides ethical standards to which the general public can hold the social work profession accountable.
5. The *Code* socializes practitioners new to the field to social work's mission, values, ethical principles, and ethical standards.
6. The *Code* articulates standards that the social work profession itself can use to assess whether social workers have engaged in unethical conduct. NASW has formal procedures to adjudicate ethics complaints filed against its members.[1] In subscribing to this *Code*, social workers are required to cooperate in its implementation, participate in NASW adjudication proceedings, and abide by any NASW disciplinary rulings or sanctions based on it.

The *Code* offers a set of values, principles, and standards to guide decision making and conduct when ethical issues arise. It does not provide a set of rules that prescribe how social workers should act in all situations. Specific applications of the *Code* must take into account the context in which it is being considered and the possibility of conflicts among the *Code*'s values, principles, and standards. Ethical responsibilities flow from all human relationships, from the personal and familial to the social and professional.

Further, the *NASW Code of Ethics* does not specify which values, principles, and standards are most important and ought to outweigh others in instances

---

[1] For information on NASW adjudication procedures, see NASW *Procedures for the Adjudication of Grievances.*

when they conflict. Reasonable differences of opinion can and do exist among social workers with respect to the ways in which values, ethical principles, and ethical standards should be rank ordered when they conflict. Ethical decision making in a given situation must apply the informed judgment of the individual social worker and should also consider how the issues would be judged in a peer review process where the ethical standards of the profession would be applied.

Ethical decision making is a process. There are many instances in social work where simple answers are not available to resolve complex ethical issues. Social workers should take into consideration all the values, principles, and standards in this *Code* that are relevant to any situation in which ethical judgment is warranted. Social workers' decisions and actions should be consistent with the spirit as well as the letter of this *Code*.

In addition to this *Code*, there are many other sources of information about ethical thinking that may be useful. Social workers should consider ethical theory and principles generally, social work theory and research, laws, regulations, agency policies, and other relevant codes of ethics, recognizing that among codes of ethics social workers should consider the *NASW Code of Ethics* as their primary source. Social workers also should be aware of the impact on ethical decision making of their clients' and their own personal values and cultural and religious beliefs and practices. They should be aware of any conflicts between personal and professional values and deal with them responsibly. For additional guidance social workers should consult the relevant literature on professional ethics and ethical decision making and seek appropriate consultation when faced with ethical dilemmas. This may involve consultation with an agency-based or social work organization's ethics committee, a regulatory body, knowledgeable colleagues, supervisors, or legal counsel.

Instances may arise when social workers' ethical obligations conflict with agency policies or relevant laws or regulations. When such conflicts occur, social workers must make a responsible effort to resolve the conflict in a manner that is consistent with the values, principles, and standards expressed in this *Code*. If a reasonable resolution of the conflict does not appear possible, social workers should seek proper consultation before making a decision.

The *NASW Code of Ethics* is to be used by NASW and by individuals, agencies, organizations, and bodies (such as licensing and regulatory boards, professional liability insurance providers, courts of law, agency boards of directors, government agencies, and other professional groups) that choose to adopt it or use it as a frame of reference. Violation of standards in this *Code* does not automatically imply legal liability or violation of the law. Such determination can only be made in the context of legal and judicial proceedings. Alleged violations of the *Code* would be subject to a peer review process. Such processes are generally separate from legal or administrative procedures and insulated from legal review or proceedings to allow the profession to counsel and discipline its own members.

A code of ethics cannot guarantee ethical behavior. Moreover, a code of ethics cannot resolve all ethical issues or disputes or capture the richness and complexity involved in striving to make responsible choices within a moral community. Rather, a code of ethics sets forth values, ethical principles, and ethical standards to which professionals aspire and by which their actions can be judged. Social workers' ethical behavior should result from their personal commitment to engage in ethical practice. The *NASW Code of Ethics* reflects the commitment of all social workers to uphold the profession's values and to act ethically. Principles and standards must be applied by individuals of good character who discern moral questions and, in good faith, seek to make reliable ethical judgments.

ETHICAL PRINCIPLES

The following broad ethical principles are based on social work's core values of service, social justice, dignity and worth of the person, importance of human relationships, integrity, and competence. These principles set forth ideals to which all social workers should aspire.

Value: *Service*

Ethical Principle: *Social workers' primary goal is to help people in need and to address social problems.*
> Social workers elevate service to others above self-interest. Social workers draw on their knowledge, values, and skills to help people in need and to address social problems. Social workers are encouraged to volunteer some portion of their professional skills with no expectation of significant financial return (pro bono service).

Value: *Social Justice*

Ethical Principle: *Social workers challenge social injustice.*
> Social workers pursue social change, particularly with and on behalf of vulnerable and oppressed individuals and groups of people. Social workers' social change efforts are focused primarily on issues of poverty, unemployment, discrimination, and other forms of social injustice. These activities seek to promote sensitivity to and knowledge about oppression and cultural and ethnic diversity. Social workers strive to ensure access to needed information, services, and resources; equality of opportunity; and meaningful participation in decision making for all people.

Value: *Dignity and Worth of the Person*

Ethical Principle: *Social workers respect the inherent dignity and worth of the person.*
> Social workers treat each person in a caring and respectful fashion, mindful of individual differences and cultural and ethnic diversity. Social workers promote clients' socially responsible self-determination. Social workers seek to enhance clients' capacity and opportunity to change and to address their own needs. Social workers are cognizant of their dual responsibility to clients and to the broader society. They seek to resolve conflicts between clients' interests and the broader society's interests in a socially responsible manner consistent with the values, ethical principles, and ethical standards of the profession.

Value: *Importance of Human Relationships*

Ethical Principle: *Social workers recognize the central importance of human relationships.*
> Social workers understand that relationships between and among people are an important vehicle for change. Social workers engage

people as partners in the helping process. Social workers seek to strengthen relationships among people in a purposeful effort to promote, restore, maintain, and enhance the well-being of individuals, families, social groups, organizations, and communities.

Value: *Integrity*

Ethical Principle: *Social workers behave in a trustworthy manner.*
Social workers are continually aware of the profession's mission, values, ethical principles, and ethical standards and practice in a manner consistent with them. Social workers act honestly and responsibly and promote ethical practices on the part of the organizations with which they are affiliated.

Value: *Competence*

Ethical Principle: *Social workers practice within their areas of competence and develop and enhance their professional expertise.*
Social workers continually strive to increase their professional knowledge and skills and to apply them in practice. Social workers should aspire to contribute to the knowledge base of the profession.

ETHICAL STANDARDS

The following ethical standards are relevant to the professional activities of all social workers. These standards concern (1) social workers' ethical responsibilities to clients, (2) social workers' ethical responsibilities to colleagues, (3) social workers' ethical responsibilities in practice settings, (4) social workers' ethical responsibilities as professionals, (5) social workers' ethical responsibilities to the social work profession, and (6) social workers' ethical responsibilities to the broader society.

Some of the standards that follow are enforceable guidelines for professional conduct, and some are aspirational. The extent to which each standard is enforceable is a matter of professional judgment to be exercised by those responsible for reviewing alleged violations of ethical standards.

1. Social Workers' Ethical Responsibilities to Clients

1.01 Commitment to Clients

Social workers' primary responsibility is to promote the well-being of clients. In general, clients' interests are primary. However, social workers' responsibility to the larger society or specific legal obligations may on limited occasions supersede the loyalty owed clients, and clients should be so advised. (Examples include when a social worker is required by law to report that a client has abused a child or has threatened to harm self or others.)

1.02 Self-Determination

Social workers respect and promote the right of clients to self-determination and assist clients in their efforts to identify and clarify their goals. Social workers may limit clients' right to self-determination when, in the social workers' professional judgment, clients' actions or potential actions pose a serious, foreseeable, and imminent risk to themselves or others.

1.03 Informed Consent

(a) Social workers should provide services to clients only in the context of a professional relationship based, when appropriate, on valid informed consent. Social workers should use clear and understandable language to inform clients of the purpose of the services, risks related to the services, limits to services because of the requirements of a third-party payer, relevant costs, reasonable alternatives, clients' right to refuse or withdraw consent, and the time frame covered by the consent. Social workers should provide clients with an opportunity to ask questions.

(b) In instances when clients are not literate or have difficulty understanding the primary language used in the practice setting, social workers should take steps to ensure clients' comprehension. This may include providing clients with a detailed verbal explanation or arranging for a qualified interpreter or translator whenever possible.

(c) In instances when clients lack the capacity to provide informed consent, social workers should protect clients' interests by seeking permission from an appropriate third party, informing clients consistent with the clients' level of understanding. In such instances social workers should seek to ensure that the third party acts in a manner consistent with clients' wishes and interests. Social workers should take reasonable steps to enhance such clients' ability to give informed consent.

(d) In instances when clients are receiving services involuntarily, social workers should provide information about the nature and extent of services and about the extent of clients' right to refuse service.

(e) Social workers who provide services via electronic media (such as computer, telephone, radio, and television) should inform recipients of the limitations and risks associated with such services.

(f) Social workers should obtain clients' informed consent before audiotaping or videotaping clients or permitting observation of services to clients by a third party.

1.04 Competence

(a) Social workers should provide services and represent themselves as competent only within the boundaries of their education, training, license, certification, consultation received, supervised experience, or other relevant professional experience.

(b) Social workers should provide services in substantive areas or use intervention techniques or approaches that are new to them only after engaging in appropriate study, training, consultation, and supervision from people who are competent in those interventions or techniques.

(c) When generally recognized standards do not exist with respect to an emerging area of practice, social workers should exercise careful judgment and take responsible steps (including appropriate education, research, training, consultation, and supervision) to ensure the competence of their work and to protect clients from harm.

1.05 Cultural Competence and Social Diversity

(a) Social workers should understand culture and its function in human behavior and society, recognizing the strengths that exist in all cultures.

(b) Social workers should have a knowledge base of their clients' cultures and be able to demonstrate competence in the provision of services that are sensitive to clients' cultures and to differences among people and cultural groups.

(c) Social workers should obtain education about and seek to understand the nature of social diversity and oppression with respect to race, ethnicity, national origin, color, sex, sexual orientation, age, marital status, political belief, religion, and mental or physical disability.

1.06 Conflicts of Interest

(a) Social workers should be alert to and avoid conflicts of interest that interfere with the exercise of professional discretion and impartial judgment. Social workers should inform clients when a real or potential conflict of interest arises and take reasonable steps to resolve the issue in a manner that makes the clients' interests primary and protects clients' interests to the greatest extent possible. In some cases, protecting clients' interests may require termination of the professional relationship with proper referral of the client.

(b) Social workers should not take unfair advantage of any professional relationship or exploit others to further their personal, religious, political, or business interests.

(c) Social workers should not engage in dual or multiple relationships with clients or former clients in which there is a risk of exploitation or potential harm to the client. In instances when dual or multiple relationships are unavoidable, social workers should take steps to protect clients and are responsible for setting clear, appropriate, and culturally sensitive boundaries. (Dual or multiple relationships occur when social workers relate to clients in more than one relationship, whether professional, social, or business. Dual or multiple relationships can occur simultaneously or consecutively.)

(d) When social workers provide services to two or more people who have a relationship with each other (for example, couples, family members), social workers should clarify with all parties which individuals will be considered clients and the nature of social workers' professional obligations to the various individuals who are receiving services. Social workers who anticipate a conflict of interest among the individuals receiving services or who anticipate having to perform in potentially conflicting roles (for example, when a social worker is asked to testify in a child custody dispute or divorce proceedings involving clients) should clarify their role with the parties involved and take appropriate action to minimize any conflict of interest.

1.07 Privacy and Confidentiality

(a) Social workers should respect clients' right to privacy. Social workers should not solicit private information from clients unless it is essential to providing services or conducting social work evaluation or research. Once private information is shared, standards of confidentiality apply.

(b) Social workers may disclose confidential information when appropriate with valid consent from a client or a person legally authorized to consent on behalf of a client.

(c) Social workers should protect the confidentiality of all information obtained in the course of professional service, except for compelling professional reasons. The general expectation that social workers will keep information confidential does not apply when disclosure is necessary to prevent serious, foreseeable, and imminent harm to a client or other identifiable person or when laws or regulations require disclosure without a client's consent. In all instances, social workers should disclose the least amount of confidential information necessary to achieve the desired purpose; only information that is directly relevant to the purpose for which the disclosure is made should be revealed.

(d) Social workers should inform clients, to the extent possible, about the disclosure of confidential information and the potential consequences, when feasible before the disclosure is made. This applies whether social workers disclose confidential information on the basis of a legal requirement or client consent.

(e) Social workers should discuss with clients and other interested parties the nature of confidentiality and limitations of clients' right to confidentiality. Social workers should review with clients circumstances where confidential information may be requested and where disclosure of confidential information may be legally required. This discussion should occur as soon as possible in the social worker–client relationship and as needed throughout the course of the relationship.

(f) When social workers provide counseling services to families, couples, or groups, social workers should seek agreement among the parties involved concerning each individual's right to confidentiality and obligation to preserve the confidentiality of information shared by others. Social workers should inform participants in family, couples, or group counseling that social workers cannot guarantee that all participants will honor such agreements.

(g) Social workers should inform clients involved in family, couples, marital, or group counseling of the social worker's, employer's, and agency's policy concerning the social worker's disclosure of confidential information among the parties involved in the counseling.

(h) Social workers should not disclose confidential information to third-party payers unless clients have authorized such disclosure.

(i) Social workers should not discuss confidential information in any setting unless privacy can be ensured. Social workers should not discuss confidential information in public or semipublic areas such as hallways, waiting rooms, elevators, and restaurants.

(j) Social workers should protect the confidentiality of clients during legal proceedings to the extent permitted by law. When a court of law or other legally authorized body orders social workers to disclose confidential or privileged information without a client's consent and such disclosure could cause harm to the client, social workers should request that the court withdraw the order or limit the order as narrowly as possible or maintain the records under seal, unavailable for public inspection.

(k) Social workers should protect the confidentiality of clients when responding to requests from members of the media.

(l) Social workers should protect the confidentiality of clients' written and electronic records and other sensitive information. Social workers should take reasonable steps to ensure that clients' records are stored in a secure location and that clients' records are not available to others who are not authorized to have access.

(m) Social workers should take precautions to ensure and maintain the confidentiality of information transmitted to other parties through the use of computers, electronic mail, facsimile machines, telephones and telephone answering machines, and other electronic or computer technology. Disclosure of identifying information should be avoided whenever possible.

(n) Social workers should transfer or dispose of clients' records in a manner that protects clients' confidentiality and is consistent with state statutes governing records and social work licensure.

(o) Social workers should take reasonable precautions to protect client confidentiality in the event of the social worker's termination of practice, incapacitation, or death.

(p) Social workers should not disclose identifying information when discussing clients for teaching or training purposes unless the client has consented to disclosure of confidential information.

(q) Social workers should not disclose identifying information when discussing clients with consultants unless the client has consented to disclosure of confidential information or there is a compelling need for such disclosure.

(r) Social workers should protect the confidentiality of deceased clients consistent with the preceding standards.

1.08 Access to Records

(a) Social workers should provide clients with reasonable access to records concerning the clients. Social workers who are concerned that clients' access to their records could cause serious misunderstanding or harm to the client should provide assistance in interpreting the records and consultation with the client regarding the records. Social workers should limit clients' access to their records, or portions of their records, only in exceptional circumstances when there is compelling evidence that such access would cause serious harm to the client. Both clients' requests and the rationale for withholding some or all of the record should be documented in clients' files.

(b) When providing clients with access to their records, social workers should take steps to protect the confidentiality of other individuals identified or discussed in such records.

1.09 Sexual Relationships

(a) Social workers should under no circumstances engage in sexual activities or sexual contact with current clients, whether such contact is consensual or forced.

(b) Social workers should not engage in sexual activities or sexual contact with clients' relatives or other individuals with whom clients maintain a close personal relationship when there is a risk of exploitation or potential harm to the client. Sexual activity or sexual contact with clients' relatives or other individuals with whom clients maintain a personal relationship has the potential to be harmful to the client and may make it difficult for the social worker and client to maintain appropriate professional boundaries. Social workers—not their clients, their clients' relatives, or other individuals with whom the client maintains a personal relationship—assume the full burden for setting clear, appropriate, and culturally sensitive boundaries.

(c) Social workers should not engage in sexual activities or sexual contact with former clients because of the potential for harm to the client. If social workers engage in conduct contrary to this prohibition or claim that an exception to this prohibition is warranted because of extraordinary circumstances, it is social workers—not their clients—who assume the full burden of demonstrating that the former client has not been exploited, coerced, or manipulated, intentionally or unintentionally.

(d) Social workers should not provide clinical services to individuals with whom they have had a prior sexual relationship. Providing clinical services to a former sexual partner has the potential to be harmful to the individual and is likely to make it difficult for the social worker and individual to maintain appropriate professional boundaries.

1.10 Physical Contact

Social workers should not engage in physical contact with clients when there is a possibility of psychological harm to the client as a result of the contact (such as cradling or caressing clients). Social workers who engage in appropriate physical contact with clients are responsible for setting clear, appropriate, and culturally sensitive boundaries that govern such physical contact.

1.11 Sexual Harassment

Social workers should not sexually harass clients. Sexual harassment includes sexual advances, sexual solicitation, requests for sexual favors, and other verbal or physical conduct of a sexual nature.

1.12 Derogatory Language

Social workers should not use derogatory language in their written or verbal communications to or about clients. Social workers should use accurate and respectful language in all communications to and about clients.

1.13 Payment for Services

(a) When setting fees, social workers should ensure that the fees are fair, reasonable, and commensurate with the services performed. Consideration should be given to clients' ability to pay.

(b) Social workers should avoid accepting goods or services from clients as payment for professional services. Bartering arrangements, particularly involving services, create the potential for conflicts of interest, exploitation, and inappropriate boundaries in social workers' relationships with clients. Social workers should explore and may participate in bartering only in very limited circumstances when it can be demonstrated that such arrangements are an accepted practice among professionals in the local community, considered to be essential for the provision of services, negotiated without coercion, and entered into at the client's initiative and with the client's informed consent. Social workers who accept goods or services from clients as payment for professional services assume the full burden of demonstrating that this arrangement will not be detrimental to the client or the professional relationship.

(c) Social workers should not solicit a private fee or other remuneration for providing services to clients who are entitled to such available services through the social workers' employer or agency.

1.14 Clients Who Lack Decision-Making Capacity

When social workers act on behalf of clients who lack the capacity to make informed decisions, social workers should take reasonable steps to safeguard the interests and rights of those clients.

1.15 Interruption of Services

Social workers should make reasonable efforts to ensure continuity of services in the event that services are interrupted by factors such as unavailability, relocation, illness, disability, or death.

1.16 Termination of Services

(a) Social workers should terminate services to clients and professional relationships with them when such services and relationships are no longer required or no longer serve the clients' needs or interests.

(b) Social workers should take reasonable steps to avoid abandoning clients who are still in need of services. Social workers should withdraw services precipitously only under unusual circumstances, giving careful consideration to all factors in the situation and taking care to minimize possible adverse effects. Social workers should assist in making appropriate arrangements for continuation of services when necessary.

(c) Social workers in fee-for-service settings may terminate services to clients who are not paying an overdue balance if the financial contractual arrangements have been made clear to the client, if the client does not pose an imminent danger to self or others, and if the clinical and other consequences of the current nonpayment have been addressed and discussed with the client.

(d) Social workers should not terminate services to pursue a social, financial, or sexual relationship with a client.

(e) Social workers who anticipate the termination or interruption of services to clients should notify clients promptly and seek the transfer, referral, or continuation of services in relation to the clients' needs and preferences.

(f) Social workers who are leaving an employment setting should inform clients of appropriate options for the continuation of services and of the benefits and risks of the options.

2. Social Workers' Ethical Responsibilities to Colleagues

2.01 Respect

(a) Social workers should treat colleagues with respect and should represent accurately and fairly the qualifications, views, and obligations of colleagues.

(b) Social workers should avoid unwarranted negative criticism of colleagues in communications with clients or with other professionals. Unwarranted negative criticism may include demeaning comments that refer to colleagues' level of competence or to individuals' attributes such as race, ethnicity, national origin, color, sex, sexual orientation, age, marital status, political belief, religion, and mental or physical disability.

(c) Social workers should cooperate with social work colleagues and with colleagues of other professions when such cooperation serves the well-being of clients.

2.02 Confidentiality

Social workers should respect confidential information shared by colleagues in the course of their professional relationships and transactions. Social workers should ensure that such colleagues understand social workers' obligation to respect confidentiality and any exceptions related to it.

2.03 Interdisciplinary Collaboration

(a) Social workers who are members of an interdisciplinary team should participate in and contribute to decisions that affect the well-being of clients by drawing on the perspectives, values, and experiences of the social work profession. Professional and ethical obligations of the interdisciplinary team as a whole and of its individual members should be clearly established.

(b) Social workers for whom a team decision raises ethical concerns should attempt to resolve the disagreement through appropriate channels. If the disagreement cannot be resolved, social workers should pursue other avenues to address their concerns consistent with client well-being.

2.04 Disputes Involving Colleagues

(a) Social workers should not take advantage of a dispute between a colleague and an employer to obtain a position or otherwise advance the social workers' own interests.

(b) Social workers should not exploit clients in disputes with colleagues or engage clients in any inappropriate discussion of conflicts between social workers and their colleagues.

2.05 Consultation

(a) Social workers should seek the advice and counsel of colleagues whenever such consultation is in the best interests of clients.

(b) Social workers should keep themselves informed about colleagues' areas of expertise and competencies. Social workers should seek consultation only from colleagues who have demonstrated knowledge, expertise, and competence related to the subject of the consultation.

(c) When consulting with colleagues about clients, social workers should disclose the least amount of information necessary to achieve the purposes of the consultation.

2.06 Referral for Services

(a) Social workers should refer clients to other professionals when the other professionals' specialized knowledge or expertise is needed to serve clients fully or when social workers believe that they are not being effective or making reasonable progress with clients and that additional service is required.

(b) Social workers who refer clients to other professionals should take appropriate steps to facilitate an orderly transfer of responsibility. Social workers who refer clients to other professionals should disclose, with clients' consent, all pertinent information to the new service providers.

(c) Social workers are prohibited from giving or receiving payment for a referral when no professional service is provided by the referring social worker.

2.07 Sexual Relationships

(a) Social workers who function as supervisors or educators should not engage in sexual activities or contact with supervisees, students, trainees, or other colleagues over whom they exercise professional authority.

(b) Social workers should avoid engaging in sexual relationships with colleagues when there is potential for a conflict of interest. Social workers who become involved in, or anticipate becoming involved in, a sexual relationship with a colleague have a duty to transfer professional responsibilities, when necessary, to avoid a conflict of interest.

2.08 Sexual Harassment

Social workers should not sexually harass supervisees, students, trainees, or colleagues. Sexual harassment includes sexual advances, sexual solicitation, requests for sexual favors, and other verbal or physical conduct of a sexual nature.

2.09 Impairment of Colleagues

(a) Social workers who have direct knowledge of a social work colleague's impairment that is due to personal problems, psychosocial distress, substance abuse, or mental health difficulties and that interferes with practice effectiveness should consult with that colleague when feasible and assist the colleague in taking remedial action.

(b) Social workers who believe that a social work colleague's impairment interferes with practice effectiveness and that the colleague has not taken adequate steps to address the impairment should take action through appropriate channels established by employers, agencies, NASW, licensing and regulatory bodies, and other professional organizations.

2.10 Incompetence of Colleagues

(a) Social workers who have direct knowledge of a social work colleague's incompetence should consult with that colleague when feasible and assist the colleague in taking remedial action.

(b) Social workers who believe that a social work colleague is incompetent and has not taken adequate steps to address the incompetence should take action through appropriate channels established by employers, agencies, NASW, licensing and regulatory bodies, and other professional organizations.

2.11 Unethical Conduct of Colleagues

(a) Social workers should take adequate measures to discourage, prevent, expose, and correct the unethical conduct of colleagues.

(b) Social workers should be knowledgeable about established policies and procedures for handling concerns about colleagues' unethical behavior. Social workers should be familiar with national, state, and local procedures for handling ethics complaints. These include policies and procedures created by NASW, licensing and regulatory bodies, employers, agencies, and other professional organizations.

(c) Social workers who believe that a colleague has acted unethically should seek resolution by discussing their concerns with the colleague when feasible and when such discussion is likely to be productive.

(d) When necessary, social workers who believe that a colleague has acted unethically should take action through appropriate formal channels (such as contacting a state licensing board or regulatory body, an NASW committee on inquiry, or other professional ethics committees).

(e) Social workers should defend and assist colleagues who are unjustly charged with unethical conduct.

3. Social Workers' Ethical Responsibilities in Practice Settings

3.01 Supervision and Consultation

(a) Social workers who provide supervision or consultation should have the necessary knowledge and skill to supervise or consult appropriately and should do so only within their areas of knowledge and competence.

(b) Social workers who provide supervision or consultation are responsible for setting clear, appropriate, and culturally sensitive boundaries.

(c) Social workers should not engage in any dual or multiple relationships with supervisees in which there is a risk of exploitation of or potential harm to the supervisee.

(d) Social workers who provide supervision should evaluate supervisees' performance in a manner that is fair and respectful.

3.02 Education and Training

(a) Social workers who function as educators, field instructors for students, or trainers should provide instruction only within their areas of knowledge and competence and should provide instruction based on the most current information and knowledge available in the profession.

(b) Social workers who function as educators or field instructors for students should evaluate students' performance in a manner that is fair and respectful.

(c) Social workers who function as educators or field instructors for students should take reasonable steps to ensure that clients are routinely informed when services are being provided by students.

(d) Social workers who function as educators or field instructors for students should not engage in any dual or multiple relationships with students in which there is a risk of exploitation or potential harm to the student. Social work educators and field instructors are responsible for setting clear, appropriate, and culturally sensitive boundaries.

3.03 Performance Evaluation

Social workers who have responsibility for evaluating the performance of others should fulfill such responsibility in a fair and considerate manner and on the basis of clearly stated criteria.

3.04 Client Records

(a) Social workers should take reasonable steps to ensure that documentation in records is accurate and reflects the services provided.

(b) Social workers should include sufficient and timely documentation in records to facilitate the delivery of services and to ensure continuity of services provided to clients in the future.

(c) Social workers' documentation should protect clients' privacy to the extent that is possible and appropriate and should include only information that is directly relevant to the delivery of services.

(d) Social workers should store records following the termination of services to ensure reasonable future access. Records should be maintained for the number of years required by state statutes or relevant contracts.

3.05 Billing

Social workers should establish and maintain billing practices that accurately reflect the nature and extent of services provided and that identify who provided the service in the practice setting.

3.06 Client Transfer

(a) When an individual who is receiving services from another agency or colleague contacts a social worker for services, the social worker should carefully consider the client's needs before agreeing to provide services. To minimize possible confusion and conflict, social workers should discuss with potential clients the nature of the clients' current relationship with other service providers and the implications, including possible benefits or risks, of entering into a relationship with a new service provider.

(b) If a new client has been served by another agency or colleague, social workers should discuss with the client whether consultation with the previous service provider is in the client's best interest.

3.07 Administration

(a) ~~Social work administrators should advocate within and outside their~~ agencies for adequate resources to meet clients' needs.

(b) Social workers should advocate for resource allocation procedures that are open and fair. When not all clients' needs can be met, an allocation procedure should be developed that is nondiscriminatory and based on appropriate and consistently applied principles.

(c) Social workers who are administrators should take reasonable steps to ensure that adequate agency or organizational resources are available to provide appropriate staff supervision.

(d) Social work administrators should take reasonable steps to ensure that the working environment for which they are responsible is consistent with and encourages compliance with the *NASW Code of Ethics*. Social work administrators should take reasonable steps to eliminate any conditions in their organizations that violate, interfere with, or discourage compliance with the *Code*.

3.08 Continuing Education and Staff Development

Social work administrators and supervisors should take reasonable steps to provide or arrange for continuing education and staff development for all staff for whom they are responsible. Continuing education and staff development should address current knowledge and emerging developments related to social work practice and ethics.

3.09 Commitments to Employers

(a) Social workers generally should adhere to commitments made to employers and employing organizations.

(b) Social workers should work to improve employing agencies' policies and procedures and the efficiency and effectiveness of their services.

(c) Social workers should take reasonable steps to ensure that employers are aware of social workers' ethical obligations as set forth in the *NASW Code of Ethics* and of the implications of those obligations for social work practice.

(d) Social workers should not allow an employing organization's policies, procedures, regulations, or administrative orders to interfere with their ethical practice of social work. Social workers should take reasonable steps to ensure that their employing organizations' practices are consistent with the *NASW Code of Ethics*.

(e) Social workers should act to prevent and eliminate discrimination in the employing organization's work assignments and in its employment policies and practices.

(f) Social workers should accept employment or arrange student field placements only in organizations that exercise fair personnel practices.

(g) Social workers should be diligent stewards of the resources of their employing organizations, wisely conserving funds where appropriate and never misappropriating funds or using them for unintended purposes.

3.10 Labor–Management Disputes

(a) Social workers may engage in organized action, including the formation of and participation in labor unions, to improve services to clients and working conditions.

(b) The actions of social workers who are involved in labor–management disputes, job actions, or labor strikes should be guided by the profession's values, ethical principles, and ethical standards. Reasonable differences of opinion exist among social workers concerning their primary obligation as professionals during an actual or threatened labor strike or job action. Social workers should carefully examine relevant issues and their possible impact on clients before deciding on a course of action.

4. Social Workers' Ethical Responsibilities as Professionals

4.01 Competence

(a) Social workers should accept responsibility or employment only on the basis of existing competence or the intention to acquire the necessary competence.

(b) Social workers should strive to become and remain proficient in professional practice and the performance of professional functions. Social workers should critically examine and keep current with emerging knowledge relevant to social work. Social workers should routinely review the professional literature and participate in continuing education relevant to social work practice and social work ethics.

(c) Social workers should base practice on recognized knowledge, including empirically based knowledge, relevant to social work and social work ethics.

4.02 Discrimination

Social workers should not practice, condone, facilitate, or collaborate with any form of discrimination on the basis of race, ethnicity, national origin, color, sex, sexual orientation, age, marital status, political belief, religion, or mental or physical disability.

4.03 Private Conduct

Social workers should not permit their private conduct to interfere with their ability to fulfill their professional responsibilities.

4.04 Dishonesty, Fraud, and Deception

Social workers should not participate in, condone, or be associated with dishonesty, fraud, or deception.

4.05 Impairment

(a) Social workers should not allow their own personal problems, psychosocial distress, legal problems, substance abuse, or mental health difficulties to interfere with their professional judgment and performance or to jeopardize the best interests of people for whom they have a professional responsibility.

(b) Social workers whose personal problems, psychosocial distress, legal problems, substance abuse, or mental health difficulties interfere with their professional judgment and performance should immediately seek consultation and take appropriate remedial action by seeking professional help, making adjustments in workload, terminating practice, or taking any other steps necessary to protect clients and others.

4.06 Misrepresentation

(a) Social workers should make clear distinctions between statements made and actions engaged in as a private individual and as a representative of the social work profession, a professional social work organization, or the social worker's employing agency.

(b) Social workers who speak on behalf of professional social work organizations should accurately represent the official and authorized positions of the organizations.

(c) Social workers should ensure that their representations to clients, agencies, and the public of professional qualifications, credentials, education, competence, affiliations, services provided, or results to be achieved are accurate. Social workers should claim only those relevant professional credentials they actually possess and take steps to correct any inaccuracies or misrepresentations of their credentials by others.

4.07 Solicitations

(a) Social workers should not engage in uninvited solicitation of potential clients who, because of their circumstances, are vulnerable to undue influence, manipulation, or coercion.

(b) Social workers should not engage in solicitation of testimonial endorsements (including solicitation of consent to use a client's prior statement as a testimonial endorsement) from current clients or from other people who, because of their particular circumstances, are vulnerable to undue influence.

4.08 Acknowledging Credit

(a) Social workers should take responsibility and credit, including authorship credit, only for work they have actually performed and to which they have contributed.
(b) Social workers should honestly acknowledge the work of and the contributions made by others.

5. Social Workers' Ethical Responsibilities to the Social Work Profession

5.01 Integrity of the Profession

(a) Social workers should work toward the maintenance and promotion of high standards of practice.
(b) Social workers should uphold and advance the values, ethics, knowledge, and mission of the profession. Social workers should protect, enhance, and improve the integrity of the profession through appropriate study and research, active discussion, and responsible criticism of the profession.
(c) Social workers should contribute time and professional expertise to activities that promote respect for the value, integrity, and competence of the social work profession. These activities may include teaching, research, consultation, service, legislative testimony, presentations in the community, and participation in their professional organizations.
(d) Social workers should contribute to the knowledge base of social work and share with colleagues their knowledge related to practice, research, and ethics. Social workers should seek to contribute to the profession's literature and to share their knowledge at professional meetings and conferences.
(e) Social workers should act to prevent the unauthorized and unqualified practice of social work.

5.02 Evaluation and Research

(a) Social workers should monitor and evaluate policies, the implementation of programs, and practice interventions.
(b) Social workers should promote and facilitate evaluation and research to contribute to the development of knowledge.
(c) Social workers should critically examine and keep current with emerging knowledge relevant to social work and fully use evaluation and research evidence in their professional practice.
(d) Social workers engaged in evaluation or research should carefully consider possible consequences and should follow guidelines developed for the protection of evaluation and research participants. Appropriate institutional review boards should be consulted.

(e) Social workers engaged in evaluation or research should obtain voluntary and written informed consent from participants, when appropriate, without any implied or actual deprivation or penalty for refusal to participate; without undue inducement to participate; and with due regard for participants' well-being, privacy, and dignity. Informed consent should include information about the nature, extent, and duration of the participation requested and disclosure of the risks and benefits of participation in the research.

(f) When evaluation or research participants are incapable of giving informed consent, social workers should provide an appropriate explanation to the participants, obtain the participants' assent to the extent they are able, and obtain written consent from an appropriate proxy.

(g) Social workers should never design or conduct evaluation or research that does not use consent procedures, such as certain forms of naturalistic observation and archival research, unless rigorous and responsible review of the research has found it to be justified because of its prospective scientific, educational, or applied value and unless equally effective alternative procedures that do not involve waiver of consent are not feasible.

(h) Social workers should inform participants of their right to withdraw from evaluation and research at any time without penalty.

(i) Social workers should take appropriate steps to ensure that participants in evaluation and research have access to appropriate supportive services.

(j) Social workers engaged in evaluation or research should protect participants from unwarranted physical or mental distress, harm, danger, or deprivation.

(k) Social workers engaged in the evaluation of services should discuss collected information only for professional purposes and only with people professionally concerned with this information.

(l) Social workers engaged in evaluation or research should ensure the anonymity or confidentiality of participants and of the data obtained from them. Social workers should inform participants of any limits of confidentiality, the measures that will be taken to ensure confidentiality, and when any records containing research data will be destroyed.

(m) Social workers who report evaluation and research results should protect participants' confidentiality by omitting identifying information unless proper consent has been obtained authorizing disclosure.

(n) Social workers should report evaluation and research findings accurately. They should not fabricate or falsify results and should take steps to correct any errors later found in published data using standard publication methods.

(o) Social workers engaged in evaluation or research should be alert to and avoid conflicts of interest and dual relationships with participants, should inform participants when a real or potential conflict of interest arises, and should take steps to resolve the issue in a manner that makes participants' interests primary.

(p) Social workers should educate themselves, their students, and their colleagues about responsible research practices.

6. Social Workers' Ethical Responsibilities to the Broader Society

6.01 Social Welfare

Social workers should promote the general welfare of society, from local to global levels, and the development of people, their communities, and their environments. Social workers should advocate for living conditions conducive to the fulfillment of basic human needs and should promote social, economic, political, and cultural values and institutions that are compatible with the realization of social justice.

6.02 Public Participation

Social workers should facilitate informed participation by the public in shaping social policies and institutions.

6.03 Public Emergencies

Social workers should provide appropriate professional services in public emergencies to the greatest extent possible.

6.04 Social and Political Action

(a) Social workers should engage in social and political action that seeks to ensure that all people have equal access to the resources, employment, services, and opportunities they require to meet their basic human needs and to develop fully. Social workers should be aware of the impact of the political arena on practice and should advocate for changes in policy and legislation to improve social conditions in order to meet basic human needs and promote social justice.

(b) Social workers should act to expand choice and opportunity for all people, with special regard for vulnerable, disadvantaged, oppressed, and exploited people and groups.

(c) Social workers should promote conditions that encourage respect for cultural and social diversity within the United States and globally. Social workers should promote policies and practices that demonstrate respect for difference, support the expansion of cultural knowledge and resources, advocate for programs and institutions that demonstrate cultural competence, and promote policies that safeguard the rights of and confirm equity and social justice for all people.

(d) Social workers should act to prevent and eliminate domination of, exploitation of, and discrimination against any person, group, or class on the basis of race, ethnicity, national origin, color, sex, sexual orientation, age, marital status, political belief, religion , or mental or physical disability.

APPENDIX

B

UNDERSTANDING AND ACCESSING THE LAW

In the preparation of this appendix, two excellent chapters in recent texts were relied on heavily; see Saltzman and Proch (1990/1994) and Swenson (1993).

LAWS

Laws are grouped into three categories: (1) criminal law; (2) civil law; and (3) case law, which evolves from court decisions rather than legislative action. Laws, or statutes, are considered and passed by federal and state legislatures as well as county and municipal governments. The vast majority of laws that directly affect social work practice and malpractice are federal and state laws. However, social workers should understand their local community's legal system and identify and consider selective parts of the local codes that could bear on if, how, and where they practice (for example, occupational licensure laws, zoning laws, and public health matters).

At both the federal and state levels, often many related but discrete statutes are packaged as one bill for the legislature's consideration. If enacted, the entire bill will become an "act" or "code," with logical groupings of statutes termed "titles," "articles," or "chapters," and with each separate statute designated as a "section" within a title, article, or chapter.

Acts or codes are archived in three main sources. Session law compilations, often called *Laws of (Name of State)* or, at the federal level, *United States Statutes at Large*, are chronological compilations of acts and subsequent changes to acts.[1] Although practitioners should be aware of the existence of session law compilations, use of these sources is likely to be rare, because the interest will be in studying laws organized in certain areas rather than reading the chronology of law in general.

Codified statutes, which are fully indexed, organize acts by subject and include all amendments up to the date of publication of the bound volumes. At the federal level, codified statutes constitute the *United States Code* (U.S.C.); they are divided into titles (groupings of acts on certain subjects), which are alphabetized and numbered (for example, Title 20 includes all acts on the

---

[1] In *United States Statutes at Large,* acts are enumerated according to volume and number rather than the number assigned to the act when it was a bill before Congress. For example, as a bill, the Education for All Handicapped Children Act of 1975 was designated P.L. 94-142 (public law of the 94th Congress, 142nd bill to be passed); in the *United States Statutes at Large,* the act is numbered 89 Stat. 773 (89th volume, 773rd law in the volume). Any change to 89 Stat. 773 would involve a new bill number for the new Congress and, if passed, a chronological location in subsequent volumes of *United States Statutes at Large.* In state session laws, the same principle may apply.

subject of education, and Title 42, public health and welfare). A title may occupy more than one bound volume of the U.S.C. However, a given statute may not be found in the most seemingly logical title; therefore, researchers can thoroughly search the detailed index to make certain all acts germane to the topic have been identified.

Changes to the code after publication of the bound volumes of codified statutes are found in supplements, which are often inserted in pockets at the end of the appropriate bound volume and referred to as "pocket parts." Periodically, the bound volumes of codified statutes are updated and republished, incorporating the existing supplements. Practitioners should make certain that they are relying on the most recently published set of volumes.

Most, but not all, state statutes are codified according to substantive topic and are fully indexed. Different names are used, such as the *Revised Statutes of (Name of State)* or *Codes of (Name of State)* or, in some cases, the name of a private publisher, such as New York's *McKinney's*. In some states, topic groupings are called "chapters" rather than "titles"; elsewhere, subject groupings are referred to by a name and not a number, such as the California Penal Code. In other states, both chapter numbers and names are used, as in Florida's Chapter 394, the Mental Health Act.

Annotated codified statutes embellish the codified statutes by including, in addition to updated and supplemented statutes, court interpretations, applicable regulations, references to pertinent journal articles and other literature, and a legislative history of the act. Two private publishers produce annotated versions of the U.S.C., *United States Code Annotated* and *United States Code Service*. Various private publishers produce "annotated codified state laws." Like codified statutes, annotated codified statutes are fully indexed by topic and include supplements.

If a law is cited in a text, it is customary to reference the codified statute. Many books of codified and annotated codified statutes provide citation information, as does the *Publication Manual of the American Psychological Association* (APA, 1994) and *A Uniform System of Citation* (Harvard Law Review Association, 1986). Generally, legal citations provide, in order, a volume number, an abbreviated title of the source, a title or chapter number, a section number, and page information (see Beebe, 1993, for NASW's preferred citation forms).

REGULATIONS

Administratively promulgated regulations are published at the federal level and, in many states, at the time they are proposed and again when they are adopted. Proposed federal regulations are found in the *Federal Register*, a daily report of actions of the executive branch of government, available in most university libraries, state and local government offices, and some large agencies in which federal grant seeking is routine.

Once adopted, federal regulations are, like laws, codified in topic areas and published in the fully indexed *Code of Federal Regulations*, or C.F.R., which is organized in titles that roughly align with the titles found in the U.S.C. For example, "45 C.F.R. 46" refers to "Title 45, Section 46 of the *Code of Federal Regulations*" and specifies the protection of human research participants.

The C.F.R. is republished annually, and an index of updates called "C.F.R. Sections Affected" is contained in each edition. The index may refer to a volume and page of an issue of the *Federal Register* that is more recent than the annual edition of the C.F.R.

State regulations and administrative codes are typically available from the appropriate state agency mandated to discharge state law in specified areas, such as mental health, substance abuse, child welfare, juvenile justice, and elder affairs. Every state has a compiled administrative code as well, which is best identified with the help of a reference librarian or state agency administrator.

COURT OPINIONS

Federal and state courts themselves or commercial publishers under contract with the government publish court opinions in books known as official "reporters." In addition, commercial publishers produce unofficial reporters. Regardless of publication auspices, the text of an opinion should be the same and the format for citation identical.

In writing, it is always preferable to cite the official reporter. If the official reporter has not yet published the opinion, a cite from an unofficial reporter is necessary. However, it is customary to precede the unofficial reporter citation with the official reporter's citation, leaving blanks for volume and page. Citations to court opinions include, in order, an abbreviated version of the official case name, the reporter's volume number, the reporter's abbreviated name, the page on which the opinion begins, and the year of the decision. For example, *Brown v. Board of Education*, 347 U.S. 483 (1954) is the cite for the landmark desegregation decision of the U.S. Supreme Court.

U.S. Supreme Court opinions are found in the official reporter, *United States Reports* (U.S.), and two unofficial reporters, *United States Supreme Court Reports, Lawyer's Edition* (L.Ed. or L.Ed.2d) and *Supreme Court Reporter* (S.Ct.). Moreover, a weekly loose-leaf service, *United States Law Week* (U.S.L.W.), rapidly captures Supreme Court decisions as well as those of selected lower courts and recently enacted statutes.

Federal district court opinions are found in two official reporters: the *Federal Supplement* (F.Supp.) and the *Federal Rules Decisions* (F.R.D.). State supreme court opinions are found in official reporters identified by an abbreviation of the state's name, for example, "Cal." or "Ida." Unofficial reporters exist in some states. State appellate court opinions are usually found in official reporters designated by an abbreviation of the state's name, plus "App.", for example, "Neb. App." Unofficial reporters exist in some states. An unofficial reporter, *National Reporter System*, published by the West Publishing Company, is organized around regions of the country and compiles most state appellate court decisions. The West reporter may be the only reporter available for appellate court decisions in some states.

Regardless of the court and the reporter, published court opinions have predictable parts or elements: the official case name indicating all parties and capacities in the case; followed by the court docket numbers, indicating the chronology of the hearing (useful if there is a need to correspond with a deciding court to obtain a court file); official name of deciding court; dates, including the date of decision; and case summary, called a "syllabus."

West reporters contain research tools called "headnotes" or "keynotes," which are excerpts from the case, headed by a sequential number, a topic, and a key number. These excerpts are inserted into the annotated codified statutes if they relate to a statute and are also compiled into books called "digests of West reporters" in alphabetical topical order using the key numbers. West digests are useful in finding cases on a given topic.

In addition, the remainder of the published court opinions contain the names of lawyers for the parties and names of deciding justices for an appellate court. The name of the judge writing the court's opinion is also indicated. The text of the court's opinions follows. For appellate courts, the court's opinion may reflect the majority of justices hearing the case; a majority opinion decides the case and may make law. If most justices concur but there are fewer than a majority, a plurality opinion will decide the case. Plurality opinions have little impact on statute. Majority or plurality opinions are presented first, followed by dissenting and concurring opinions. A dissenting opinion is written by a justice who disagrees with the majority or plurality opinion; there may be multiple dissenting opinions. A concurring opinion is written by a justice who agrees with the result of the majority or plurality opinion but disagrees with the supporting reasoning or wishes to stress certain points; there may be multiple concurring opinions. Majority or plurality opinions can be expected to contain certain predictable elements, including procedural history—a detailed record of actions, rulings, motions, appeals, and decisions of lower courts; facts determined to be significant in deciding what law to apply and how to apply it in deciding the case; issues—questions of law the court distills from the array of issues discussed and ways of framing issues; holdings—statements of law made by the court that form the basis for the court's decision; the decision or the procedural action taken or directed by the court; and the reasoning—the logical process by which the court arrives at its opinion or decision.

SECONDARY LEGAL SOURCES

Many additional sources can aid in understanding law and locating primary sources. Two legal encyclopedias, *American Jurisprudence* (Am.Jur.) and *Corpus Juris* (C.J.), are fully indexed, comprehensive, national overviews of laws on given topics. Either is a recommended place to begin legal research. A less comprehensive encyclopedia, *American Law Reports* (A.L.R.), presents selected court opinions along with pertinent articles. Some states also have legal encyclopedias, which can be found at a university law school library or a courthouse library.

Practice manuals summarizing the law on given topics and instructing attorneys on taking cases to court under these laws can be helpful in understanding probable proceedings. Continuing education series for attorneys on various topics are also available at law schools.

Almost every law school publishes a periodical of articles written by scholars or students that include extensive references. Called "law reviews," these publications are often extremely scholarly, legalistic, detailed, and abstract. However, law reviews can be sources of comprehensive analytical surveys on the law in a given topic area.

Just as there are professional journals for social workers, there are topical as well as general-interest professional journals for attorneys, including but not limited to those published by local, state, or national bar associations. These publications may provide more pragmatic, helpful treatments of topics of interest to social workers. Journal and law review articles are indexed in *Index to Legal Periodicals*, *Current Law Index*, and *Legal Resource Index*.

As noted earlier, the U.S. Supreme Court is chronicled in *United States Law Week* (U.S.L.W.), a weekly loose-leaf service. Sometimes called "topical reporters," other similar services compile bills, statutes, proposed and adopted regulations, and case decisions on selected topics.

Westlaw and Lexis are the two best-known legal databases. Both include most court cases, some regulations and statutes, and some journal articles and are accessible primarily in libraries that subscribe to the systems.

Hornbooks are summaries of the law in a topic area, designed for practicing attorneys and students. These are found in university law libraries. *Shephard's Citations,* which will probably require a law librarian's assistance to use, provides a way to locate cases that interpret a given statute, rely on a given precedent, or overrule a given case.

RESEARCHING A LEGAL ISSUE

What is the logical process of investigating a legal matter to guide social work practice? Social workers can confer with experienced colleagues and can consult with the local area offices of pertinent state agencies, from which they can usually obtain copies of germane statutes and regulatory codes. All licensed social workers know that copies of their state's licensure law and regulations are available from the respective state department charged with professional regulation of social workers. Alternatively, legal questions can be taken to an attorney.

However, social workers may want to develop an understanding of the legalities of a situation to enrich what an attorney discusses or to prepare to confer with an attorney. Social workers may want to be assured that they have examined an issue fully and broadly.

The five research steps that follow assume that social workers may not be accustomed to using law schools and professional law librarians:

1. **Identify the best sources of legal materials.** If a university law school library is not available in the community, social workers can explore other university libraries, public libraries, courthouses, and attorneys who might permit the use of their personal collections. However, many university law library documents are accessible through computer search mechanisms and interlibrary loan.
2. **Establish whether federal, state, or local law is pertinent.** Social workers will be concerned most with state laws, unless an issue relates to immigration, federally administered benefits programs, Native American matters, or federal crime. When in doubt, begin with state law.
3. **Determine what type of law is pertinent.** Usually state statutes are the most helpful. When possible, use the annotated codified statutes, because these volumes include all that the codified statutes do and also add important references to other laws, court cases, and secondary legal sources. In looking for relevant terms in the index to a collection of statutes, allow for the possibilities of unfamiliar, obsolete, or "politically incorrect" terms and the potential that a statute will be contained in a less-than-obvious title, chapter, or code. If no relevant state statutes can be found, try case law and regulations or consult a reference law librarian.
4. **Follow up references to court cases and citations to secondary legal sources found in the annotated statutes.** Secondary sources such as

legal encyclopedias and journal articles may be the best place to begin. Legal writing is vastly more precise than much communication in the social and behavioral sciences. Do not hesitate to seek help in interpreting statutes, and know the importance of such grammatical nuances as those distinguishing "and" versus "or" and "shall" versus "will."

5. **Search for regulations at the public agency granting authority under the statute or the state's published administrative code.** Applicable regulations will rarely be noted in the annotated statutes.

REFERENCES

American Psychological Association. (1994). *Publication manual of the American Psychological Association* (4th ed.). Washington, DC: Author.

Beebe, L. (Ed.). (1993). *Professional writing for the human services.* Washington, DC: NASW Press.

Harvard Law Review Association. (1986). *A uniform system of citation* (14th ed.). Cambridge, MA: Author.

Saltzman, A., & Proch, K. (1994). Locating and using the law. In *Law and social work practice* (pp. 63–90). Chicago: Nelson-Hall. [Originally published in 1990]

Swenson, L. C. (1993). Law and the legal system for psychological professionals. In *Psychology and law for the helping professions* (pp. 31–53). Belmont, CA: Brooks/Cole.

Appendix

C

Sample Fact Sheets
and Forms

Sample Fact Sheets

File Name	Title
Worktog.doc	How We Will Work Together
Expert.doc	About This Setting and My Background
Appoints.doc	Appointments
Relat.doc	The Special Nature of the Service Relationship
Ending.doc	Ending the Service Relationship

Sample Forms

File Name	Title
Billrts.doc	Client Rights
Grievanc.doc	How to File a Complaint in this Setting
Staffcon.doc	Confidentiality Agreement and Notice to Employees/Volunteers
Chtrevu.doc	Request for Interpretive Chart Review
Avconsnt.doc	Consent to Professional Use of Clinical Record Data and Audio–Visual Recordings of Service
Eval&qa.doc	Informed Consent to Participate in Evaluation Studies
Research.doc	Informed Consent to Participate in Research
Release.doc	Release of Confidential Information

NOTE: In the development of the sample fact sheets and forms in this appendix, several generous colleagues allowed us to adapt materials from their settings: Dan Brady, LCSW, Executive Director, Douglas Gardens Community Mental Health Center, Miami; Larry Auerbach, LCSW, Port St. Lucie, FL; James Meyer, Jr., PhD, Montague Psychological Associates, Turners Falls, MA; Ron Zimmet, Esq., Behavioral Health Services, Daytona Beach, FL. In addition, the extremely helpful work of Edward L. Zuckerman, PhD, and Irving P.R. Guyett, PhD, in *The Paper Office 1* was instructive in many stylistic ways. Zuckerman and Guyett convey legally oriented material to clients with a tone of warmth, sincerity, and commitment to the client's well-being. We appreciated that manner of communication, learned from it, and sought to emulate it.

All releases of information and other legal documents should always be examined by a lawyer.

Sample fact sheets in this appendix are written in the first-person singular. By changing the language to "we" or "social workers in this setting," you can tailor the fact sheets to agencies and group practices.

SAMPLE FACT SHEET:
HOW WE WILL WORK TOGETHER

File Name: *Worktog.doc*

Our work will rely on two types of agreements. The first one is our *working agreement to begin services*. First, I will ask you to read a set of fact sheets, including this one. They are yours to keep, so feel free to jot down any questions on the sheets. As soon as you have read the fact sheets, we will talk about all the topics that they describe.

It's important for our work together that we both are clear on topics such as how this setting operates, my credentials and abilities, appointments, the confidentiality of the information you give me, and fees. This information appears on the fact sheets you have been asked to read. You have specific rights and responsibilities in service, which you must understand. It is also important for you to know what to expect of service and of a relationship with a social worker.

The confidential nature of information you share with me is one of the most important things to understand. Ordinarily, anything and everything you share with me or any other staff member in this setting is strictly confidential—whether you say it in person, say it on the telephone, or write it. Significant parts of the information you give me about yourself and matters that we discuss will be recorded in your clinical record. Other parts of our conversations may not relate specifically to your treatment and thus may not be included in the clinical record. In all cases, however, anything you tell me is treated with the strictest of confidence, including the fact that you are receiving services at this setting.

If we mutually decide that, in your interests, I should provide some part of your confidential information to another professional, your insurance company, your attorney, or even you, you will sign a specific and time-limited release of information. You will know exactly what is to be released, to whom, and how the information will be used. You will be able to stipulate the time period in which the release is to be in effect. There is only one open-ended release that I will ask you for, and that is your permission to provide information about you to my professional back-up colleague in the event that you have an emergency need to be seen and I cannot be reached.

There are four circumstances in which I would be required by law to reveal confidential information about you without your consent. The first situation would be if I learned that you were in serious danger of harming yourself or at serious risk for harming another person. The second situation would be if I learned that you were abusing or neglecting a child, an elderly person, or a disabled person in your care. The third situation would be in the event of a court order compelling me to release your clinical record to a court of law. The fourth situation would be *(specify any other conditions mandated under law, for example, some states mandate the reporting of criminal acts)*.

After you have read the fact sheets and have had a chance to question me and clarify everything, I will ask you to read and sign a *working agreement* to begin service. I will also sign it, because I also have responsibilities. I will also ask you to sign a *fee agreement* once you understand my charges, when payment is expected, and my procedures for working with health plans.

Depending on your situation, our first few sessions will be spent clarifying your problems and assessing the reasons for them. There is a possibility that I will ask you to have a physical examination with your primary care physician before we begin service.

Once we understand your issues, we will agree on the goals you want to accomplish in service. We will also identify some ways to measure your progress. At this point, we will be ready to work out a specific, *individual service plan* for you. You and I will develop this plan jointly. When we have come to an agreement about what methods I will use and what your responsibilities and tasks will be, then I will ask you to sign a *service contract*. I will also sign it, because I, too, agree to follow our plan.

Although every client's service plan is individualized, there are usually some basic things you can expect. I will carefully measure your progress to make certain the service plan is working for you. Some of the "yardsticks" I use include asking you to fill out brief questionnaires about your feelings and activities, asking you to keep certain kinds of diaries, or asking someone else to rate you. Your own opinion of how you are doing is also important. Discussion of your progress, based on all such yardsticks, will be a central part of our work.

Successful service requires a commitment from you *(as an individual, as a family, as a couple)* for optimal outcomes to be achieved. There can be many benefits to our working together. For example, you may learn to communicate better, resolve or lessen the severity of interpersonal problems at home or elsewhere, and improve your methods of coping with problems in daily life. Be aware, however, that in the course of treatment you will work hard and sometimes feel uncomfortable.

There are some risks involved in service. At times, counseling requires the sharing of painful feelings and thoughts. As a result, you may experience unpleasant feelings. Growth is difficult, and things may get worse before they get better during our work together. Finally, although scientific research persuasively shows how helpful social work treatment can be, there is always the possibility that in your specific case, our work will not result in the progress we hope to make.

There are alternatives that you or I may want to consider in addition to or instead of our working together. You could decide, now or after we have agreed to begin service, not to seek any services; I could refer you to another setting or agency; or you could decide that you would benefit from a change in individual, family, or group counseling. It is important for you to know that it is your choice to engage my services and to continue with them; it is also my professional choice, which I will make in your best interests, to engage you as my client and to continue working with you.

If we discover that, despite our best efforts, you are not making progress in meeting your goals, we will talk about several options. I regularly consult with my supervisor, an experienced, licensed clinical social worker whom I know well and respect highly. I will seek guidance from my supervisor if we reach a "roadblock." I may ask you for permission to talk with a consultant if that seems to be indicated. As an additional part of your service, I may refer you directly to someone else for further assessment or for specific services that I am unable to provide. Finally, if I determine that your best interests are not being served in working with me, then we will end our service relationship. In that event, we will work closely together to connect you with professional help that will meet your needs.

SAMPLE FACT SHEET: ABOUT THIS SETTING AND MY BACKGROUND

File Name: *Expert.doc*

About (Name of Setting)

(Sample Text)
The Family Practice Center opened in 1990 with the mission of providing quality counseling services to families with children. The Center is based on the belief that in today's world, all families may encounter problems in daily living. Our mission is to help families improve the quality of their family life.

The Center has a team of seven licensed clinical social workers and three clinical psychologists with a wide range of expertise. The Center provides a range of services to families and children, including

- play therapy
- parent education
- family therapy
- group counseling for parents and children
- marital counseling
- psychological and educational testing.

About My Background

(Sample Text)
I am _____, a licensed clinical social worker who specializes in working with families who have adolescent children. I have worked at the Family Practice Center for the past five years. Also, I have worked as a certified school social worker in secondary schools for four years. I am a member of the National Association of Social Workers Academy of Certified Social Workers, and I am licensed as a clinical social worker in the states of _____. I received my master of social work degree in 19_____ at _____ _____University. Also, I have com-pleted the postmaster's Family Therapy Certification Program of _____ University. I have specialized training in practice with adolescents and regularly attend relevant continuing education courses. I have written pamphlets entitled *Understanding Your Teenager in Today's World* and *A Teenager's Guidebook: Learning to Cope with Your Parents.*

(Elaborate on your special expertise and training, additional credentials, awards, or achievements pertinent to your role as a clinician. Consider attaching anything you have written and published, such as pamphlets or journal or magazine articles.)

I take a family approach to understanding individuals. My role is to help you find a solution to your problems, not to tell you the solution. *(Elaborate on your practice philosophy, your theoretical orientation, and techniques or strategies that you use.)*

SAMPLE FACT SHEET:
APPOINTMENTS

File Name: *Appoints.doc*

As part of your service plan, you and I will decide how long and how often we will meet. We will also decide the day and time of the meetings, and I will make every effort to accommodate your schedule. Usually, sessions are *(give frequency)* and last *(give length of time)*. A service program usually will require *(give number)* sessions. If your situation is very complicated, we may decide that more sessions are needed. We will often reassess and re-evaluate your needs.

Late Arrivals for Appointments

If I am late for our appointment. It is rare that I would be late starting a session. In the unlikely event that this happens, if your schedule permits, I will try to see you for your full session. If I cannot do this, I will see you for the time remaining of your session and adjust your fee. If my lateness can be anticipated, I will make every effort to contact you so that you can adjust your schedule accordingly. If you choose to reschedule your appointment due to my lateness, I will be happy to do so and will not bill you for the session we miss.

If you are late for our appointment. We will begin when you arrive and continue until the end of your planned session. You will be charged for the full session, unless you give me 24 hours' notice of your late arrival. Even if you cannot give me 24 hours' notice, I urge you to let me know that you are running late and the approximate time when you will arrive.

Cancellations of Appointments

When I must miss our appointment. There are times that I will be away for planned absences. Usually I am away for no more than a week or two for a conference or personal leave. I will tell you about these absences as far ahead as I know about them, and you will always know at least two weeks in advance. We will always discuss how you can use my absence to continue working toward your service goals.

In addition, I will always have a reliable professional colleague available to you as back-up in the event that you have an emergency need for service. An important part of our setting's policy is that back-up clinicians are closely informed about our clients. Part of our working agreement is that you will permit me to share your full clinical record with the back-up clinician and to discuss your situation with that person before any of my planned absences. A session with the back-up clinician will be billed at the regular fee.

In the rare event that I am called away for an emergency or I have a sudden illness or an accident, this office will make every effort to contact you as soon as possible, to apprise you of my circumstances, and to reschedule our appointment. If you need to be seen during these times, the back-up clinician will be available to you at your usual appointment time at the usual fee.

When you miss our appointment. There are times that you will be away for planned absences. Please inform me about these absences as far ahead as you know about them. We will discuss how you can use your absence to continue working toward your service goals. We will also discuss our next appointment to resume service after you return.

If you find that you cannot keep your appointment, please contact me as soon as possible so that I can offer the time to another client. You will not be charged for canceled sessions if I have 24 hours' notice. Otherwise, as stated in our fee policy, you (and not your health plan) will be billed for the session.

In the event that you are called away for an emergency or have a sudden illness or an accident, please make every effort to contact me or have someone else contact me as soon as possible. I will be concerned about you and will want to know your circumstances. I will want us to reschedule our appointment if possible.

SAMPLE FACT SHEET: THE SPECIAL NATURE OF THE SERVICE RELATIONSHIP

File Name: *Relat.doc*

A service relationship with a clinical social worker or any other professional psychotherapist has only one purpose—the client's emotional, psychological, and personal well-being. Because clients disclose to their clinicians many deeply felt personal thoughts and experiences, the relationship becomes very close and very important. Sometimes clients come to want the relationship to become more than a professional service relationship: a friendship, a dating relationship, or a business association. Although these feelings are understandable, it is necessary for all clients to recognize that there is only one relationship with the clinician and that is a service relationship.

I cannot at any time, during or after your course of treatment, be anything but your therapist. I cannot ever, now or in the future, be your friend, your client or customer, your supervisor, your teacher, or your date. I cannot ever, now or in the future, become sexually involved with you. I cannot accept goods or services from you in exchange for my services. If any of these things occurred, I would lose my ability to be objective about your needs and to serve you with only your well-being in mind.

As part of our initial conversations, I will explore whether we have any situations that would put us into social or business contact with each other. I will also be concerned about social or business ties I may have with your close relatives or even friends. We will discuss such situations thoroughly. If we cannot guarantee that we can manage these existing situations without conflict of interest or threats to your privacy, I will offer to refer you to another professional.

I will not enter into a working agreement with any person on whom I cannot concentrate totally and objectively as my client. In addition, it is my professional and ethical obligation to ensure that once we begin your treatment, our relationship remains solely professional. If, after we begin working together, either of us experiences difficulties in maintaining the singular focus of our work, we will discuss the issues as part of therapy. If they cannot be resolved, it will be necessary to end our service relationship, and I will refer you to another source of service.

I want you to understand how seriously my profession—as well as the professions of psychology, psychiatry, and others—takes the exclusivity of the service relationship. The *Code of Ethics* of the National Association of Social Workers requires that I not exploit our relationship to meet my own needs, that I avoid any conflict of interest with your needs, and that under no circumstances do I engage in sexual activities with any client. Were I to violate any of these rules, I would be heavily sanctioned by the social work profession. *(In our state, I would be likely to lose my license and could be charged with a criminal offense.)* Thus, it is in both of our interests to be just one thing to each other: You are *only* my client, and I am *only* your social worker.

Finally, in the same way that you can expect total professionalism from me, you can expect the same from everyone associated with this setting: support staff, emergency back-up clinicians, and anyone else you might encounter here. We are all committed to providing our clients a setting in which they maintain dignity and experience freedom from any form of disrespect or inequitable treatment, including sexual harassment in any form and any other form of discrimination. If ever you, as my client, have concerns about any of these issues, please bring them to my attention at once, or, if you prefer, to my supervisor's attention.

SUPERVISOR'S NAME _____

TELEPHONE NUMBER _____

SAMPLE FACT SHEET:
ENDING THE SERVICE RELATIONSHIP

File Name: *Ending.doc*

The central reason our service relationship will exist is to help you meet goals. When you have achieved those goals and if no new issues have arisen, then it is my ethical duty to end our work together. The *NASW Code of Ethics* says, "Social workers should terminate services to clients and professional relationships with them when such services and relationships are no longer required or no longer serve the clients' needs or interests."

During our work together, we will continually review your progress. When we both agree that your objectives have been achieved, we will stop meeting. We may agree that you should be referred for additional services that I cannot provide, and I will work with you to find the resources you need. I will also encourage you to call for a future appointment if you feel it would be helpful. If new issues arise, you will always be welcome and encouraged to begin service again.

State law requires that we keep your records for _____ years. However, we will preserve your files indefinitely. They remain in our offices, in secured file cabinets, for _____ years. After that, they are stored in a secure specialized document warehouse. With a few days' notice, the records can be made accessible.

The vast majority of service relationships end because the client achieved his or her goals and agreed with the social worker to end service. However, there could be circumstances in which you or I will end our relationship regardless of the other's preferences.

You are free to end service at any time for any reason, whether or not I feel it is advisable. I ask that you tell me that you plan to stop rather than just not returning. I ask that you schedule one final appointment so we can review your progress and discuss any referrals that might be beneficial to you. You will also be obliged to honor any unsettled financial obligations to this setting.

There are a few situations in which I am allowed to end service regardless of your wishes:

- If I am convinced that you no longer need service and cannot benefit from continuing, I must end service.
- If I am convinced that your needs surpass my ability to help you, I must refer you to a source of suitable help. However, I will remain closely involved with you until you are settled with a new professional.
- If you do not comply with our mutually developed service plan, there is no benefit in continuing service.
- If you do not abide by the policies and procedures of this setting as set forth in our working agreement, I must end service. This includes

missing appointments and arriving late without 24 hours' notice or failing to be current in payments or other arrangements.

- If our service relationship becomes compromised, troubled, or deteriorates, I must end service. This includes situations in which your confidentiality could be compromised (for example, if we are unavoidably going to be together socially); conflicts of interest arise (for example, if you change jobs and my spouse becomes your supervisor); tensions and disagreements result in your harming or threatening to harm me or anyone close to me; and difficulties arise in maintaining our focus on your service (for example, if we develop sexual attractions that we cannot resolve professionally within the context of your service).

In any of these cases, I will make every effort to discuss my decision with you in the hope that we can come to a mutually agreed-on ending. I will also work with you to find other sources of services you need or desire and make referrals in your interest.

Finally, you can be reassured that, even in the above circumstances, if you are in crisis, I will make every effort not to end our relationship until the crisis is resolved, and I will do so only in a severe situation of danger to one of us and only with the consultation of my supervisor.

SAMPLE FORM: CLIENT RIGHTS

File Name: *Billrts.doc*

As a client served at *(name of setting)*, you have specific rights. The purpose of this form is to inform you of your rights as our client.

I. Right to Voluntary Services

If you are a legal adult (_____ years old in this state), you have the right to request voluntary services. You have a right to

- have a staff person assigned specifically to work with you in resolving your problems and ensuring that your service is properly provided
- a personal, individualized assessment of your needs
- an individualized service plan, which will be reviewed regularly, developed with your input, and implemented with your consent
- services beginning within a reasonable time and ending when they are no longer needed or effective
- services even when you are unable (not unwilling) to pay (Ability to pay is determined by certain standard criteria.)
- another opinion regarding services provided (However, seeing someone outside of this setting is done at your own expense.)
- referrals to other competent professionals and sources of help as indicated by your service plan
- terminate service if your circumstances require it or you feel it is in your best interests, unless doing so puts you or others in grave danger
- resume service following termination.

II. Right to Refuse Services

You have a right to
- refuse any form of service or treatment unless it has been ordered by the court or in emergency situations when necessary to prevent harm to yourself and others (If you must receive services not by your own choice, you have the right to a lawyer, a court hearing, and an appeal of the decision to a higher court. If you cannot afford a lawyer, the court will appoint one for you.)
- refuse service with your primary clinician and request another practitioner in this setting or a referral to another setting
- be informed that without services, your situation may get worse
- refuse to be filmed or audiotaped without your written permission
- refuse to take part in research studies without your written permission.

III. Right to Confidentiality/Privacy

All information about you is understood to be confidential to protect your privacy. This information includes the fact that you have or have not received services. All professionals and other staff associated with this setting are obligated to preserve your privacy to the extent permitted by law. You have a right to

- determine the amount of information to be released, whether to or from anyone outside this setting, by signing a permission form
- sign a permission form to release information that is specific to each situation when information is to be released (You will not be asked to sign a "blanket" permission for release of information.)
- determine the length of time that information may be released and cancel your permission at any time (However, information may be released without your permission in a medical emergency to save lives, to prevent injury to yourself or others, or when required by law or ordered by the court.)

IV. Right to a Humane Mental and Physical Environment

You have a right to
- courtesy, respect, and professionalism from everyone involved in your service in this setting
- facilities that are comfortable and safe, promote dignity, ensure privacy, and contribute to positive outcomes of your service.

V. Right to Information

You have a right to verbal and written information about
- your rights, role, and responsibilities as a client in this setting
- your primary clinician's rights, role, and responsibilities in this setting
- what you can expect during your service process—appointments, costs, handling of emergencies, and other practices and procedures of this setting as they affect you
- any rights that are taken away and your right to a review of this action by requesting a Grievance Procedure
- your primary clinician's credentials and professional code of ethics
- means to contact your primary clinician in both emergency and nonemergency situations
- the name of and means to contact your primary clinician's supervisor
- procedures for reviewing your clinical records.

VI. Rights Pertaining to Medication (*if applicable in your setting*)

You have a right to
- the administration of medication only under the written order of a physician

- a complete explanation, in language you can understand, of the purpose of any medication, possible side effects, and possible results of long-term use
- full consideration of your opinions and reactions to the medications
- a regular review of your medication for the purpose of adjustment, as a check for possible side effects, and for possible reduction or elimination
- have accurate records kept noting your medication history, including any adverse reactions or drug allergies
- have medication prescribed for you only when necessary.

VII. Right to a Grievance Procedure

Any client or legal representative of a client may file a grievance as a formal notice of dissatisfaction regarding the operation of this service and the actions or omissions of staff. If you wish to file a formal complaint, ask any staff member in this setting for the handout, "How to File a Complaint in This Setting." The state regulatory board or the practitioner's professional association also processes grievances. Information about how to contact these organizations can be provided.

I have read and understood my rights as a client of *(name of setting)*.

CLIENT NAME (PRINT) _____

CLIENT SIGNATURE _____

DATE _____

CLINICIAN NAME (PRINT) _____

CLINICIAN SIGNATURE _____

DATE _____

NOTE: This form is reproduced, with minor modifications, with permission from Douglas Gardens Community Mental Health Center, 701 Lincoln Road, Miami Beach, FL 33139.

This document can easily be edited to suit various practice settings. It is effective as a handout, as a section of a client information handbook, or as part of a fact sheet set. The signature lines can be retained or deleted according to your preferences. A version of the bill of rights reduced to the main headings makes an effective office sign and reminder for clients.

SAMPLE FORM:
HOW TO FILE A COMPLAINT IN THIS SETTING

File Name: *Grievanc.doc*

Step 1. If you feel you have been treated unethically or unfairly, bring your grievance to the attention of your clinician verbally or in writing. *(Or, request the procedures to file a formal grievance.)*

Step 2. If your clinician cannot resolve the problem satisfactorily, seek his or her supervisor and present your complaint verbally or in writing. *(Or, fulfill the requirements of the formal process.)*

Step 3. Your grievance should be reviewed by our executive director, and he or she may seek a hearing with you and other parties involved. The decision of the executive director may be the final step in the process. *(If your setting has alternative processes, state them here.)*

Step 4. If you continue to be dissatisfied, you may contact several external professional and regulatory bodies verbally or in writing. *(List state professional regulatory agencies, state and national professional organizations, and public and private oversight agencies germane to your setting.)*

Step 5. If you think your clinician may have been unethical, you may file a complaint with the professional association to which he or she belongs or the relevant state regulatory board. Information about how to contact these organizations *(appears below on this form, may be requested from our office manager, or may be requested from your clinician's supervisor).*

Every effort will be made to resolve your grievance at the lowest possible step in the procedure so as not to prolong any difficulty or problem.

NOTICE OF A CLIENT COMPLAINT

For your convenience, this form can be used to put your grievance in writing. You are also free to write your own letter or to present your complaint verbally.

Please print.

DATE _____

TO _____
　　　　　　(to clinician, supervisor, or setting director)

FROM _____
　　　　　　　　　　　(your name)

DATE OF BIRTH _____

SOCIAL SECURITY NUMBER _____

This is my written statement of a complaint about events that occurred on
_____
(Give date or dates that the cause for the complaint began and ended or is continuing.)

The following occurred or has been occurring: _____
_____
_____
(Explain the events, actions, remarks, circumstances, and the individuals involved.)

Optional: The ways in which I have been affected by the problem are
_____
_____
_____
(Explain the ways in which you feel that you have been harmed, inconvenienced, or otherwise troubled by the situation.)

Optional: The solution or remedy I am seeking is _____
_____
_____
(Explain what you would like us to do to correct the situation.)

CLIENT SIGNATURE _____

SAMPLE FORM:
CONFIDENTIALITY AGREEMENT AND
NOTICE TO EMPLOYEES/VOLUNTEERS

File Name: *Staffcon.doc*

The identities of our current and former clients, their personal communications to us, and their records are confidential by law. This office requires that confidentiality laws be strictly followed. We cannot expect to treat our clients effectively unless they feel that they can talk freely without concern that their confidences will be revealed to others. Any employee or volunteer of this organization who violates a client's confidentiality is subject to immediate dismissal. Further, that employee or volunteer, as well as the organization, is subject to a lawsuit brought by a client.

Do Not
- reveal a client's identity in any way
- address a client by name when others are in the office
- disclose that a person is a client to anyone, including a client's spouse
- leave a client's file unattended on your desk or anywhere else in the workplace
- have files or appointment books on your desk or anywhere else in the workplace in a manner that allows a client's name to be seen by others
- have a client's information visible on a computer screen when you are away from your desk
- leave computers and file cabinets that store client information unsecured when you are not in the work area
- remove client files from the workplace for reasons other than authorized functions (for example, a home visit or court appearance)
- repeat anything a client tells you to anyone other than your supervisor
- disclose anything in a client's chart to anyone other than your supervisor
- talk about a client with anyone other than your supervisor in a private situation, even if you do not use the client's name
- talk about a client with your spouse or other members of your family or friends
- give copies of anything in a client's chart to anyone other than your supervisor
- retrieve messages from your voice mail or answering machine within earshot of others.

Do
- address clients in the workplace by "Sir" or "Ma'am" or other courteous address without the use of a client's name when other people are present

- keep files and appointment books face down or otherwise out of view on your desk and throughout the workplace so that a client's name cannot be seen by others
- safeguard your computer password to prevent unauthorized people from accessing client information
- strictly comply with a client's permission to disclose identity, confidences, or records when permission has been properly obtained in writing
- observe all limits and conditions a client places on any permission to disclose confidential information
- discard confidential materials properly by shredding them
- consider a client's confidentiality on the receiving end of fax communications, e-mail, and telephone message-taking devices; ensure that the intended recipient is the only recipient of such communications.

It is possible that requests for information—including subpoenas—about our clients may come to you from the police or other law enforcement personnel, lawyers, or the courts. Tell your supervisor immediately when you receive these types of requests and determine with your supervisor how to proceed. Note that "following orders" may not be sufficient justification in a court of law for breaching confidentiality.

Some exceptions to confidentiality may require or authorize certain disclosures about our clients. Immediately inform your supervisor of any information you obtain about our clients that leads you to believe that you, the client, or anyone else may be endangered by the client. Immediately inform your supervisor of any information you obtain that leads you to believe that a client may be involved in some way, directly or indirectly, in the abuse or neglect of a child, elderly person, or disabled person. Meet with your supervisor at once and determine how to proceed. Note that "following orders" may not be sufficient justification in a court of law for breaching confidentiality.

I, _____, hereby acknowledge that I have read this confidentiality agreement and notice to employees/volunteers. I understand it fully, and I will strictly follow its terms.

SIGNATURE _____

DATE _____

NOTE: This form is reproduced, with minor modifications, from "Confidentiality Agreement for Clerical Staff," *Mental Health Legal Review,* Vol. 2, No. 4, July 1993, p. 2, with permission of the publisher, Behavioral Health Services, Inc., P.O. Box 1788, Daytona Beach, FL 32115.

SAMPLE FORM:
REQUEST FOR INTERPRETIVE CHART REVIEW

File Name: *Chtrevu.doc* _____

I, _____, am hereby requesting access to my clinical record by means of an interpretive chart review.

In requesting this review, I understand that I am releasing all *(employees, associates, and so forth)* of this organization and any agencies or individuals whose correspondence has been made a part of the clinical record from liability for any damages, material or psychological, resulting from this interpretive chart review.

I understand that some of the information in my clinical record may be sensitive and that there is risk that it may invoke strong emotions on my part. Therefore, if my clinician judges it to be beneficial, he or she will meet with me in person before the review to prepare me. I understand that I will be allowed to read all or any portion of my record only while in the presence of designated staff members of this organization. I understand that my clinician will be present to debrief me after I have completed my review. I understand that portions of my record may be withheld from me if allowing my access would breach the confidentiality of someone else who has not given consent to my reading the information they have provided.

I understand that I can add statements in writing to clarify or correct information in the record.

The interpretive chart review will be scheduled within 14 working days of the date of this signed request at a time convenient for me and the staff.

I thoroughly understand the interpretive chart review process described above, and I agree to abide by the requirements set forth by the records access policy of this organization.

SIGNATURE _____

RECORD ID NO. _____

DATE OF REQUEST _____

WITNESSED BY _____

REVIEW DATE _____

STAFF MEMBER ASSIGNED TO BE PRESENT _____

NOTE: This form is reproduced, with minor modifications, from Douglas Gardens Community Mental Health Center, 701 Lincoln Road, Miami Beach, FL 33139.

Sample Form:
Consent to Professional
Use of Clinical Record Data
and Audio–Visual Recordings
of Service

File Name: *Avconsnt.doc*

By checking items that are acceptable to me and signing below I,_____, am agreeing to the indicated procedures associated with my service in *(name of setting)* by *(name of clinician)*.

I am agreeable to my clinician making audiotapes of our sessions for his or her use in

_____ supervision, case consultation, and routine staffings in this setting
_____ consultation about my case with an expert outside this setting
_____ in-service training of other professionals or interns in this setting
_____ scientific presentations or publications as long as the data are presented anonymously and in a manner that would completely protect my identity.

I am agreeable to my clinician making videotapes of our sessions, as long as the camera focuses on my clinician and I cannot be viewed or identified by sight, for his or her use in

_____ supervision, case consultation, and routine staffings in this setting
_____ consultation about my case with an expert outside this setting
_____ in-service training of other professionals or interns in this setting
_____ scientific presentations or publications as long as the data are presented anonymously and in a manner that would completely protect my identity.

I am agreeable to my clinician using information from my written clinical record for purposes of

_____ supervision, case consultation, and routine staffings in this setting
_____ consultation about my case with an expert outside this setting
_____ in-service training of other professionals or interns in this setting
_____ scientific presentations or publications as long as the data are presented in grouped statistical form, so that no individual information is reported, or individual data are presented anonymously and in a manner that would completely protect my identity.

I understand that anyone who hears and views material from my clinical record and tapes of our sessions made by my clinician is a professional or trainee in a bona fide profession and that these individuals are ethically obligated to protect my confidentiality just as rigorously as my clinician is bound.

Any further use of audiotaped, videotaped, or written material from my treatment for other professional, scholarly, or research purposes or by professionals other than my clinician will require separate discussion with me and additional informed consent.

NAME (PLEASE PRINT) _____

SIGNATURE _____

DATE _____

NAME OF LEGALLY RESPONSIBLE PARENT OR GUARDIAN (PLEASE PRINT)

_____

SIGNATURE _____

DATE _____

NAME AND TITLE OF WITNESS (PLEASE PRINT)

_____

_____

SIGNATURE _____

DATE _____

Sample Form:
Informed Consent to Participate in Evaluation Studies

File Name: *Eval&qa.doc*

In the course of your intake to *(name of setting)*, we asked you to answer a number of questions. Your clinician also completes forms regarding your care, and you may also at times be asked to complete forms about your circumstances, feelings, and activities. All of this information is kept strictly confidential by the staff and will not be released to anyone unless we have your permission, receive a court order, or in the event that preserving your confidentiality puts your life or someone else's life in jeopardy.

This organization conducts scientific evaluation studies to help improve our services. This involves surveying our clients by telephone, in person, or with a mailed questionnaire. Research interviews by telephone or in person are done by specially trained staff or consultants, other than your clinician, who are prepared to maintain your confidentiality just as strictly as your clinician. If you decide to participate, we will contact you later in the course of service and within six months after you have ended service to ask you to answer again some of the same questions we asked when you began service. This helps judge the effectiveness of our service. When we mail questionnaires or ask you questions by telephone, we will not use this organization's name to prevent any possible breach of your confidentiality. We will refer only to "the study of community services you agreed to participate in."

When the results would help other service providers, the studies may be published in professional journals. Data from the studies may also be required by funding agencies and presented in the form of technical reports. Such studies report only averages and group results. Information on individual clients is never revealed.

We would like your permission to include data from your service in these group data. If you agree to participate, you will be helping advance scientific knowledge and will indirectly help other clients, as well as yourself, benefit from improved services and techniques. Other than the possible inconvenience of our follow-up contacts and asking you about progress on the personal issues that brought you here, we are aware of no risks to you inherent in this research. Should you determine that some aspect of the research does, in fact, pose problems, hardships, or risks to your well-being, please advise us immediately.

If you do not agree to participate, we will leave your data out of the study group. Not agreeing to participate in no way affects your right to receive services. Also, if you agree to participate and later change your mind, you are free to withdraw this consent at any time without consequence to you and your service. If not previously revoked, this consent will terminate on *(date, event, or condition)* _____

_____.

If at any time during or after your service you want information about this evaluation research or wish to discuss any aspect of it with us, please contact *(name of research director/coordinator)* _____

_____

at *(telephone number)* _____.

CLIENT NAME (PLEASE PRINT) _____

SIGNATURE _____

DATE _____

SIGNATURE OF PARENT OR GUARDIAN (WHERE REQUIRED)

_____

DATE _____

SIGNATURE OF PERSON AUTHORIZED TO SIGN IN LIEU OF THE CLIENT (WHERE REQUIRED)

_____

DATE _____

NOTE: This form is reproduced, with minor modifications, with permission from Douglas Gardens Community Mental Health Center, 701 Lincoln Road, Miami Beach, FL 33139.

Sample Form:
Informed Consent to
Participate in Research

File Name: *Research.doc*

This setting is at times involved in scientific research that helps us better understand clients and helps us improve treatment methods and services. We may invite our clients to participate in this research. It is important you understand that you are completely free to say no or yes; your participation is voluntary. Your decision will have no effect on your treatment or your relationship with your clinician or this organization. Furthermore, even if you volunteer for the study and change your mind later, you can stop participating and ask that your data be withdrawn.

We are now conducting a study with the purpose of *(summarize the study's purpose, the research question, or the hypotheses)* _____ _____ .

The researcher(s) (is, are) *(state names, degrees, titles, organizational bases, business addresses, and telephone numbers)* _____ _____ .

The research procedures involve *(explain the research methods, the role participants play or the tasks they perform, how long tasks take, how often tasks have to be repeated, and the duration of their participation. Indicate whether participants will be asked to remain involved with the study after treatment ends for follow-up purposes)* _____ _____ .

The benefits of this research include *(indicate the expected general benefits for knowledge, service improvement, or understanding of people and, if any, the advantages or benefits to the client)* _____ .

The risks of this research to you include *(indicate any foreseeable risks to physical or emotional comfort or well-being)*_____ _____ .

If, after agreeing to participate, you determine that some aspect of the research does in fact pose problems, hardships, or risks to your well-being, please advise us immediately. If the situation cannot be adjusted to your satisfaction, you have the right to withdraw from participation *(indicate as appropriate provisions for compensation or treatment in the event of harm or injury resulting from participation in the study)*.

The confidentiality of data you provide to the research project will be strictly protected. Research interviews and clinical record reviews are done by specially trained staff or consultants, other than your clinician, who are obligated to maintain your confidentiality just as strictly as your clinician. The research data will be given a code number that could be connected with you only through a master file that will be kept secured *(explain where)*. At the end of the study, the master file will be destroyed. Data will be analyzed by computer, with only your code number appearing. No one but the principal researcher will have access to the master file, and even that person will have no reason to know or pay attention to your name.

Results of this study is likely to be published in professional journals. Data from the study is also required by the funding agency *(specify if there is an external funder)* presented in the form of technical reports. Such reports present only averages and group results. Information on individual participants is never revealed in written reports and articles.

If, at any time during or after your treatment, you want information about this research or wish to discuss any aspect of it with us, please contact *(name of research director/coordinator)* _____
at *(telephone number)* _____ .

CLIENT NAME (PLEASE PRINT) _____

SIGNATURE _____

DATE _____

SIGNATURE OF PARENT OR GUARDIAN (WHERE REQUIRED)

_____

DATE _____

SIGNATURE OF PERSON AUTHORIZED TO SIGN IN LIEU OF THE CLIENT (WHERE REQUIRED)

_____

DATE _____

cc: Client
     Principal Researcher
     Client file

Sample Form:
Release of Confidential
Information

File Name: *Release.doc*

Note to Practitioners:

Many, but not all, records of mental health and substance abuse treatment are confidential under federal regulations (Code of Federal Regulations 42, Part 2). Disclosure of confidential information is, of course, allowed with the client's consent. However, many requests for information will come to you with client consent forms that do not comply with federal regulations. Federal law imposes an affirmative duty on you to refuse to disclose records if the request for disclosure is based on a consent form that is not legal.

The regulations are addressed in the sample forms that follow. You may add additional information. The forms should be used either to respond to requests for disclosure or whenever you request copies of a client's records from other sources.

When reviewing a consent form received with a request for disclosure, validate the client's signature. Check to determine the expiration date and if the consent has been revoked (for example, a client may have told a secretary or other professional that the consent has been revoked). The regulations require that the person disclosing records make a reasonable effort to determine if the consent is false. Therefore, depending on the circumstances, it may be prudent to call the client to verify the accuracy of the consent or to ask that the consent be notarized. In addition, consider whether it might be necessary to review the content of the record with the client to make certain that the client's consent is truly informed.

A signed consent to release information to a specific entity, for a specific purpose, assumes the following:

- Information will be released once. If the entity requires additional information, even within the consent's valid period, a new consent form must be executed.
- Information released will be selective and specific to the purpose. For example, if only a psychosocial history is requested, added elements of the clinical record are not to be released.

REQUEST FOR INFORMATION

NAME OF CLIENT _____

DATE OF BIRTH _____

ADDRESS _____

Dear Colleague:

The above-named client is currently receiving services from *(name of setting)*. In the best interests of client care, it would be appreciated if you would release to us the information specified below pertaining to care and services received from your organization between *(give month/year to month/year)*. Attached is a signed authorization for release of this information. Thank you for your prompt attention and response.

Sincerely,

AUTHORIZATION FOR RELEASE OF
CONFIDENTIAL INFORMATION TO CURRENT PROVIDER

I, *(name of client)* _____, ( ) request

( ) authorize *(name of program that is to make the disclosure)* _____

_____

to disclose *(type, amount of, and time period of information to be disclosed)*

_____

to *(name and practice setting to which disclosure is to be made)* _____

_____

for the purpose of *(purpose)* _____

_____ .

The designated information about me ( ) may ( ) may not be transmitted by fax, electronic mail, or other electronic file transfer mechanisms. The provider of the information and the recipient designated above ( ) may ( ) may not discuss by telephone the content of the information released.

This request and authorization to release information is based on my understanding of the content of my records, the use of the information once it is released, and my understanding that the source providing the information cannot be responsible for the protection of my privacy once the information is conveyed. I release the source of information from all liability arising from the release. I understand that the willingness to treat me of the party requesting information is not affected by the response of the source of the requested information. I understand that the recipient of the requested information is prohibited by federal law (Code of Federal Regulations 42, Part 2) from making any further disclosure of it without my specific written permission.

I understand that this release of information is intended to allow me to provide my informed consent for an exception to my confidentiality and the protection of my privacy guaranteed under federal law, including but not limited to the Privacy Act of 1974 (P.L. 93-579), the Freedom of Information Act of 1974 (P.L. 93-502), and the Code of Federal Regulations 42, Part 2.

This consent is subject to revocation at any time except to the extent that the program instructed to make the disclosure has already taken action in reliance on it. If not previously revoked, this consent will terminate on *(date, event, or condition)* _____

_____ .

If this consent is to be renewed after its expiration, it may be photocopied, but it must be signed again by me and by a witness.

SIGNATURE OF CLIENT _____

DATE _____

SIGNATURE OF PARENT OR GUARDIAN (WHERE REQUIRED)

_____

DATE _____

SIGNATURE OF PERSON AUTHORIZED TO SIGN IN LIEU OF THE CLIENT (WHERE REQUIRED)

_____

DATE _____

SIGNATURE OF WITNESS _____

DATE _____

AUTHORIZATION TO A
CURRENT PROVIDER FOR
RELEASE OF CONFIDENTIAL INFORMATION

I, (name of client) _____, ( ) request

( ) authorize (name of clinician and setting) _____

_____

to disclose (type, amount of, and time period of information to be disclosed)

_____

_____

to (name and organization to which disclosure is to be made) _____

_____

for the purpose of (purpose) _____

_____ .

(If the intended recipient is the client's attorney, add a statement that covers the client's willingness to allow the attorney to further question you and to have you testify in depositions and in court and that holds you harmless from claims related to the release of information to the judicial system. As appropriate, add a clause in which the client instructs the attorney to reimburse you for assessment and treatment services provided by you at the request of an attorney.)

(If the intended recipient is the client's insurance company, use a specially tailored release form such as the one in this book or add a statement that stipulates that the material released is strictly confidential and intended for use only by mental health professionals who are competent to understand and use the information. Add a statement that you assume no responsibility if the third-party payer allows untrained, nonprofessional persons access to the information. In addition, add a statement allowing payment of benefits to you.)

The designated information about me ( ) may ( ) may not be transmitted by fax, electronic mail, or other electronic file transfer mechanisms. The provider of the information and the recipient designated above ( ) may ( ) may not discuss by telephone the content of the information released.

This request and authorization to release information is based on my understanding of the content of my records, the use of the information once it is released, and my understanding that the source providing the information cannot be responsible for the protection of my privacy once the information is conveyed. I release the source of information from all liability arising from the release. I understand that the willingness to treat me of the party requesting information is not affected by the response of the source of the requested information. I understand that the recipient of the requested information is prohibited by federal law (Code of Federal Regulations 42,

Part 2) from making any further disclosure of it without my specific written permission.

I understand that this release of information is intended to allow me to provide my informed consent for an exception to my confidentiality and the protection of my privacy guaranteed under federal law, including but not limited to the Federal Privacy Act of 1974 (P.L. 93-579), the Freedom of Information Act of 1974 (P.L. 93-502), and the Code of Federal Regulations 42, Part 2.

This consent is subject to revocation at any time except to the extent that the program instructed to make the disclosure has already taken action in reliance on it. If not previously revoked, this consent will terminate on *(date, event, or condition)* _____

_____ .

SIGNATURE OF CLIENT _____

DATE _____

SIGNATURE OF PARENT OR GUARDIAN (WHERE REQUIRED)

_____

DATE _____

SIGNATURE OF PERSON AUTHORIZED TO SIGN IN LIEU OF THE CLIENT (WHERE REQUIRED)

_____

DATE _____

SIGNATURE OF WITNESS _____

DATE _____

REPLY TO A REQUEST FOR CONFIDENTIAL INFORMATION

NAME OF CLIENT _____

DATE OF BIRTH _____

ADDRESS _____

Dear Colleague:

We are responding to your recent request for information on the above-named individual.

(If you can fulfill the request, use the following paragraph.)

The requested information is enclosed. We wish to emphasize that it is strictly confidential and under federal regulations (Code of Federal Regulations 42, Part 2) it may not be disclosed by or transferred from you to anyone else without the client's further consent. Hence, do not release this material to any other party, including the client, without written consent of the client. In addition, this information is intended only for the use of professional persons capable of understanding and acting on it. We assume no responsibility if this information is conveyed to individuals not professionally prepared to interpret and use it, including the client.

(If you cannot fulfill the request, use the following paragraph.)

We are unable to provide the requested information because you did not send a legally executed release of information. *(Specify the problem.)* Enclosed is a form that, when properly completed and signed by indicated parties, will allow us to fulfill your request. *(Enclose a copy of your version of Authorization to a Current Provider.)*

Please contact us if we can be of further assistance.

NOTE: Introductory information and forms reproduced with minor modifications from "A Form for Consent to Release Confidential Information," *Mental Health Legal Review,* Vol. 2, No. 6, November 1993, with permission of the publisher, Behavioral Health Services, Inc., P.O. Box 1788, Daytona Beach, FL 32115.

SAMPLE FORM: RELEASE OF CONFIDENTIAL INFORMATION TO A THIRD-PARTY PAYER

File Name: *Insurrel.doc* _____

I, *(name of client)* _____ ( ) request

( ) authorize *(name of clinician and setting)* _____

_____

to disclose *(type, amount of, and time period of information to be disclosed)*

_____

_____

to *(name and organization to which disclosure is to be made)* _____

_____

for the purpose of *(purpose)* _____

_____ .

The designated information about me ( ) may ( ) may not be transmitted by fax, electronic mail, or other electronic file transfer mechanisms. The provider of the information and the recipient designated above ( ) may ( ) may not discuss by telephone the content of the information released.

This request and authorization to release information is based on my understanding of the specific items of information to be released, my understanding of the use of the information by qualified mental health professionals once it is released, and my understanding that the source providing the information cannot be responsible for the protection of my privacy once the information is conveyed. I release the source of information from all liability arising from the release. I understand that I am not required by law to grant this release of information and that if I choose to assume responsibility for payments for my own treatment, this release is not required for my treatment. I understand that the recipient of the requested information is prohibited by federal law (Code of Federal Regulations 42, Part 2) from making any further disclosure of it without my written permission.

I understand that this release of information is intended to allow me to provide my informed consent for an exception to my confidentiality and the protection to my privacy guaranteed under federal law, including but not limited to the Federal Privacy Act of 1974 (P.L. 93-579), the Freedom of Information Act of 1974 (P.L. 93-502), and the Code of Federal Regulations 42, Part 2.

(As appropriate, depending on the client's form of health coverage)

_____ I authorize payment of my health benefits to the above-named *(clinician and setting)*.

_____ I have reimbursed the above-named *(clinician and setting)* and request payment of my health benefits to myself.

This consent is subject to revocation at any time except to the extent that the person instructed to make the disclosure has already taken action in reliance on it. If not previously revoked, this consent will terminate on *(date, event, or condition)* _____

_____ .

SIGNATURE OF CLIENT _____

DATE _____

SIGNATURE OF PARENT OR GUARDIAN (WHERE REQUIRED)

_____

DATE _____

SIGNATURE OF PERSON AUTHORIZED TO SIGN IN LIEU OF THE CLIENT (WHERE REQUIRED)

_____

DATE _____

SAMPLE FORM:
RELEASE OF CONFIDENTIAL
INFORMATION FROM A SCHOOL

File Name: *School.doc* _____

NAME OF CHILD _____

DATE OF BIRTH _____

ADDRESS _____

I, (*name of parent/guardian/custodial caretaker*) _____

_____ ,

( ) request ( ) authorize (*name of staff member and school*) _____

_____

to release information regarding my child named above to (*name and organization to which disclosure is to be made*) _____

_____ .

I authorize the above-named staff member and school to disclose (*type,
amount of, and time period of the information to be disclosed*) _____

_____

for the purpose of (*purpose*) _____

_____ .

The designated information about my child ( ) may ( ) may not be transmitted electronically by fax, electronic mail, or other electronic file transfer
mechanisms. The provider of the information and the recipient designated
above ( ) may ( ) may not discuss by telephone the content of the information released.

(If indicated, for example, for custody evaluations)

I also grant permission for (*name of clinician*) _____

_____

to visit with my child during school hours. I ask that the school cooperate
with him or her in his or her efforts to determine the degree of difficulty,

anxiety, stress, and so forth that my child may be experiencing. I ask that any relevant information regarding my child's behavior and performance while in school be provided to him or her on my behalf.

This request and authorization to release information is based on my understanding of the content of my child's records, my understanding of the use of the information once it is released, and my understanding that the source providing the information cannot be responsible for the protection of my child's privacy once the information is conveyed. I release the source of information from all liability arising from the release. I understand that the willingness to serve my child of the party requesting information is not affected by the response of the source of the requested information. I understand that the recipient of the requested information is prohibited by federal law (Code of Federal Regulations 42, Part 2) from making any further disclosure of it without my written permission.

I understand that this release of information is intended to allow me to provide my informed consent for an exception to my child's confidentiality and the protection of his or her privacy guaranteed under federal law, including but not limited to the Federal Privacy Act of 1974 (P.L. 93-579), the Freedom of Information Act of 1974 (P.L. 93-502), and the Code of Federal Regulations 42, Part 2.

This consent is subject to revocation at any time except to the extent that the program instructed to make the disclosure has already taken action in reliance on it. If not previously revoked, this consent will terminate on (*date, event, or condition*) _____

_____ .

If this consent is to be renewed after its expiration, it may be photocopied, but it must be signed again by me and a witness.

SIGNATURE OF PARENT, GUARDIAN, OR CUSTODIAL CARETAKER

_____

DATE _____

SIGNATURE OF WITNESS _____

DATE _____

NOTE: This form has been adapted with modifications from a school release used by Larry Auerbach, LCSW, Hillmoor Professional Plaza, 1801 S.W. Hillmoor Drive, Suite B-103, Port St. Lucie, FL 34952.

PRUDENT PRACTICE

SAMPLE FORM: WORKING AGREEMENT FOR INDIVIDUALS

File Name: *Workindv.doc*

I, *(name of client)* _____, hereby agree
to begin service in *(name of setting)* _____
with *(name of clinician)* _____.
I have read the *(client handbook, practice brochure, or fact sheets)*. I have
discussed with my social worker the operating policies and procedures of this
practice setting, the role and responsibilities of my social worker, and my role
and responsibilities as a client. I understand my rights to receive and refuse
services, to privacy and confidentiality, to respectful treatment, to be informed about all aspects of my service, to read and amend my clinical record,
and to file a complaint if I feel I have been unfairly or unethically or disrespectfully treated. I have asked all questions that have occurred to me. I
know that I can contact my social worker's supervisor *(name of supervisor)*

_____

at *(telephone number)* _____.
I understand the purposes of this setting, the service approaches and
methods used, and the qualifications of my social worker.

I understand that after my situation is assessed, I and my social worker
will develop a service plan and that we will make another agreement to
follow through with the service plan. As part of a complete assessment, I
understand that I may be asked to have a physical examination with my
personal physician and to request that his or reports be sent to my social
worker in this setting.

I understand my financial responsibilities, arrangements with my insurance payer or payers, the rules about notifying my social worker if I have to
miss an appointment or be late, the charges for broken appointments and
late arrivals without prior notification, and the consequences if my account
is past due.

I understand what to do in an emergency and what happens if I have an
emergency and my social worker cannot be reached. In the event that my
social worker is not available, his or her back-up professional is *(name,
telephone numbers, office address if appropriate)* _____

_____.

In the event that the back-up professional cannot be reached, I understand
that I should contact *(name and telephone number of crisis line; name, address,
and telephone number of mental health center; and/or name, address, and telephone number of hospital with psychiatric services)* _____

_____.

I understand that staff of this setting other than my social worker must have access to confidential information about me because of *(give reasons)*. I understand that my social worker and all others involved in this setting will protect my privacy and that confidential information about me will be revealed only if I give my written consent, if my safety or the safety of someone else is threatened, or if a court orders the information released.

I understand that I will be asked to furnish the name of someone close to me to be contacted in the event of an emergency. I understand that in contacting that person, my social worker will have to identify his or her relationship to me and my whereabouts and condition. However, I am assured that no details of my service will be provided to that person. My contact person is *(name, address, and telephone number)* _____

_____ .

I understand that my written consent will be obtained if information about me is to be used for research or training purposes or if my social worker wishes to audiotape or videotape our sessions for any reason.

I understand that my relationship with my social worker is now and will be in the future solely a professional relationship and that we will have no shared interests or activities outside my service.

I realize that, although service is recommended for me and will probably be helpful, there are no guarantees that any or all of my problems will be remedied. I further understand that service involves possible risks as well as benefits. Hence, I may experience difficulties as a result of the service process.

I understand that service will terminate when the goals of the service plan that I agree to have been fulfilled. However, I also understand that I may end service at any time I wish or feel that I need to do so and that my social worker may also end service if we do not make progress, if our relationship becomes too strained to continue our work, or if I and/or my insurer are no longer able to pay for services. If my service is ended before the goals of my service plan have been accomplished, I understand that my social worker will do everything possible to refer me to an alternative source of care.

Finally, I understand that any time I have questions about this setting, the evaluation process, or any policy or procedure, I should promptly bring my questions or concerns to my social worker, his or her supervisor, or managerial staff.

CLIENT NAME (PLEASE PRINT) _____

SIGNATURE _____

DATE _____

NAME OF LEGALLY RESPONSIBLE PARENT OR GUARDIAN (WHERE REQUIRED)

_____

SIGNATURE _____

DATE _____

NAME AND TITLE OF WITNESS _____

SIGNATURE _____

DATE _____

By signing below, I, *(name of clinician)* _____ ,
am indicating that I agree to begin the process of assessment and service with
(name of client) _____ , who
I believe has read and comprehended the *(client handbook, practice brochure,
or fact sheets)*. I have discussed the content of our written client information
thoroughly with the client and am satisfied, by his or her comments and
questions, that he or she is clear in his or her understanding and is prepared
to begin service.

SIGNATURE _____

DATE _____

SAMPLE FORM:
WORKING AGREEMENT FOR
COUPLES OR FAMILIES

File Name: *Workcpfm.doc*

We, *(names of clients)* _____ ,
hereby agree to begin service in *(name of setting)* _____

with *(name of clinician)* _____ .
We have read the *(client handbook, practice brochure, or fact sheets)*. We have discussed with our social worker the operating policies and procedures of this practice setting, the role and responsibilities of our social worker, and our roles and responsibilities as clients. We understand our rights to receive and refuse services, to privacy and confidentiality, to respectful treatment, to be informed about all aspects of our service, to read our clinical record and amend it if we find errors, and to file a complaint if we feel we have been unfairly or unethically or disrespectfully treated. We have asked all questions that have occurred to us. We know that we can contact our social worker's supervisor *(name of supervisor)* _____
at *(telephone number)* _____ .

We understand the purposes of this setting, the service approaches and methods used, and the qualifications of our social worker.

We understand that after our situation is assessed, we and our social worker will develop a service plan and that we will make another agreement to follow through with the service plan. As part of a complete assessment, we understand that we each may be asked to have a physical examination with our respective personal physicians and to request that their reports be sent to our social worker in this setting.

We understand that the social worker will not keep secrets with individual family members. Hence, we are expected as a family to talk about our respective individual sessions.

We understand our financial responsibilities and arrangements with our insurance payer or payers, the rules about notifying our social worker if we have to miss an appointment or will be late, the charges for broken appointments and late arrivals without prior notification, and the consequences if our account is past due.

We understand what to do in an emergency and what happens if we have an emergency and our social worker cannot be reached. In the event that our social worker is not available, his or her back-up professional is *(name, telephone numbers, office address if appropriate)* _____

In the event that the back-up professional cannot be reached, we understand that we should contact *(name and telephone number of crisis line; name, address,*

*and telephone number of mental health center; and/or name, address, and tele-
phone number of hospital with psychiatric services)* _____

_____ .

We understand that staff in this setting other than our social worker must
have access to confidential information about us because of *(give reasons)*.
We understand that our social worker and all others involved in this setting
will protect our privacy and that confidential information about us will be
revealed only if we give our written consent, if our safety or the safety of
someone else is threatened, or if a court orders the information released.

In granting consent for the release of confidential information about us
from one professional to another or to our health plan, we stipulate that

_____ We each wish to sign our own release of information and, if we
are legal adults, each reserve the right to withhold permission to
release part or all of the information sought that is specifically
about us as individuals; or

_____ We grant to one party, *(name)* _____ ,
the right to consent to the release of confidential information
about us as a family.

We understand that we will be asked to furnish the name of someone
close to us to be contacted in the event of an emergency. We understand that
in contacting that person, our social worker will have to identify his or her
relationship to us and our whereabouts and condition. However, we are
assured that no details of our service will be provided to that person. Our
contact person is *(name, address, and telephone number)* _____

_____ .

We understand that our written consent will be obtained if information
about us is to be used for research or training purposes or if our social worker
wishes to audiotape or videotape our sessions for any reason.

We understand that our relationship with our social worker is now and
will be in the future solely a professional relationship and that we will have
no shared interests or activities outside our service.

We realize that, although service is recommended for us and will probably
be helpful, there are no guarantees that any or all of our problems will be
remedied. We further understand that service involves possible risks as well
as benefits. We understand that as individuals we may have to set aside our
individual goals and needs to achieve the goals of the family and to resolve
our family problems. Hence, we know that we may experience stress, strained
relationships, or other difficulties as a result of the service process.

We understand that service will terminate when the goals of the service
plan that we agree to have been fulfilled. However, we also understand that
we may end service at any time we wish or feel that we need to do so. If one
or some of us wish to continue while the other or others wish to end service,
we understand that our social worker will initiate a new working agreement
and a new service plan and contract with the one or those of us wishing to
continue. We further understand that our social worker may also end service

if we do not make progress, if our relationship becomes too strained to continue our work, or if we and/or our insurer are no longer able to pay for services. If our service is ended before the goals of our service plan have been fulfilled, we understand that our social worker will do everything possible to refer us to an alternate source of care.

Finally, we understand that any time we have questions about this setting, the evaluation process, or any policy or procedure, we should promptly bring our questions or concerns to our social worker, his or her supervisor, or managerial staff.

CLIENT NAME (PLEASE PRINT) _____

SIGNATURE _____

DATE _____

CLIENT NAME (PLEASE PRINT) _____

SIGNATURE _____

DATE _____

CLIENT NAME (PLEASE PRINT) _____

SIGNATURE _____

DATE _____

CLIENT NAME (PLEASE PRINT) _____

SIGNATURE _____

DATE _____

CLIENT NAME (PLEASE PRINT) _____

SIGNATURE _____

DATE _____

NAME OF LEGALLY RESPONSIBLE PARENT OR GUARDIAN (WHERE REQUIRED)

_____

SIGNATURE _____

DATE _____

NAME AND TITLE OF WITNESS _____

SIGNATURE _____

DATE _____

By signing below, I, *(name of clinician)* _____ ,
am indicating that I agree to begin the process of assessment and service with
(names of clients) _____ ,
who I believe have read and comprehended the *(client handbook, practice brochure, or fact sheets)*. I have discussed the content of our written client information thoroughly with the clients and am satisfied, by their comments and questions, that they are clear in their understanding and are prepared to begin service.

SIGNATURE _____

DATE _____

SAMPLE FORM:
WORKING AGREEMENT FOR PARENTS WHEN A CHILD IS THE PRIMARY CLIENT

File Name: *Workchil.doc*

We, *(names of parents)* _____ ,
hereby agree to our child, *(name of child)* _____ ,
beginning service in *(name of setting)* _____

_____
with *(name of clinician)* _____ .
We have read the *(client handbook, practice brochure, or fact sheets)*. We have discussed with our child's social worker the operating policies and procedures of this practice setting, the role and responsibilities of our child's social worker, and our roles and responsibilities as parents. We understand that we are consenting to begin our child's treatment, not our own, and that although our consent is important and necessary, our role is to help provide information, to plan, to assist in measuring progress, and to coordinate our child's treatment. We understand our rights to receive and refuse services, to privacy and confidentiality, to respectful treatment, to be informed about our child's treatment, to have reasonable access to the clinical record and amend it if we find errors, and to file a complaint if we feel we have been unfairly or unethically or disrespectfully treated. We have asked all questions that have occurred to us. We know that we can contact the social worker's supervisor *(name of supervisor)* _____
at *(telephone number)* _____ .

We understand the purposes of this setting, the service approaches and methods used, and the qualifications of our child's social worker.

We understand that after our child is assessed, our child and our child's social worker will develop a service plan and that we will make another agreement to follow through with the service plan. As part of a complete assessment, we understand that we may be asked to have our child have a physical examination with his or her pediatrician and to request that his or her reports be sent to our child's social worker in this setting.

We understand our financial responsibilities and arrangements with our insurance payer or payers, the rules about notifying the social worker if our child has to miss an appointment or will be late, the charges for broken appointments and late arrivals without prior notification, and the consequences if our account is past due. We understand that sessions we request with our child's social worker or that he or she requests with us will be charged at the same hourly fee as our child's service.

We understand what to do in an emergency and what happens if our child has an emergency and the social worker cannot be reached. In the event that

our child's social worker is not available, his or her back-up professional is (*name, telephone number, office address if appropriate*) _____
_____ .

In the event that the back-up professional cannot be reached, we understand that we should contact (*name and telephone number of crisis line; name, address, and telephone number of mental health center; and/or name, address, and telephone number of hospital with psychiatric services*) _____
_____
_____ .

    We understand that staff in this setting other than our child's social worker must have access to confidential information about us and our child because of (*give reasons*). We understand that our child's social worker and all others involved in this setting will protect our privacy and that confidential information about us will be revealed only if we give our written consent, if our child's safety or the safety of someone else is threatened, or if a court orders the information released.

    We also understand that our child's social worker will keep discussions he or she has with us in the absence of our child confidential and will keep material discussed with our child in our absence confidential. However, we understand that the social worker may breach confidentiality with our child if our child talks about harming himself or herself and (*specify any conditions about which social workers are required by law to inform the parents or that you believe should be shared with them*). We will be encouraged, as a family, to talk about our respective sessions with the social worker. However, our child's social worker will not transmit information from one of us to the other(s).

    In granting consent for the release of confidential information about our child from one professional to another or to our health plan, we stipulate that

      _____ We each wish to sign our own release of information, and we each reserve the right to withhold permission to release part or all of the information sought; or

      _____ We grant to one party, (*name*) _____ , the right to consent to the release of confidential information about our child.

    We understand that our written consent will be obtained if information about our child is to be used for research or training purposes or if our child's social worker wishes to audiotape or videotape the sessions for any reason.

    We understand that our and our child's relationship with the social worker is now and will be in the future solely a professional relationship and that we will have no shared interests or activities outside of our child's treatment.

    We realize that, although service is recommended for our child and will probably be helpful, there are no guarantees that any or all of his or her problems will be remedied. We further understand that service involves possible risks as well as benefits. Hence, we and our child may experience stress, strained relationships, or other difficulties as a result of the service process.

We understand that service will terminate when the goals of the service plan have been fulfilled. However, we also understand that we may end service at any time we wish or feel that we and/or our child need to do so. We further understand that our child's social worker may also end service if our child does not make progress, has needs that the social worker cannot meet, or if we and/or our insurer are no longer able to pay for services. If our child's service is ended before the goals of the service plan have been accomplished, we understand that the social worker will do all possible to refer our child to an alternative source of care.

Finally, we understand that at any time we or our child have questions about this setting, the service process, or any policy or procedure, we should promptly bring our questions or concerns to our child's social worker, his or her supervisor, or managerial staff.

NAME OF LEGALLY RESPONSIBLE PARENT OR GUARDIAN (PLEASE PRINT)

_____

SIGNATURE _____

DATE _____

NAME OF LEGALLY RESPONSIBLE PARENT OR GUARDIAN (PLEASE PRINT)

_____

SIGNATURE _____

DATE _____

NAME AND TITLE OF WITNESS _____

SIGNATURE _____

DATE _____

By signing below, I, *(name of clinician)* _____ , am indicating that I agree to begin the process of assessment and service with *(names of clients)* _____ , who I believe have read and comprehended the *(client handbook, practice brochure, or fact sheets)*. I have discussed the content of our written client information thoroughly with them and am satisfied, by their comments and questions, that they are clear in their understanding and are prepared to begin service.

SIGNATURE _____

DATE _____

SAMPLE FORM:
WORKING AGREEMENT FOR GROUPS

File Name: *Workgrup.doc*

I, *(name of client)* _____ , *(am seeking social group work treatment or have been referred for social group work treatment)* in *(name of setting)* _____ with *(name of clinician)* _____ .

Before proceeding with a service contract, I hereby indicate that I have read the *(client handbook, practice brochure, or fact sheets)*. I have discussed with the group social worker the operating policies and procedures of this practice setting, the role and responsibilities of the group social worker, and my role and responsibilities as a client and group member. I understand my rights to receive and refuse services, to privacy and confidentiality, to respectful treatment, to be informed about all aspects of my service, to have reasonable access to my individual clinical record and amend it if I find errors, and to file a complaint if I feel I have been unfairly or unethically or disrespectfully treated. I have asked all questions that have occurred to me. I know I can contact the group social worker's supervisor *(name of supervisor)* _____ at *(telephone number)* _____ .

I understand the purposes of this setting, the purpose of the group, the group service approaches and methods used, and the qualifications of the group social worker.

I understand that my participation in the group will be based on a *(individualized, if appropriate)* plan that will be developed between *(me or the group)* and the group social worker. The goals and plan will be elaborated in another agreement, the service contract. As part of a complete assessment, I understand that I may be asked to have a physical examination with my personal physician and to request that his or her reports be sent to the group social worker in this setting.

I understand that the group social worker is responsible for helping me set personal goals and identifying ways that I can apply what happens during the group to my daily life. Also, I will have the opportunity to talk about my concerns and discuss any unfinished business.

I understand my financial responsibilities and arrangements with my insurance payer or payers, the rules about notifying the group social worker if I have to miss a session or be late, the charges for missed sessions and late arrivals without prior notification, and the consequences if my account is past due.

I understand that if I experience a mental health emergency I should contact *(the group social worker or my individual therapist)*. I further understand what happens if I have an emergency and *(the group social worker or my individual therapist)* cannot be reached. In the event that the group social worker is not available, his or her back-up professional is *(name, telephone number, office address if appropriate)* _____

_____ .

In the event that the back-up professional cannot be reached, I understand that I should contact *(name and telephone number of crisis line; name, address, and telephone number of mental health center; and/or name, address, and telephone number of hospital with psychiatric services)* _____

_____ .

I understand that staff in this setting other than the group social worker must have access to confidential information about me because of *(give reasons)*. I understand that the group social worker and all others involved in this setting will protect my privacy and that confidential information about me will be revealed only if I give my written permission, if my safety or the safety of someone else is threatened, or if a court orders the information released.

I understand that I will be asked to furnish the name of someone close to me to be contacted in the event of an emergency. I understand that in contacting that person, our group social worker will have to identify his or her relationship to me and my whereabouts and condition. However, I am assured that no details of my group treatment will be provided to that person. My contact person is *(name, address, and telephone number)* _____

_____ .

I understand that my written consent will be obtained if information about me is to be used for research or training purposes or if the group social worker wishes to audiotape or videotape our sessions for any reason.

I understand that my relationship with the group social worker is now and will be in the future solely a professional relationship and that we will have no shared interests or activities outside group sessions.

I agree to abide by the following group rules:

- **First,** I will attend all of the *(number)* _____ group sessions and be on time. I understand that I can miss *(number)* _____ sessions for a prearranged vacation. I have chosen the following dates: _____ . Also, I understand that if I am late or absent the effectiveness of the group process is diminished.
- **Second,** I understand that I am expected to be an active group participant, although I can choose what and how much information I want to discuss in the group. I understand that my responsibilities include being truthful about what I say in the group, not monopolizing the group, and making certain that I resolve any unfinished business before the end of the session.
- **Third,** I understand that confidentiality and privacy are basic to building trust among group members. I agree to keep confidential what other group members share, and I will not talk about what is shared during the group with others outside the group.
- **Fourth,** I understand that I have the right to leave the group. However, I understand that it is very important not to leave any unfinished business with other group members. Hence, it is my responsibility to

explain to other members my reasons for wanting to leave the group before I leave.

- **Fifth,** I agree that I will not socialize with group members outside our sessions.

I realize that, although group work service is recommended for me and will probably be helpful, there are no guarantees that any or all of my problems will be remedied. I further understand that service will involve possible risks as well as benefits. I understand that I might experience group pressure from the other members. Hence, I know that I may experience stress, strained relationships, or other difficulties as a result of the group work process. However, it is my right to decide how I will participate in the group and whether to accept the suggestions of the other members.

I understand that my participation in my group will terminate when the goals of my individualized plan and/or the goals of the group have been fulfilled. However, I also understand that I will be free to end my participation at any time I wish or feel that I need to do so. If other members of the group wish to discontinue the group and I am among those wishing to continue, I understand that the group social worker will offer to initiate a new working agreement and a new service plan and contract with those of us wishing to continue.

I further understand that the group social worker will be obligated to end my participation in the group if I do not make progress, if my relationship with the group social worker or other group members becomes too strained to continue our work, or if I and/or my insurer are no longer able to pay for services. If my group participation is ended before the goals of my service plan have been accomplished, I understand that the group social worker will do all possible to refer me to an alternative source of care.

Finally, I understand that any time I have questions about this setting or any policy or procedure, I should promptly bring my questions or concerns to the group social worker, his or her supervisor, or managerial staff.

CLIENT NAME (PLEASE PRINT) _____

SIGNATURE _____

DATE _____

NAME OF LEGALLY RESPONSIBLE PARENT OR GUARDIAN (WHERE REQUIRED)

_____

SIGNATURE _____

DATE _____

NAME AND TITLE OF WITNESS _____

SIGNATURE _____

DATE _____

By signing below, I, *(name of clinician)* _____ ,
am indicating that I agree to begin the process of assessment and group work
service with *(name of client)* _____ ,
who I believe has read and comprehended the *(client handbook, practice
brochure, and fact sheets)*. I have discussed the content of our written client
information thoroughly with the client and am satisfied, by his or her comments and questions, that he or she is clear in understanding and prepared to
begin service.

SIGNATURE _____

DATE _____

SAMPLE FORM:
CUSTODY EVALUATION POLICY
AND AGREEMENT

File Name: *Custeval.doc*

If this setting has been asked to provide a child custody and home evaluation study on your behalf, you are asked to read this policy carefully and discuss it with your social worker in detail. This policy explains our expectations for office visits, home visits, charges, and payments. If you agree to abide by the policy, both you and your social worker will affirm your understanding by signing on the bottom of the last page.

You have selected this setting to provide a child custody and home evaluation in a divorce situation. It is understood that separations and divorces are emotionally painful to all parties concerned, and not just the adults. We have been contracted to examine both home environments and the parenting skills and capabilities of both caretakers and then prepare a report for the mediator and the court, giving a recommendation for the individual most likely to provide a stable, nurturing, and role-appropriate environment for the child(ren). Each caretaker will be charged exactly half of the costs for the full evaluation.

Your social worker will interview both caretakers as follows. There will be two visits for each parent: one in the office with the child(ren) and one at the proposed custodial home. The first visit will be in your social worker's office and will last about 1° hours, depending on the number of people to be interviewed and the information to be obtained. This visit will be charged at our office rate, which is $_____ per hour. The second visit will be scheduled at the time of the first visit, will be in the family home, and will last about 1° hours, depending on the number of people to be interviewed and the information to be obtained. This visit will be charged at our out-of-office rate, which is $_____ per hour, from our office door back to our office door. This means that if it takes 30 minutes to get to your home and your social worker is there for 1° hours, you will be charged for a 2°-hour visit.

The report will take from 1 to 2 hours to prepare; both caretakers will divide the cost evenly. Charges for any time your social worker spends on the telephone calling witnesses or gathering other resources will also be divided evenly. Three copies of the report (one to each party's attorney and one to the mediator of record) will be mailed, all at the same time. The reports will be mailed only after both caretakers have paid their bills in full. Neither caretaker will be given his or her copy, nor will the mediator, until the entire balance due is paid in full, regardless of whether one caretaker has paid his or her respective share in full. Neither caretaker will be given advance notice or preview copies of the report or its recommendations.

Your social worker and all others involved in this setting will protect your privacy, and confidential information about you and your child(ren) will be revealed only to your attorney, the attorney of the other caretaker, the mediator for the court, and the court, based on your affirmation of this policy and your written informed consent to the release of confidential information for purposes of this custody evaluation. You may supply telephone numbers and releases of information for individuals you wish us to contact, but we make no guarantee that they will be called.

Nothing that anyone says in confidence to your social worker will be identified in the written report by name of the party making the statement. Any and all comments made by the parties or the child(ren) will be kept confidential. No sources of information will be identified to either caretaker. Your confidentiality is thus assured with the following specific exceptions governed by state law: if your safety or the safety of someone else is found to be threatened; if we suspect abuse, neglect, or exploitation of a minor, elderly person, or disabled adult; or if a court other than your family court ordered the information released.

We try to complete the evaluation report within three weeks of the first telephone contact by the mediator, because we know that both caretakers are anxious for a quick resolution of the issue. After the report is mailed, your social worker will not return any telephone calls or respond to any correspondence from either party. The wishes of your child(ren) will be given consideration insofar as they do not conflict with their best interests.

Payments may be made as you go or as a lump-sum payment in advance or as a single, final payment. We accept cash, money orders, personal checks (which must clear before your report is released), and major credit cards.

By signing below I, *(name of client)* _____ , am indicating that I agree to begin the above-described evaluation in *(name of setting)* _____ with *(name of clinician)* _____ .
I have read and understand this statement and agree with its terms. I will comply with all the points in this agreement. I understand that I am responsible for all payments due, and neither my attorney nor the mediator will receive my report until all payments are made. I also acknowledge that I have received a copy of this policy statement.

I have discussed with my social worker the operating policies and procedures of this practice setting with respect to custody evaluations, the role and responsibilities of my social worker, and my role and responsibilities as a client. I understand my rights to receive the agreed-on services, to refuse or to terminate these services at any time, to privacy and confidentiality, to respectful treatment, and to file a complaint if I feel I have been unfairly or unethically or disrespectfully treated. I have asked all questions that have occurred to me.

Finally, I understand that any time I have questions about this setting, the evaluation process, or any policy or procedure, I should promptly bring my questions or concerns to my social worker or any other staff member of this setting.

NAME OF CLIENT (PLEASE PRINT) _____

SIGNATURE _____

DATE _____

NAME OF LEGALLY RESPONSIBLE PARENT OR GUARDIAN (WHERE REQUIRED)

_____

SIGNATURE _____

DATE _____

NAME AND TITLE OF WITNESS _____

SIGNATURE _____

DATE _____

By signing below, I, *(name of clinician)* _____ ,
am indicating that I agree to provide the above-described custody evaluation
with *(name of client)* _____ ,
who I believe has read and comprehended the foregoing statement of policy
and procedure. I have discussed the content of the statement thoroughly
with the client and am satisfied, by his or her comments and questions, that
he or she is clear in his or her understanding and is prepared to undertake the
evaluation process.

SIGNATURE _____

DATE _____

_____

NOTE: This text is adapted, with minor modifications, from an information statement provided to clients by Larry Auerbach, LCSW, Hillmoor Professional Plaza, 1801 S.W. Hillmoor Drive, Suite B-103, Port St. Lucie, FL 34952.

SAMPLE FORM:
CONSENT TO SERVICE PLAN AND SERVICE CONTRACT FOR INDIVIDUALS

File Name: *Rxconind.doc*

I, *(name of client)* _____, hereby agree to the service plan developed in *(name of setting)* _____ _____ by myself and my clinician, *(name of clinician)* _____. I understand that this is not a legally binding contract; rather, it is an agreement between us that we can amend as needed. I further understand that my treatment will take place based on my earlier consent to accept the general operating and financial policies and procedures of this setting.

As a result of the assessment of my problems done by my clinician and myself, the following goals and objectives have been agreed on: *(list desired goals and specific objectives with time lines)*. Accordingly, my clinician has recommended the following service procedures and explained the reasons for preferring them: *(list the interventions selected and a brief justification of why these and not other approaches have been chosen; also list expected benefits of the recommended service and prognosis)*. I am, however, aware that I am not guaranteed the benefits we expect. Additionally, I understand that there are specific risks associated with the recommended service process: *(list any emotional, situational, relationship, or other possible difficulties; side effects; or discomforts or losses that may reasonably occur as a result of service)*.

(Note: Any listing should not purport to be all-inclusive.)

I understand that other procedures and sources of help are available to me and also could be helpful, such as *(list possible alternatives)*. However, I have decided to pursue my clinician's recommendations, realizing the potential benefits, risks, and possible alternatives.

To work toward our goals and objectives, we have agreed to meet *(list how often, on what day and time, for how long, and where)* _____ _____.

I have been made aware of the financial policies of this setting, and I understand that I will pay for each service session $ _____ *(dollars per unit)*.

My responsibilities include *(list assigned duties, activities, things or situations to avoid or pursue, and so forth)*. My clinician's responsibilities include providing his or her best efforts to implement and facilitate this service plan, monitoring my progress, giving me feedback, safeguarding my privacy, keeping me informed of my rights, meeting with me promptly at appointed times, being available to me in emergencies or providing appropriate back-up, making thoughtful referrals when I need adjunct services, not prolonging my treatment unnecessarily, and ensuring that our relationship is conducted professionally and ethically.

I understand that my treatment is a time-limited, focused procedure and that to know whether our goals and objectives are being reached, my clinician and I will systematically study my progress and record our observations. Specifically, my clinician will *(indicate procedure for empirically measuring client progress)*. Additionally, I agree to *(indicate any logs, diaries, and so forth that the client is expected to keep)*. Any time either of us feels we are not making satisfactory progress, either of us may and should ask to renegotiate the service plan. If either of us feels we cannot identify a way to make progress on the goals and objectives of my treatment, then my clinician is responsible for referring me to alternative sources of help.

Finally, I understand that background information about me, this service contract, my service plan, and information about my progress and treatment outcomes will be part of my clinical record. My clinical record is strictly confidential with very specific exceptions:

- I can request and/or give consent to the release of information about me to others (for example, my insurance company, HMO, EAP, and family doctor) with whom I want to share it.
- I can request access to my own clinical record.
- Confidential information will be selectively revealed to proper authorities in instances when I am in danger or I put someone else in danger or when a court of law orders disclosure.

CLIENT NAME (PLEASE PRINT) _____

SIGNATURE _____

DATE _____

NAME OF LEGALLY RESPONSIBLE PARENT OR GUARDIAN (WHERE REQUIRED)

_____

SIGNATURE _____

DATE _____

NAME AND TITLE OF WITNESS _____

SIGNATURE _____

DATE _____

SAMPLE FORM:
CONSENT TO SERVICE PLAN AND SERVICE CONTRACT FOR COUPLES OR FAMILIES

File Name: *Rxconc&f.doc* _____

We, *(names of clients)* _____ ,
hereby agree to the service plan developed in *(name of setting)* _____
_____ by ourselves and our
clinician *(name of clinician)* _____ .
We understand that this is not a legally binding contract; rather, it is an
agreement between us that we can amend as needed. We further understand
that our service will take place based on our earlier consent to accept the
general operating and financial policies and procedures of this setting.

As a result of the assessment of our problems done by our clinician and
ourselves, the following goals and objectives have been agreed on: *(list desired
goals and specific objectives with time lines)*. Accordingly, our clinician has
recommended the following service procedures and explained the reasons for
preferring them: *(list the interventions selected and a brief justification of why
these and not other approaches have been chosen; also list expected benefits of the
recommended service and prognosis)*. We are, however, aware that we are not
guaranteed the benefits we expect. Additionally, we understand that there
are specific risks associated with the recommended service process: *(list any
emotional, situational, relationship, or other possible difficulties; side effects; or
discomforts or losses that may reasonably occur as a result of service)*.

(Note: Any listing should not purport to be all-inclusive.)

We understand that other procedures and sources of help are available to
us and also could be helpful, such as *(list possible alternatives)*. However, we
have decided to pursue our clinician's recommendations, realizing the potential benefits, risks, and possible alternatives.

To work toward our goals and objectives, we have agreed to meet *(list how
often, on what day and time, for how long, and where)* _____
_____ .

We have been made aware of the financial policies of this setting, and
we understand that we will pay for each treatment session $_____
(dollars per unit).

Our responsibilities include *(list assigned duties, activities, things or situations to avoid or pursue, and so forth)*. Our clinician's responsibilities include
providing his or her best efforts to implement and facilitate this service plan,
monitoring our progress, giving us feedback, safeguarding our privacy, keeping us informed of our rights, meeting with us promptly at appointed times,

being available to us in emergencies or providing appropriate back-up, making thoughtful referrals when we need adjunct services, not prolonging our service unnecessarily, and ensuring that our relationship is conducted professionally and ethically.

We understand that our service is a time-limited, focused procedure and that to know whether our goals and objectives are being reached, our clinician and we will systematically study our progress and record our observations. Specifically, our clinician will *(indicate procedure for empirically measuring client progress)*. Additionally, we agree to *(indicate any logs, diaries, and so forth that the clients are expected to keep)*. Any time any of us feels we are not making satisfactory progress, any of us may and should ask to renegotiate the service plan. If any of us feels we cannot identify a way to make progress on the goals and objectives of our service, then our clinician is responsible for referring us to alternative sources of help.

Finally, we understand that background information about us, this service contract, our service plan, and information about our progress and service outcomes will be part of our clinical record. Our clinical record is strictly confidential with very specific exceptions:

- We can request and/or give consent to the release of information about ourselves to others (for example, our insurance company, HMO, EAP, and family doctor) with whom we want to share it.
- We can request access to our own clinical record.
- Confidential information will be selectively revealed to proper authorities in instances when any of us is in danger or we put someone else in danger or when a court of law orders disclosure.

CLIENT NAME (PLEASE PRINT) _____

SIGNATURE _____

DATE _____

CLIENT NAME (PLEASE PRINT) _____

SIGNATURE _____

DATE _____

CLIENT NAME (PLEASE PRINT) _____

SIGNATURE _____

DATE _____

CLIENT NAME (PLEASE PRINT) _____

SIGNATURE _____

DATE _____

CLIENT NAME (PLEASE PRINT) _____

SIGNATURE _____

DATE _____

NAME OF LEGALLY RESPONSIBLE PARENT OR GUARDIAN (WHERE REQUIRED)

_____

SIGNATURE _____

DATE _____

NAME AND TITLE OF WITNESS _____

SIGNATURE _____

DATE _____

SAMPLE FORM:
CONSENT TO SERVICE PLAN AND SERVICE CONTRACT FOR GROUPS

File Name: *Rxcongrp.doc*

I, *(name of client)* _____, hereby agree to the group treatment plan developed in *(name of setting)* _____ _____ by myself and my clinician *(name of clinician)* _____. I understand that this is not a legally binding contract; rather, it is an agreement between us that we can amend as needed. I further understand that my treatment will take place based on my earlier consent to accept the general operating and financial policies and procedures of this setting.

As a result of the assessment of my problems done by my clinician and myself, the following goals and objectives have been agreed on: *(list desired goals and specific objectives with time lines)*. Accordingly, my clinician has recommended the following group service procedures and explained the reasons for preferring them: *(list the interventions selected and a brief justification of why these and not other approaches have been chosen; also list expected benefits of the recommended service and prognosis)*. I am, however, aware that I am not guaranteed the benefits we expect. Additionally, I understand that there are specific risks associated with the recommended service process: *(list any emotional, situational, relationship, or other possible difficulties; side effects; or discomforts or losses that may reasonably occur as a result of service)*.

(Note: Any listing should not purport to be all-inclusive.)

I understand that other procedures and sources of help are available to me and also could be helpful, such as *(list possible alternatives)*. However, I have decided to pursue my clinician's recommendations, realizing the potential benefits, risks, and possible alternatives.

To work toward my goals and objectives, I have agreed to meet with a *(specify type of group and how often, on what day and time, for how long, and where)* _____ _____ .

I have chosen the following dates for my prearranged absence: _____ _____. I have been made aware of the financial policies of this setting, and I understand that I will pay for each group treatment session $ _____ *(dollars per unit)*.

My responsibilities include participating actively in the group, although I can choose what information and how much information I want to discuss; being truthful about what I say; attending all group sessions and arriving on time; keeping the confidentiality of other members; resolving any unfinished business; and not socializing with other group members outside our sessions. I agree to follow the group rules (*described in the agreement to initiate service*) and understand that if I do not follow the rules, the consequences will be (*specify consequences*). In addition, my responsibilities include (*list other assigned duties, activities, things or situations to avoid or pursue, and so forth*).

My clinician's responsibilities include providing his or her best efforts to implement and facilitate this group service plan, giving us opportunities to resolve unfinished business, helping us apply what is done in the group to our personal goals, monitoring our progress, giving us feedback, safeguarding our privacy, keeping us informed of our rights, meeting with the group promptly at appointed times, being available in emergencies or providing appropriate back-up, making thoughtful referrals when we need adjunct services, not prolonging service unnecessarily, and ensuring that our relationship is conducted professionally and ethically.

I understand that my service is a time-limited, focused procedure and that to know whether our goals and objectives are being reached, my clinician and I will systematically study my progress and record our observations. Specifically, my clinician will (*indicate procedure for empirically measuring clients' progress*). Additionally, I agree to (*indicate any logs, diaries, and so forth that the client is expected to keep*). Any time either of us feels we are not making satisfactory progress, either of us may and should ask to renegotiate the service plan. If either of us feels we cannot identify a way to make progress on the goals and objectives of my treatment, then my clinician is responsible for referring me to alternative sources of help. If, at any time, I am thinking about quitting the group, it is my responsibility to talk to the group members about my reasons before I leave the group.

Finally, I understand that background information about me, this service contract, my service plan, and information about my progress and service outcomes will be part of my clinical record. My clinical record is strictly confidential with very specific exceptions:

- I can request and/or give consent to the release of information about me to others (for example, my insurance company, HMO, EAP, and family doctor) with whom I want to share it.
- I can request access to my own clinical record.
- Confidential information will be selectively revealed to proper authorities in instances when I am in danger or I put someone else in danger or when a court of law orders disclosure.

CLIENT NAME (PLEASE PRINT) _____

SIGNATURE _____

DATE _____

NAME OF LEGALLY RESPONSIBLE PARENT OR GUARDIAN (WHERE REQUIRED)

_____

SIGNATURE _____

DATE _____

NAME AND TITLE OF WITNESS _____

SIGNATURE _____

DATE _____

SAMPLE FORM:
FEE POLICY AND AGREEMENT

File Name: *Feeagree.doc*

This setting is committed to providing the most effective and efficient social work treatment and services possible. To do so, we need your understanding of our fee policy and the reasoning behind it, as well as your cooperation.

Payment Schedule

Payment is due at the time services are rendered, unless other arrangements have been approved in advance by your clinician. By having you pay at each session, we eliminate the need to bill you. This helps keep our costs as low as possible, prevents the accumulation of large debts on your part, and avoids possible risks to your privacy that occur when invoices for service are mailed to you.

We encourage you to contact us immediately for assistance if temporary financial problems affect the timely payment of your account.

Insurance Procedures

If you have medical insurance, we do all we can to assist you in receiving your maximum allowable mental health benefits. If you wish, we will submit your claim, or you may file your own claim. In either instance, your insurer will reimburse you directly. Regardless of whether you or we file your claim, your insurer will require a completed insurance form, and we will require your signed consent permitting us to provide confidential information to your insurer or even to you.

Our fees are considered usual, customary, and reasonable by most insurance companies. Some insurance companies, however, reimburse on a "schedule" that is below the current standard. Depending on your insurance, you may be required to pay out of pocket the difference between our charges and their reimbursement. We will accept assignment of benefits from a few large insurance companies, which include *(names of companies)* _____

_____ .

We emphasize that our relationship is with you and not with your insurance company. Although we file insurance claims as a courtesy to our clients, all charges are your responsibility from the date the service is rendered.

HMOs and Managed Care Provider Networks

We also belong to the following HMOs and managed care provider networks: *(names of networks)* _____

_____ .

These third-party payer systems require a referral from your primary care physician and a copayment at each session. Under no circumstances can the copayment be waived, and it must be paid at the time of service. However, the copayment is your only out-of-pocket expense, and our reimbursement is directly from the third-party payer. In this instance, our relationship is with the HMO or provider network as well as with you.

Services Not Covered

Regardless of the nature of your third-party payer, some of the services you receive may not be covered under your mental health benefit. Responsibility for payment for those services rests with you. However, nonreimbursable services will be thoroughly discussed with you before they are provided, and you will have full opportunity to refuse such services and to consider alternatives.

Payment Methods

We accept cash, money orders, personal checks, and the following credit and debit cards: *(names of cards)* _____ .
Returned checks will be subject to a $_____ charge, which will be added to your bill. Balances older than _____ days will be subject to interest charges of _____% per month. Unpaid balances older than _____ days and in excess of $_____ will be the basis for terminating service. In this unfortunate event, we will make every effort to help you locate alternative affordable care; however, we will be unable to continue to work with you in the face of financial default.

(If applicable, also note that the law allows the referral of unpaid bills to a collection agency or the utilization of small-claims court procedures. Note that this is not the preferred course of action, but may become necessary if the problem of a delinquent account cannot be resolved otherwise.)

Charges for Late and Canceled Appointments

We require 24 hours' advance notification if you are not able to keep a scheduled appointment. This notice permits us to offer that time to someone else. If you have given 24 hours' notice, you will not be charged for the appointment. However, if you break your appointment and do not call this office within 24 hours, you may be charged for the session.

We understand that there may be occasional emergencies when you will not be able to keep your appointment and also will not be able to notify us within 24 hours. We will take these circumstances into account.

Charges for broken appointments and appointments canceled without 24-hours' notice cannot be billed to your third-party payer. You will be personally responsible, therefore, for the full amount of the session.

If you are late for your appointment without 24 hours' notice, you will be seen for the balance of your time but charged for a full session. If you provide 24 hours' notice of an expected late arrival, your fee will be prorated.

Charges for Home Visits, Telephone Contacts Emergency Appointments, and Collateral Contacts

Occasionally, it is advisable for a session to be held in your home. Our out-of-office fee is $_____ per hour, from our office door back to our office door. Thus, a one-hour home visit and travel time of 30 minutes each way would result in a charge of two hours.

Brief telephone calls in which you advise us of a schedule change or ask for a specific piece of information are encouraged. If the duration of the call is less than five minutes, you will not be charged. If the situation requires telephone consultation that exceeds five minutes, there will be a charge of $_____ for each 15-minute segment or partial 15-minute segment of the telephone contact.

If your need is more urgent and complex and it cannot be postponed until a scheduled appointment, an immediate emergency appointment will be arranged and billed at (the usual fee or an emergency fee) $_____.

If, with your permission, we contact other people on your behalf—such as family members, teachers, or other health care professionals—and consult with them in person or by telephone, then the above fees for scheduled in-office and out-of-office sessions, as well as telephone contacts, will apply.

Questions

If you have any questions about the financial policy of our setting or third-party coverage, please ask us for assistance.

FEE AGREEMENT

By signing below I am indicating that I have read the above statements on fees and payment policies. I have discussed these conditions with my social worker and have had the opportunity to ask any questions I have had. My questions have been answered to my satisfaction. I understand and agree to meet my financial responsibilities in receiving treatment and services in this practice setting.

I agree to

_____ remit to *(the office manager, secretary, or clinician)* at the beginning of each session a fee of \$_____, which is based on a rate of \$_____ per treatment hour.

_____ remit to *(the office manager, secretary, or clinician)* a copayment in the amount of \$_____ in keeping with the policies of my health benefits.

_____ the assignment of my health insurance benefit to this *(setting, clinician, or provider)*.

CLIENT NAME (PLEASE PRINT) _____

SIGNATURE _____

DATE _____

NAME OF LEGALLY RESPONSIBLE PARENT OR GUARDIAN (WHERE REQUIRED)

_____

SIGNATURE _____

DATE _____

NAME AND TITLE OF WITNESS _____

SIGNATURE _____

DATE _____

NOTE: This fee agreement is reproduced with permission and with minor modifications from the statement of "Patient Rights and Responsibilities" of Montague Psychological Associates, 52 Main Street, Turners Falls, MA 01376.

SAMPLE FORM:
MISSED APPOINTMENT NOTICES

File Name: *Dropout.doc*
_____

NOTE TO A PROSPECTIVE CLIENT
WHO FAILS TO KEEP THE FIRST APPOINTMENT

Dear _____ :

I regret that it was not possible for you to meet with me at *(appointment date and time)* _____ as we had agreed. If you would like to reschedule our appointment, please call me. I would also be pleased to refer you to other sources of service, if that is your preference. Let me know how I can assist you now or at any time in the future.

Sincerely,

NOTE TO AN ACTIVE CLIENT
WHO FAILS TO KEEP APPOINTMENTS

Dear _____:

You have now missed _____ appointments. (*Summarize number and content of follow-up telephone calls.*)

    I am concerned about your well-being and the fact that the goals and objectives we agreed on seem to be off course. I believe that you can still benefit from the services we planned. If you would prefer to pursue your treatment with another professional or in another setting, I can assist you with a referral. However, it is important for both of us that we have closure on our work together and that we discuss alternative referrals.

    I must also remind you that appointments missed without notification are charged to you. I cannot invoice your health insurer for services not provided. If you will come in to see me, we can discuss a workable payment plan if that would suit you better than a lump-sum payment in the amount of $_____ for _____ missed sessions. Please contact me so we can determine the best ways to meet your needs and keep up the momentum of your treatment.

Sincerely,

SAMPLE FORM:
DELINQUENT ACCOUNT NOTICES

File Name: *Collect.doc*

Note to Practitioners:
If an active client is in arrears, confront the problem in a session and strive for a payment schedule. Alternatively, have a support staff person call the client to determine if there has been "a problem in our records or if the clinician has not collected fees as agreed upon." Coach the caller to convey supportiveness and nonjudgmentality and to communicate that the problem is very possibly on "your end."

Most situations of significant delinquent accounts will involve clients whose service was terminated for default on fees or clients who terminated on their own volition, often against professional advice. If the amount is small (for example, the cost of one or two sessions) or if the client was upset when the service relationship ended, it may be wise to make one or two efforts to collect and, these failing, to write off the debt. Larger debts may warrant more-intensive efforts on your part and ultimately the use of small-claims court or a collection agency. Always consider the possibility that your collection efforts will spur a malpractice suit by an unhappy former client.

You might start a collection attempt with a former or a current client with a very informal and pleasant communication. Send via registered mail an invoice suitable for the client to submit to his or her third-party payer, along with a separate note that might read:

INITIAL NOTICE

Dear _____ :

Our accounts show an unpaid balance of $ _____ for services rendered to you between *(beginning and ending dates of service)* _____ _____ . An invoice is attached. Please remit the unpaid balance.

If you cannot settle your account at this time, please send some portion of the balance and call our office or send a note letting us know how you wish to schedule and make the remainder of your payments. We will be happy to work out a payment system that is suitable to you.

If you think we are in error about this outstanding balance, please call *(the office manager, secretary, or clinician)* promptly to discuss the situation.

Best regards,

SECOND NOTICE

Dear_____:

We are still waiting for your response to our letter of *(date of initial letter)*. In the event that you did not receive that communication, another copy of the letter and invoice is enclosed, indicating an unpaid balance of $_____.

We need to receive your payment at this time or, alternatively, to hear from you about payment arrangements that are suitable for you. You can rely on our willingness to work with you concerning your financial obligation to us. However, if you do not communicate with us and you do not pay by *(date)*, we will have no choice but to *(reluctantly end our relationship with you and/or turn to our collection agency/small-claims court)*.

We remind you that your privacy will be protected in the event that you press us to use outside collection services. We will provide only your identity and the amount you owe for services rendered on specified dates.

We genuinely hope that the problem we are experiencing with your delinquent account can be resolved without outside collection services and that you will contact us before *(date)*.

Sincerely,

SAMPLE FORM:
POSTTERMINATION FOLLOW-UP

File Name: *Followup.doc*

Dear_____ :

You may recall that when you sought our services _____ months ago, our working agreement explained that we routinely contact our clients about _____ months after our final appointment. We do this out of interest in your well-being and because we would like to know how you are. Additionally, we would like to know how you feel about your service with us. Your thoughts can help us improve our services.

We hope you will be willing to complete the brief survey we have enclosed. Like any other information you have shared with us, your response to our survey will be completely confidential within the limits of the law. Your completed survey *(will/will not)* be filed in your clinical record. Your social worker will review it to learn how you are doing and to help him or her evaluate the service choices that were made. Otherwise, the information will be used only to compile some statistics of use to the practice setting. If any reports are written based on this survey data, only group statistics will be presented. No individual identities will be used.

By returning the survey in the enclosed stamped envelope, you will be indicating your informed consent to participate in our follow-up process.

If you have any questions about this follow-up survey, we urge you to call your social worker at *(telephone number)*. We thank you for your help and extend our best regards. Please let us know if we can be helpful to you in the future.

Sincerely,

NOTE: This letter can be adjusted if your procedure is to telephone clients at the designated posttermination time. Or, you may use an anonymous survey that is not used by clinicians for individual feedback and thus is never seen by the treating professional. There are so many variations in follow-up protocol that any letter should be customized. However, from a risk reduction perspective, you will want to protect the client's confidentiality, being clear that participation is optional and about the uses of the data and how privacy is assured.

SAMPLE FORM:
REFERRAL ACKNOWLEDGMENT
AND REQUEST

File Name: *Referral.doc*

ACKNOWLEDGMENT OF
REFERRAL FROM A PROFESSIONAL

NAME OF CLIENT _____

DATE OF BIRTH _____

SOCIAL SECURITY NUMBER _____

Dear Colleague/Referral Source:

Thank you for your recent referral of the above-named client to our setting. With *(name of client's)* _____ permission, I am letting you know that we have initiated contact, and our first appointment is scheduled for *(date)* _____ .

　　(If appropriate, include: If, at the end of our treatment effort, you are still involved in a relationship with our client, I will provide you with a summary of our work together and recommendations for subsequent care, assuming that our client grants me consent to release this information.)

Sincerely,

NOTE: To acknowledge a referral from a current or former client, you could write a brief note on your letterhead; for example, "I appreciate your recent referral. I hope all is going well with you."

REFERRAL TO ANOTHER PROFESSIONAL

NAME OF CLIENT _____

DATE OF BIRTH _____

SOCIAL SECURITY NUMBER_____

Dear Colleague:

I am referring the above-named client to you for the following reasons: *(problems, services desired, and so forth)* _____ .
I and my client *(or former client)* have thoroughly discussed this referral, and he or she has consented to the referral. If you accept my client, I have enclosed a release of information. If my client and you complete the form, I will be pleased to furnish you with requested information from my records that may facilitate your work together.

    If you find you cannot accept my client, please advise me and encourage him or her to return to me for alternative referrals.

    Thank you for your consideration.

Sincerely,

SAMPLE FORM: TERMINATION

File Name: *Termltrs.doc*

Note to Practitioners:

When you terminate service consensually because service goals have been met and further services are not needed, send a brief letter to the client that includes the following points:

- Briefly summarize the service that has taken place, including when you began and ended, central goals, interventions, accomplishments, and final recommendations.
- Thank the client for the opportunity to serve him or her. Indicate you will be available in the future should the need for service arise again, and invite the client to refer others to your setting.
- Remind the client that you will retain his or her clinical record (*state where*) for (*state period of time*) and that those records or parts of them will be provided to another entity only if you receive a legal release of information signed by the client, if you receive a court order, or if you are required by law to release information.
- Include as an attachment a final statement of the satisfied account or a final invoice if appropriate.

When the client terminates service against professional advice, your letter should include the following points:

- Briefly summarize the service that has been completed, including when you began and ended, central goals, interventions, accomplishments, unrealized objectives, final recommendations, and referrals.
- Emphasize your judgment that continued service is advisable, and encourage the client to consider returning to treatment. Indicate you would be pleased to resume your work with the client or to discuss alternative sources of care and referrals.
- If you believe that not receiving service seriously jeopardizes the client or endangers others, say so.
- If the client refused a final session with you, encourage him or her to make a final appointment so that you both can be satisfied that you achieved closure.
- Thank the client for the opportunity to serve him or her, indicate that you regret the circumstances that have interrupted your relationship, and reiterate that you will be available in the future should he or she reconsider and wish to resume service.

- Remind the client that you will retain his or her records *(state where)* for *(state period of time)* and that those records or parts of them will be provided to another entity only if you receive a legal release of information signed by the client, if you receive a court order, or if you are required by law to release information.
- Include as an attachment a final statement of the satisfied account or a final invoice if appropriate.

When you terminate service with the client against her or his wishes, your letter should include the following points:

- Briefly summarize the service that has been completed, including when you began and ended, central goals, interventions, accomplishments, unrealized objectives, reasons for your decision to terminate the relationship, final recommendations, and referrals.
- Emphasize your judgment that continued service is either advisable *(or not indicated)*, and encourage the client to consider your final recommendations for alternative services or use of other resources. Provide explicit information about other appropriate sources of service. Offer to discuss alternative sources of service and additional referrals by telephone, but remain clear that the service relationship has ended.
- If you believe that not receiving service seriously jeopardizes the client or endangers others, say so.
- Thank the client for the opportunity to serve him or her, and indicate that you regret the circumstances that have interrupted your relationship.
- Remind the client that his or her records will be retained by you *(state where)* for *(state period of time)* and that those records or parts of them will be provided to another entity only if you receive a legal release of information signed by the client, if you receive a court order, or if you are required by law to release information.
- Include as an attachment a final statement of the satisfied account or a final invoice if appropriate.

SAMPLE FORM:
COMMUNICATION WITH A
MANAGED CARE COMPANY

File Name: *Mngdcare.doc*

Note to Practitioners:
The *Mental Health Legal Review* points out that practitioners can be held liable for failing to advocate for their clients' bona fide service needs when third-party payers and managed care companies deny payment for initial care or move to discontinue reimbursement for continued care. Hence, as the *Review* urges, document your efforts to persuade care managers that service is indicated. First, talk by telephone with the representative of the company that denied payment. Confirm that telephone call with a letter including the elements in the sample below but customized to the client's circumstances.

The *Review* also highlights a dilemma. Note that

> This letter makes a strong case for continued treatment. Once the letter is written, it may be difficult to justify a termination of treatment as within the standard of care. Therefore, the professional should consider whether to provide treatment without charge or on a reduced fee basis. No court has yet ruled that a mental health professional is obligated to work without charge. However, if a strong case is made in writing that additional treatment is needed, there is a possibility that a future claim might be made alleging inappropriate termination of treatment. Any decision to terminate treatment after writing the . . . letter should be made only in consultation with other professionals and only after attempts have been made to arrange other treatment. (p. 3)

DATE _____

RE _____

NAME OF CLIENT _____

DATE OF BIRTH _____

SOCIAL SECURITY NUMBER _____

Dear Third-Party Payer or Utilization Review/Managed Care Company:

This is to confirm our telephone conversation of *(date)*.

As I have indicated, I am the licensed clinical social worker responsible for the care of the above-named client, who has a diagnosis of *(DSM-IV diagnosis)*. A brief description of this client's history is as follows: *(summary of the client's psychosocial, medical, and service history)*. I have enclosed a copy of my clinical chart for this client, along with a copy of his/her written consent for me to release this information to you.

It is my opinion that this client needs the following service in accordance with the service plan set forth in the enclosed record and recapitulated here: *(service plan)*. This service is needed for the following reasons: *(specific reasons)*.

I understand your company has decided to deny payment for this care. The client has told me that *(he/she)* has no money to pay for the required care. It is my opinion that this denial of payment could cause serious damage to the client as follows: *(specific concerns)*.

Please write to let me know what, if any, rules apply regarding how decisions are made to authorize service and by whom those decisions should be made. For instance, do your rules provide that I as the provider have input into the decision? Do you have an appeals procedure? If so, please consider this letter as a formal appeal of the decision to deny payment for service for my client. If there is a particular procedure that I or my client need to follow in order to appeal, please advise me at once what is necessary to comply.

Please advise as to whether you will continue payment while the appeal is pending. Please also advise about whether you have any time limits to respond to this appeal.

If you have questions or if you need further information, please contact me promptly.

Sincerely,

NOTE: This form is reproduced, with minor modifications, from "Preventing Liability in the Managed Care Setting," *Mental Health Legal Review,* Vol. 3, No. 1, January 1994, pp. 1–3, with permission of the publisher, Behavioral Health Services, Inc., P.O. Box 1788, Daytona Beach, FL 32115.

INDEX

About the Authors

Mary Kay Houston-Vega, PhD, ACSW, MSW, LCSW, is associate professor at the School of Social Work, Barry University, Miami Shores, FL. An experienced practitioner as well as educator, Dr. Houston-Vega has published and presented frequently about social work malpractice risks, crisis intervention, suicide, violence, and HIV. She has coauthored a risk management paper with Elane M. Nuehring published in *Managers' Choices: Compelling Issues in the New Decision Environment* (1992) and coauthored with John Wood, "Suicide and Treatment of Persons Infected with HIV" in *Community Mental Health and HIV* (in press).

Elane M. Nuehring, PhD, MSSW, is professor at the School of Social Work, Barry University, Miami Shores, FL. Dr. Nuehring's background includes extensive social work consultation and scholarship in the areas of community mental health, homelessness, violence, and program evaluation.

Elisabeth R. Daguio, MBA, is membership benefits analyst for the National Association of Social Workers Insurance Trust, Washington, DC. Ms. Daguio has more than 15 years of experience in the marketing and administration of group insurance programs and, among other duties, has analyzed and compiled data from the Trust-sponsored social workers' professional liability program.

PRUDENT PRACTICE:
A GUIDE FOR MANAGING MALPRACTICE RISK

Designed by The Watermark Design Office

Composed by CC Graphic Connections, in Goudy Old Style

Printed by Boyd Printing Company, Inc.

PRACTICE RESOURCES
FOR SOCIAL WORKERS

Prudent Practice: A Guide for Managing Malpractice Risk, *by Mary Kay Houston-Vega and Elane M. Nuehring with Elisabeth R. Daguio.* Social workers and other human services professionals face a heightened risk of malpractice suits in today's litigious society. The NASW Press now offers practitioners a complete practice guide to increasing competence and managing the risk of malpractice.

ISBN: 0-87101-267-7. Item #2677. Price $42.95

Clinical Practice with Individuals, *by Mark A. Mattaini.* Practitioners and educators alike will find this guidebook invaluable. Mattaini presents practice guidelines that are firmly rooted in contemporary state-of-the-art knowledge and are both accessible and immediately applicable to practice.

ISBN: 0-87101-270-7. Item #2707. Price $28.95

Person-in-Environment Systems: The PIE Classification System, *by James M. Karls and Karin E. Wandrei, Editors.* Demonstrates how to use PIE to facilitate social work practice. Helps clinicians better understand their clients. A valuable teaching tool for social work practice courses. Used by administrators to develop agency and community programs. Also available in a set with the *PIE Manual.*

ISBN: 0-87101-240-5. Item #2405A. Price $28.95

PIE Manual, *by James M. Karls and Karin E. Wandrei, Editors.* Lists the descriptions, classifications, and codes used in PIE and includes case examples to help familiarize readers with the PIE system. Also available in a set with the *Person-in-Environment System.*

ISBN: 0-87101-254-5. Item #2545. Price $28.95

Person-in-Environment System (2-Volume Set)

When purchased together, the *Person-in-Environment System* and *PIE Manual* serve as a major tool for classifying and codifying problems in social functioning. Applications are useful for social work practitioners, students, administrators, researchers, and educators, as well as social policymakers and community organizers.

Item # 2405. Price $38.95

Managed Care Resource Guides, *by Vivian H. Jackson, Editor.* These guides provide essential information to help practitioners advance social work within a managed care environment. Each guide contains an overview of the issues and information on the knowledge and skills necessary for effective practice in a specialized environment

—for Agency Settings (Item #2456)
—for Social Workers Who Are Private Practitioners (Item #2472)
$50 each

(Order form on reverse side)

ORDER FORM

Title	Item #	Price	Total
__ Prudent Practice (Word for Windows disk)	Item 2677	$42.95	_____
__ Prudent Practice (Macintosh disk)	Item 2677A	$42.95	_____
__ Clinical Practice with Individuals	Item 2707	$28.95	_____
__ Person-in-Environment System Book	Item 2405A	$28.95	_____
__ Person-in-Environment System Manual	Item 2545	$28.95	_____
__ Person-in-Environment System (book and manual)	Item 2405	$38.95	_____
__ Managed Care Resource Guide— Agency Setting	Item 2456	$50.00	_____
__ Managed Care Resource Guide— Private Practice	Item 2472	$50.00	_____
		Subtotal	_____
	+ 10% postage and handling		_____
		Total	_____

❐ I've enclosed my check or money order for $ _____.

❐ Please charge my   ❐ NASW Visa*   ❐ Other Visa   ❐ MasterCard

_____   _____

Credit Card Number   Expiration Date

Signature _____

Use of this card generates funds in support of the social work profession.

Name _____

Address _____

City _____ State/Province _____

Country _____ Zip _____

Phone _____   _____

NASW Member # (if applicable)

(Please make checks payable to NASW Press. Prices are subject to change.)

NASW PRESS

NASW Press
P.O. Box 431
Annapolis JCT, MD 20701
USA

Credit card orders call
1-800-227-3590
(In the Metro Wash., DC, area, call 301-317-8688)
Or fax your order to 301-206-7989
Or e-mail nasw@pmds.com

Visit our Web site at http://www.naswpress.org   PPBI96